A

STRANGE BREED OF CAT

(An Encounter
in
Human Sexuality)

A

STRANGE BREED

OF CAT

(An Encounter in Human Sexuality)

by

B. Mark Schoenberg

An ETC Publication

1975

C̲I̲P̲

Library of Congress Cataloging in Publication Data

Schoenberg, B.   Mark, 1928 —
   A strange breed of cat (an encounter in human sexuality)

   1. College students — Sexual behavior. 2. Group relations training. I. Title.

HQ27.3.S35   301.11   74-5281

ISBN 0-88280-015-9

Copyright   © 1975 by ETC PUBLICATIONS
18512 Pierce Terrace
Homewood, Illinois 60430

CONTENTS

*For only the light which we have
kindled in ourselves can illuminate others.*

Schopenhauer

INTRODUCTION

A beginning, like an ending, is a pretty nebulous thing. It is extremely chancy to select a spot in time where a thing starts up, but it can be done if you're willing to forgive and forget such minor nuisances as precipitating and predisposing influences. An ending presents more of a problem in that a judge of the situation must be able to state categorically that the matter is at a dead end, that nothing more will come of it, and that further movement and growth is impossible. The student of Alpha and Omega deals in terms which are presumptuous at the outset, and he soon learns to discard them. Thus it is the approximation of the beginning and the speculation of the ending which must capture interest chiefly because these are the realms of the possible. It is an exercise in futility to seek a beginning or an ending unless both these dimensions are contrived.

An ending, unlike a beginning, is a hoped for bit of prettiness. This is not to say that an ending point cannot be symbolically done up in a neat little box with a gorgeous wrap and a flamboyant bow. Yet to hope is to court disillusionment; but if we abandoned our grand expectations, life would be the more colorless for it. For those who will live it, life is colorful enough without the overtones of platitudinous crap.

Thus it is that these words begin with a statement that the beginning of the group was occasioned by a visit to the psychologist's office by two of the members-to-be, and that this caused the formation of a group whose shared concerns were the yeast that fermented group action and involvement, and the adhesive that bound them together. There is no ending; nor will there be as long as any of us may live. Even the death of the members will not decisively indicate the terminal point, for the experiences which they shared one with another are like the rippling wave spreading from the center of an impact. All humanity can benefit from one human's example of humanity.

The sessions were not taped, and in retrospect this proved to be unfortunate. Nonetheless, written notes and sketchy observations allowed continuity of recall. The author has taken few liberties with the content and process of the sessions; any omission or changed emphasis is a result of a lack of total recall, and is not due to any other factor. The truncated notes furnished a kind of continuity; it is from these notes that the book evolved.

The first concern of the membership of the group was secrecy. Without exception, each of the young men was highly anxious that not only their identity but the main thrust of the group be kept confidential. Their worries included the maintenance of confidentialitiy by the group leader as well as by every other member of the group. In retrospect, it can be observed that several initial traumatic experiences within and without the group membership provided early cohesion; much more in the way of role-playing and gamesmanship was logically to have been expected. However the process of the group was saved the early sparring and swordplay, and deliberations quickly moved into a comfortable high gear.

It is safe to say that membership in (and belonging to) the group did not come easy for any of its members. Even though each individual was personally invited by the group leader, commitment to the group as a whole and to each other as individuals was made extremely difficult because of felt societal pressures. But as the young men learned to lean on each other the pressures contracted and each learned to cope more satisfactorily with his own feelings. No member came out of the group feeling the same as he went into it, but then all experiences tend to alter the personality. It becomes believable that humans change greatly after an intensive experience; thus it comes as no surprise to learn that the individual members did change due to the group experience. That they changed for better or worse is of no immediate consequence, for in terms of each individual's perception the alteration in manifest behavioural patterns became a result of rational deliberation. With regard to reality and possible protestations that the changes in lifestyle for several members of the group are so unreal as not to be believable, my sole rejoinder is that human beings are capable of just about anything; and it is only the sublime jackass who dares to question the direction in which the individual and collective man may move.

These pages are a result of a change in attitude by the members of the group. Although their earlier wishes bordered on an exclusive veil of secrecy, the collective wish now is that the experiences of the group be shared in order that others might benefit. The anonymity of group members must be continued, but their collective sharing is the meat of these pages.

THE PARTICIPANTS

Todd Callahan   A third year university student, majoring in Architecture. Todd is 21 years old and measures exactly at 6'2". An all-city hockey player in high school, Todd is now at least twenty-five pounds over his best weight. He would have liked to have gone into professional hockey, but he lacked the killer instinct which would have earned him a spot on a professional team. Todd lives at home with his father, mother, a younger brother and a younger sister.

Joe Chambers   Although he hasn't fully decided on a career, Joe is in his second year at University and has given much thought to going on to law school. Joe was all-city hockey from the same school as Todd Callahan. Unlike Todd, Joe has kept himself in top physical condition. He continues to live at home with his parents where, as an only child, he is free to come and go as he pleases.

Rick Rischer   Rick went to the same school as Joe and Todd, but he wasn't a hockey player. He was a star swimmer however and hopes that when he gets through law school he can do a bit of swimming coaching on the side. Rick and Joe have been very good friends throughout high school.

Jim Harris   Jim lives at home, but it's a toss-up as to who is most unhappy about his being there: himself or his father. He considers living at home too restrictive. Although he is not definite about it, he thinks sometimes that the answer for him is to go to Toronto to study fashion design. He doesn't like university, and sees little future in staying either at home or in university.

Mike Stewart   Mike had been in the Navy prior to entering university. He also is athletic in build, but is much shorter than either Joe or Todd. He hasn't decided on a major yet, but figures since he's only in his second year that there is no great need for deciding on a career. Mike is 24 years old but wants to keep his options open a while longer yet. Rooms with Carlos Vaca.

Carlos Vaca   Mike's room-mate, Carlos, is a Mexican-American from Brownsville, Texas. He is about 5'8", and he tends to be short and fat. Carlos is only 18, and he's in his first year at university. He doesn't know what he wants to study, and the only real reason he is in university is that he's the first one in his family ever to go beyond high school. He has mixed feelings about being so far from home.

Frank Westcott   Frank will get his Bachelor's degree in Psychology at the end of term, and then he plans to enter graduate school and work for a Ph.D, in Counselling Psychology. Frank did a tour in the Air Force prior to entering university. He is married. His wife works a full-time job so this allows him to attend classes in all terms. Frank is 23 years old. He's tremendously interested in the study of Psychology, and considers himself to be an excellent student.

Denton White   Officially the trainer or leader of the group, Denton is a registered psychologist and is associate director of the University Counselling Centre. Denton is in his mid-thirties, is married, and he and his wife have two children.

PROLOGUE

Without a shadow of a doubt, Mike Stewart and Todd Callahan were the prime movers in the formation of the group.

The first time Denton White saw Mike remained an experience which words can but inadequately describe. One should be able to empathize and relate to an experience, if he is to know it at all. But even if the case is truly one which defies description, still an attempt should be made to particularize the details. In short, Mike was a study in contrast. Righteous indignation seemed to be his number one feeling, but there was xenophobic reaction as well. From his slouched posture one might suspicion cowardice, but a more talented and experienced observer could well select a false bravado as the label to hang onto him. There was more. Bloody, he was not beaten; threatened, he was not cowed.

Todd Callahan presented himself to Denton as no cool study of conflicting emotions. Todd was in a rage, and every measure of his being shouted this feeling. A tall boy, his external appearance could best be described as an out-of-condition high school football player. Probably he played at one of the heavier spots, possibly center or guard. Todd was red of face and his breath came heavy. One of his big hands firmly gripped the collar of Mike's shirt while the other fist was poised at Mike's face, obviously in readiness for contact.

The students' entry into the Counselling Office created something of a stir. As later reported by the receptionist, the door was practically kicked open. The noise caused her to look up. A young male student stood seemingly immobile in the doorway, and at first glance he appeared to be alone. Scant seconds passed before he came flying into the room, the receiver of a heavy shove in the back. A second student rushed in after him.

"I want to see a counsellor," the shover told her.

Janet, the receptionist, was ready to frame the usual 'do you have an appointment' question when a second thought intervened to cause her to buzz for Dr. Denton White. White was a psychologist attached to the Counselling Office. "Can you come out right away, Doctor?" she inquired.

Some tone in her voice made White respond instantly. He moved quickly from his office down the corridor to the receptionist's desk. Todd continued to glare at Mike.

1

"Come on back to my office, fellows," he told them cheerfully. He stepped out of the way so Mike, followed by a determined Todd, could lead the way.

Inside his office and after he closed the door, Denton extended his hand to the two young men. "I'm Denton White," he said, giving his name.

"Pleased to meet you. I'm Todd Callahan." His eyes shifted around the room. "You are a doctor, aren't you?"

"Well, I'm a psychologist," he replied. He shook hands with the other student. "And your name?"

"My name's Mike," he replied in a noncommital fashion.

"Good, Mike," the psychologist said as he moved to sit in his chair behind the desk. "How about you and Todd sitting down and telling me about the disagreement you two are having?"

Before he got seated, Todd blurted out: "Some disagreement." He turned to Mike: "You want to tell him or do you want me to?"

Mike had sat down. He gave a long cold stare at the other boy, but didn't reply.

"He's going to hear the whole story whether you tell him or not, buddy," Todd warned. "I'm just giving you the chance to tell your story first."

"Big deal," came the reply. "Look, you're so uptight, man. Why don't you just go and get it off your chest." He took his eyes off Todd for a minute, then returned them. "That's right. You tell him. I bet you'll even get your jollies that way."

"You son-of-a-bitch," Todd roared. "I ought to belt you again."

Mike replied evenly. "Look, guys. This is no good. You came in with a loud gripe. Now let's hear it. Okay?" He stabbed a finger at Todd. "You first, Todd."

In a few brief moments the two students had been seated in the office, Denton got a chance to make a few observations. Todd was the larger of the two, and appeared to be twenty or twenty-one years of age. He had dark good looks, a good hard physique, but seemed a good fifteen or twenty pounds over his best weight. Todd probably carried six feet two. Mike was shorter, about five feet eleven. He also had a year or two of age on Todd. His physique was good, meaning he definitely did not tend to the delicate, and he had better control of his weight than Todd. Mike wasn't light skinned, but he wasn't to be considered dark either. He had eyes that appeared to Denton to be brown, and he had brown hair worn in that present style where it is combed forward and then brought in half-circle over the forehead before it swoops back on the other side.

Todd looked as if he was about to burst. Impatient as he was to relate the details, something seemed to be holding him back. "Well, like I said, my name is Todd Callahan."

"Okay, Todd," Denton replied softly, "and you're a student?"

"Yes, sir. I'm carrying six courses."

Denton turned to the other young man. "And you're a student, Mike?"

"Yeah," he replied. "I'm a student. Full name is Michael T. Stewart." He shrugged, "I guess I'm going to have to give it sooner or later." It was a type of a question.

"It might come to that, Mike," White advised him. "It sure doesn't hurt to give a name, does it?"

"Guess not," he replied. "Anyway, I'm enrolled in classes."

Denton turned inquisitively to Todd. "Do you want to continue?"

"Well, sir. I'm glad you're a psychologist. You'll know what to do. This guy's got problems," Todd intoned.

White caught Mike's response out of the corner of his eyes. It wasn't much, but he rolled his eyes heavenward in such a manner that caused Denton to inwardly chuckle.

But Todd was very serious. "Dr. White," he continued. He stopped short, then resumed. "It's just embarrassing as hell. I don't really know how to say it, but this guy kind of did something to me that I don't like. I guess he's got to be punished, and maybe even kicked out of school or something like that. But I guess he's sick too." Todd took a deep breath, obviously relieved that he had at least broken into the subject.

3

"I'm not sure I understand," Denton told him. "Can you go into a little more detail?"

"Well, sir, he said something to me too."

"Okay," White pressed. "He did something and he said something. Go on."

"Well, actually, he didn't say something. He wrote something."

"Look, brown eyes," Mike interrupted. "Spit it out, will you. You're acting like a virgin queen."

White said nothing. Todd turned quickly to Mike, and looked as if he fully intended to physically assault him. Instead, he shook his head and again faced the psychologist. He made a swipe at a strand of hair that had fallen over his eyes. "The guy's a queer," he spit out. "He wrote me a note and wanted me to leave the campus with him. Go over to his place and have a couple of drinks is what he said."

Mike's eyes met with those of the psychologist, but he did not rise to any defense.

White looked back at Todd. "Writing you a note asking you to come over to his place for a couple of drinks doesn't mean anything, Todd."

"But there was more, Doctor White," he insisted. "He did enough and said enough. I've been around enough to know one of these guys."

"I'll bet you have," Mike spat out, overtones of heavy sarcasm in his voice.

Todd jumped halfway from his chair. This time Mike rose to meet him, his fists clenched.

"There'll be no fighting," White said calmly. "Both of you sit back down, please."

"It's still not too late for me to beat the hell out of you," Todd told Stewart. "Keep that up and I will."

"Like I said a minute ago, try it baby. Besides, if all you want to do is beat me up, why did you bring me down here to do it?"

"I didn't want to beat you up," Todd told him. "I wanted to see if somebody could talk some sense into you. Somebody should be able to tell you how mixed-up you are."

"Oh, yeah? Well, what about you? What about how mixed-up you are?"

"I'm not like you," Todd sneered.

Mike needled him. "You also said you were going to get me thrown out of school. Remember? You promised that," Mike shouted through gritted teeth. "Doesn't sound to me like you want to talk."

"Forget what it sounds like to you," Todd replied heatedly. "I thought a psychologist might know what to do with you. What should I have done?"

Mike started to reply, but Denton intervened. "I guess Todd felt someone else might be able to help him make a decision about what to do. Is that about it, Todd?"

"Yes, that's right. Truth of the matter is I didn't know what to do. But I had to do something."

"Just why did you have to do anything, you clown!" Mike roared. "Why in hell did you have to start screaming at the top of your lungs? Why, for Christ's sake, did you have to keep screaming down the hall how you were going to take care of this bloody queer and see that he got kicked out of school?" Mike's outburst had a calming effect on him. He paused for a second, but then continued in a slow but deliberate manner. "It sure seemed to me that you knew what in hell you are doing. You went so ape that it's still hard for me to believe that it all happened." He pointed his finger at Todd. "You're sick, you know. You've got a goddam sick mind."

Todd seemed to be taken aback for a second. Then he continued, "I still think something ought to be done about you guys."

"Yeah, you screamed that point out loud and clear coming down the corridor. Thank God only half of Arts and Sciences heard you roaring like a madman, and not the whole god damned University."

Denton pressed his palms together, and studied Mike for a second. "Does that bother you, Mike?"

"Yeah, it does, doc. You know, why couldn't the guy just say get lost or something like that?" Mike cleared his throat. "Why did he have to make such a big deal out of it?"

"Can you answer that, Todd?"

"Don't you think I should have, Dr. White? After all, somebody's got to do something. Right?"

"But is this something you did the right thing?" Denton asked.

"Heck, I think so," Todd replied. "What else could I have done?"

"A lot of things," Mike told him. "You know, doc, there are a hell of a lot of so-called straight guys thinking they have to go around beating up on the gays. Does something for their masculinity, I suppose." Mike stared at Todd. "What does it do for you, buddy?"

"That's not what I do at all," Todd replied defensively.

"Yeah, I'm certain of that," Mike told him. "But that's what you thought you were going to be doing when you grabbed hold of me."

"Maybe I didn't really know what I was doing."

"Maybe is right," Mike said evenly.

"Look, Dr. White," Todd continued. "All I know is that these guys are in all the rest rooms. Hell, even the Student Union is running over with them. The administration doesn't seem to be doing anything about getting them off campus."

"Do you think the administration should be getting involved in that kind of thing, Todd?" Denton's words were being weighed very carefully by both of the young men, but no less than by Denton himself. "In other words, what would you have the administration do?"

"Are you administration?" Todd asked.

Denton laughed, "No way."

Todd looked confused, "Well, all I know is that somebody ought to be doing something. These guys are all over the place." His voice became very earnest. "No kidding. Everywhere you look."

"Right, baby," Mike intoned gleefully. "And now may I ask where else you have been looking?"

Todd jumped to his feet. "That does it," he roared. "This time I'm calling a cop. That's what I should have done right away. Instead, I tried to be nice to you; give you a chance."

"Oh, sit down," Mike replied, not moving a muscle. "Or do you just like making an ass of yourself?"

Todd towered over the seated Mike, who simply ignored the fury being directed at him.

Denton moved to Todd's side, and took hold of his elbow. "Sit down, Todd," he said forcefully. "Come on now. I mean it."

Todd allowed himself to be pulled back, and he seated himself.

"Two things I have to say," the psychologist noted quietly. "One, to both of you. There'll be no more of this arguing. If you two want to fight, I've got a room down the hall. I'll even hold your coats, but that will be only as a last resort so that you can work off some of your steam. Number two; and this goes especially to you, Todd. Nobody's going to be called, not the police or anyone else. Understand? When you brought what you considered a problem to my attention, you more or less left everything up to me. Now, you're going to give me a chance to get to the bottom of this. Okay?"

Todd nodded his head agreeably.

"Mike?" White asked. "No more arguing?"

He grinned his infectious smile. "I make love, not war."

"Good," the psychologist said. "Now maybe we can get on with it. Todd? You want to continue?" White took a pipe from his desk and began playing with it, but his eyes framed in on Todd Callahan.

"Well, it all happened in the men's restroom. You know the one on the fourth floor?"

Every floor had several restrooms, but White nodded. He didn't know which one Todd was referring to, but he pretended to know nonetheless.

"Well, I was using the restroom. Like I said. I was using the end stall." Todd looked at Mike, almost as if he were seeking some kind of agreement that such was the case. Mike returned the glance but no sign of agreement or disagreement was in his posture. He simply looked blank. "Gee, you know it's kind of hard to talk about it," Todd continued.

"Why?" Denton wanted to know.

"Well, it's embarrassing for the first thing."

"Oh, aren't we being coy?" Mike intoned sarcastically.

Denton moved quickly to avoid another confrontation. "Knock it off," he said none too kindly to Mike. "But one thing Mike's right about, Todd, is that you shouldn't be coy. If that's what you're trying to be."

"Hell, that's not what I'm trying to be, Doctor White. It's just that it's pretty damn difficult to sit around and spit out a bunch of words."

"For what it's worth, Todd," Denton told him in what he hoped was the kindliest way possible, "I doubt anything you say is going to embarrass any one of us. Sure, sometimes it is hard to say certain things. But if we are going to look into this matter like you say you want to . . ." Denton allowed his voice to fade away. He kept quiet for a few seconds before continuing. "Well, if we are going to look into the matter you simply are going to have to come up with the words. Okay?"

Todd lowered his head, refusing to look either Stewart or White in the eyes. "Okay. Well, his head came in under the partition."

"His head came under the partition?" Denton looked inquiringly at Mike Stewart. Mike returned the stare, but said nothing.

"That's right. That guy stuck his head under the partition."

"And what did you do?" the psychologist asked. "Or did you say anything?"

"No, sir. I didn't say or do anything."

"Nothing?"

Todd shifted in the chair. "I guess there was nothing to say," he continued.

"And Mike?"

"Well, he just kept looking. That's all."

"What was he looking at?"

"Well, he was looking at me."

"You mean he was looking at you straight in your eyes."

Todd shifted uncomfortably. "No, he was looking at my penis."

"Oh, my God," Mike hurled the expression out like he was throwing a fastball. "You've got to be kidding with that penis bit!"

"You shut up," Todd told him. "That's exactly what you were doing."

Mike rolled his eyes heavenward as if asking for strength.

Denton White reached for the humidor on his desk and began stuffing tobacco into his pipe. "All right, Todd, continue. You say Mike was looking at your penis?"

"Yes, sir. That's what he was doing." Todd took a deep breath. "It was then that he tried to put his hand on it, only I moved back on the seat so that he couldn't reach it. But he kept his hand moving around, and finally grabbed hold of my leg. He rubbed my leg for a few seconds, I guess, and then it seemed like he was trying to pull me off the seat toward him. But I stood up and that broke the hold he had on my leg."

"Was that all there was to it?" Denton asked.

Todd looked surprised. "No. What happened then was that when he let go of my leg, I simply sat back down again. Only this time I pulled my shorts up around me so he couldn't see me." He cleared his throat. Well, after a while he seemed to give up. He just quit looking at me."

White took a match to his pipe while waiting for Todd to continue. "Go on."

"Well, it was than that he passed the note to me." Todd reached into his pocket and pulled out a very rumpled and very soiled piece of paper. White could make out some writing on it. "I've got it right here in case you want some evidence."

Mike Stewart broke his silence. "Big deal," he said flatly. "All it says is for you to come over to the place with me for a couple of drinks."

"Yeah, but there's more to it than just coming over for a couple of drinks. And you know it."

"I don't know anything," Mike told him.

"Like hell you don't. Like what comes after a couple of drinks?"

"I'll leave that for your filthy little mind to figure out," Mike sneered.

"It's not me with the filthy mind," Todd shot back. "Hell, you don't even try to deny that you reached over and grabbed hold of my leg."

Mike Stewart said nothing, but fixed Callahan with a stare.

"Or that you were trying to play with me."

"It means nothing," Mike told him. "Only your word against mine that it even happened that way."

"Oh, yeah?" Todd screamed at him. "How about all those bloody witnesses?"

"Look, fellow. You don't have any bloody witnesses. Unless you're talking about all those people in the hall who watched you make such a god-awful fool of yourself. A first class show, I must say. That is, if you enjoy watching a guy make a complete ass of himself." Mike pointed a finger at Callahan. "Look, all those people know is what you were yelling when we were coming down the hall. They didn't see anything going on. So it's your word against my word. Okay?"

Todd sputtered in reply. "But you've got to admit to Dr. White . . ."

Mike cut him off sharply. "I don't have to admit to one goddamn thing." He turned to White. "I don't mean to be disrespectful to you, Dr. White. But I think this guy needs to be told that he has only his word against mine."

"But it's the way it happened," Todd insisted.

"Is it, Mike?" Denton asked.

"Well, let me ask you something," he said to Denton White. "Is this considered a confidential conversation?"

"As far as I'm concerned," Denton replied evenly, "it is. Of course, what you and Todd do with it is your business." He puffed several times on his pipe. "But as far as I'm concerned, it's all confidential."

Mike turned to Todd. "Okay, as far as I'm concerned it's all in this room too." He waited to give Todd a chance to say something; but when Todd failed to make a response, Mike continued. "Okay, What you've said so far is true. Okay?"

"Sure, it's true," Todd muttered. "But I didn't think you were going to admit it."

"Hell, why not?" he wanted to know. "It's not like it's any big crime."

"Well, I think it is."

"Do you, Todd?" Mike asked very softly. "Do you really?"

"Well, I told you I did."

Mike moved to the offense. "Yeah, I know you told me you did. But that's not all the story, is it?"

"Well, more or less it is," Todd insisted.

"No," Mike said softly, "that's not true at all."

Todd sat very quietly, saying nothing.

The room was very still. There was a great undercurrent going on, and the tension showed particularly on Todd's face. Mike continued to look at Todd, but Todd stared at the floor. At last, Denton White moved in to break the heavy mood. "Is there more that needs telling?"

"Only that after I got the note and read it I grabbed him and made him come down here with me."

"Mike?" Denton asked.

"No more from me, doc," Mike replied. "He can say more if he wants. I tried, but he wants to leave it alone."

Denton said nothing, and neither did Mike. The pressure of the room bore heaviest on Todd. He shuffled in his chair, but seemed to be making an effort to remain quiet also. At last it was too much, and Todd's voice broke the electric quiet. He tried to sound cheerful, but it didn't come across that way. "I don't know what else to say, Doctor White. I just thought if I brought him to you that you would know what to do. I sure as hell don't." He swallowed with great difficulty. "I guess I'm sorry I brought him in. God knows I don't want to get him or anybody else in trouble." He stole a look at Mike out of the corner of his eye. "I don't guess he can help it, but you know more about that than I do." Todd stood up. "I've got to go now," he apologized. "I've got some studying to do."

"Todd," Denton told him, "I think you'd better sit down for a moment. Okay? I think we ought to hear if Mike has anything he wants to say before you leave."

Mike seemed at first not to hear Denton's words, but Todd sat back down in the chair.

"Mike?" Denton prodded.

"Like I said, I guess we might as well forget it. Todd doesn't seem to want to say anything else. And as far as I'm concerned, he's the one who should be saying something."

"I simply don't know what to say," Todd replied evenly.

"Okay," Mike said. "You don't know what to say. So let's forget it, eh?"

"For what it's worth," Denton said to the two boys, "I think we ought to go on with it if there's anything more to say." He looked squarely at Todd. "What do you think?"

"I don't know what else to say."

"Mike?"

"It's not that I don't think there's more that should be said," he replied. "I just don't think that I'm the one who should be saying anything."

"Well," Denton intoned in even terms, "maybe we could begin by getting you to at least tell us what you think happened, Mike. You know, everyone perceives things differently. Maybe if Todd heard you say what happened in the restroom he would have something more to say on the subject."

"Why not?" Mike laughed. "What do you think, Todd?"

"What can I say? He can tell his story. It's okay with me."

"Well, there's not really much more to tell," Mike began. "Todd told basically what happened. I was in the stall next to him. I did look under the partition. I tried to get a feel of his cock." He laughed loudly. "See, buddy. The word is cock," he told Todd. "Cock. Not that phony sounding word penis. Okay?"

White smiled, "I'm sure you know that that's the anatomical word, Mike."

"Sure it is, doc," Mike replied returning the smile. "But it's not the household word that cock is." He turned to Todd. "Is it?" Even as tense as Todd appeared to be couldn't prevent a shy smile from breaking all over his face. "Well," Mike told him, "I'm glad to see you can smile. Welcome to the world of the living."

The smile left Todd's face. "Get on with it, will you?"

"Sure," Mike replied evenly. "But penis still sounds phony. Okay? At any rate, I did try to get a feel of him. But he backed off. I didn't know why he did, so I wrote him the note. Asked him to come over to my place. I thought he was nervous in that place. And that's the only reason. I don't think I misjudged that he wanted some action." Mike let his eyes land on Todd, but Todd averted the glance. "As a matter of fact, I still think he wants the action." His words had a special impact on Todd, who noticeably tightened his facial muscles in reply. "But I thought he was nervous. I thought if we went over to my place and had a few drinks that he'd get over it."

"Okay, you wrote him the note," Denton stated. "Then what?"

"Well, at first nothing. I wasn't looking over at him or anything by that time, but it seemed to me that he was weighing whether to come with me or not. But then all of a sudden he started screaming things about having the evidence now and that he was going to come over and get me. All of his screaming and ranting and roaring got to me, I guess. I don't know that I was scared, but it occurred to me that I better get the hell out of there. That I was dealing with a lunatic of some kind sure did occur to me. So I hurried to get my pants up and I took off for the door. I had just gotten the door open and was going out into the hall when he grabbed me from behind. He began pounding on me like a madman. Hell, for some damn fool reason I couldn't even fight back. Something happened to me. I could have taken him," he said with conviction in his voice. "I could do it right now for that matter. At least I think I can. But that's no big matter now. The point is that then and there it seemed like I couldn't move a goddamn muscle. I didn't even try to fight back. So from there on he kept pounding on me. He kind of pushed me down the hall in between punches, and he was screaming all kinds of crazy things about me being a goddamn queer and that he was going to see that I got what was coming to me. In front of all those goddamned people he was yelling like crazy. Anyway, all I know is that I didn't fight him back. For Christ's sake, I don't even know what got into me. The next thing I know we were here and he shoved me in the door so hard that I almost fell down out there." Mike shook his head in bewilderment. "I just don't know what the hell got into me that I let him push me around like that."

"Did you realize how upset you were, Todd?" Denton wanted to know.

"Sure I did," came the reply. "But didn't I have reason to be?"

"You were plenty uptight, baby," Mike told Todd, while a wide grin creased his face. "I don't know why in hell I think it's so goddamned funny now, but I swear to Christ this boy treated those people out in the hall to a sight they'll never see again even if they all live to be a hundred and fifty." Mike gave a huge burst of laughter. "Hell, their grandkids will be chuckling about it."

Denton smiled, and when he looked at Todd he wasn't surprised to see that Todd was smiling as well, albeit sheepishly. Todd nodded his head. "They're going to remember all right."

"And what about you, Mike?" Denton asked. "Will you remember?"

Mike laughed. "You bloody well know I will. I hope to God none of those people will remember me. On the other hand, I guess I really don't care. The thing is that it all happened so damned quickly that probably noone will really be able to recall anything other than how goddamned noisy Todd was." The smile left his face quickly. "The thing I really can't understand is how I let him pound on me and I didn't raise a hand to protect myself. It really bugs me that I let him beat on me without me doing one goddamned thing. And, Jesus, that's not like me at all. Believe it or not, I'm damned good with my fists."

"I wouldn't worry about it, Mike," Denton told him. "You were probably taken by surprise and didn't react as you normally would."

"That's for sure," Mike agreed.

"Anyway," Denton continued, "you don't look too much the worse for wear."

"No," Mike admitted. "I suppose I'm not."

"And you, Todd. How do you feel?"

"I guess more than anything I'm sorry I caused all the commotion. Still, at the time it seemed like the thing I had to do."

"Are you saying you're sorry this happened, Todd?" Denton wanted to know.

"Well, seeing how it turned out I guess I am."

"What do you mean by that?" Denton asked.

"I really don't know." He buried his face in his hands. "I don't know what I thought or what I expected. I thought I was doing right, but it seems that all I've done is to make a lot of damn noise out in the hall. Maybe what he said is right. Maybe I did make a bloody ass of myself." He raised his eyes so that he looked squarely at Denton. "I don't really know what to do now; or what to say now. I guess maybe I am sorry after all."

"But sorry for what?" Mike demanded. "Sorry that you pounded on me? Sorry that you made such a loud scene in the hall? Sorry that you even went into that restroom when you did?"

"I guess all that is true," Todd admitted.

"Or," Mike drawled, "are you sorry that you didn't come on over to my place after all?"

"Mike, I wonder if it wouldn't be better not to put words in his mouth," Denton said firmly.

"That's the point, doc. I don't think I'm putting words into his mouth."

Todd returned to his erstwhile occupation of staring at the floor.

"Todd," Denton said, "is there anything elese you would like to say?"

"I don't think so, Doctor White. I'm just all mixed up."

"We can let it drop at this point if you want to," Denton told him.

Mike interrupted: "I don't think we ought to let it drop at this point, doc. That is, if you want my honest opinion."

"What do you mean by that?"

"Well, I think there's a hell of a lot more to it than Todd is saying."

"But Todd doesn't want to say anything more."

"Could I say it for him?"

Denton fiddled with his pipe. "That wouldn't be up to me, Mike. Todd would have to go along with it. If you're going to talk for somebody, you have to have his permission first. Don't you think that's how it should be done?"

"Yes, I guess it is the right way," Mike admitted. "Only he's never going to get the nerve up to do anything about his problem."

"Right, but is it up to you to say that Todd has a problem?"

"Maybe yes, maybe no. I do think he owes me after all the hell he's caused me today. And I think the one way he can pay what he owes me is by telling you a lot about himself that he hasn't come up with yet. Hell, I'm trying to do him a favour. But like you say, it's up to him. I guess."

"And Todd is sitting there and we're talking about him almost like he wasn't here," Denton observed.

"Like a damned statue," Mike agreed.

"I just don't know what to do," Todd mumbled.

"Is it okay if I try to help him, doc?"

"It's up to Todd, don't you think?"

Todd shrugged his shoulders. "It's okay with me," he said.

"Well," Mike began, "I thought I'd get Todd over to my place. Yeah, I did have ideas about what we'd do once we got there. But like I said, I thought he was nervous about the restroom. At my place and after a few drinks he'd get over being nervous. Pure and simple. Then I thought we could have a little fun."

"I don't know why you'd think that," Todd said defensively.

"Oh, hell, Todd," Mike said. "Give up on that crap. Believe me, I'm trying to help. Look, I've been through all this myself. It's a tough go. But you're so damned stupid that you don't see I'm giving you a golden opportunity to talk to a man who can help you to know yourself better. If nothing else, Doctor White can probably help you to understand some of the ways you feel." Mike was almost pleading. "For Christ's sake, Todd. This man is a psychologist. He can help."

Denton sat back quietly, allowing the action to unfold before him. Denton could actually feel the tension rising in the room and felt a deep appreciation for the emotions both young men were experiencing. He knew that Mike was sincerely trying to help Todd, and Denton felt that Todd was beginning to react to a very special kind of hell he had been living in. But he didn't know this for a certainty, because Todd had yet to give words to his feelings. But all the nonverbal cues were there. As a psychologist Denton could be of most help by sitting back and allowing the tension to rise to a fast boil.

"Todd, tell me," Mike continued. "And be honest. Didn't you have a hard on while you were sitting on that seat? And didn't you show it to me?"

Todd continued to stare at the floor, refusing to answer Mike.

"Well, it's true. Todd had a hard on, and when I first looked under the partition he did everything but jack it off so I could get a better look. He crouched on the floor, but he didn't seem to want for me to touch him. I thought he needed a little more encouragement, so that's why I made a grab at him. Then he got back on the seat. And that's all there was to it. Except of course that I wrote him a note asking him to come over to my place." Mike turned to Todd. "Now isn't that what happened?"

Todd nodded, eyes glued to the floor.

Mike turned again to Denton White. "You know, doc, I guess I've got a lot of sympathy for Todd. I've been scared like he was many times. I guess maybe I was scared this afternoon and that caused me to let him beat on me the way he did. And sure, I would have liked to have gotten him to my place. Why the hell not? I've come to terms with myself. I've got damn few complexes. I guess I'm saying it right, because God knows I've spent enough hours with a psychiatrist who thought he could cure me of the sexual dysfunction he said I was manifesting. Shit. That dumb shrink!" Mike laughed. "He thought sure to god that he could cure me. Only his dumb cure wouldn't work because there sure as hell is nothing wrong with me. He just couldn't understand that I like sex with a man because there's aboslutely no responsibility over the long haul. What really screws it up is that I like women too. Sometimes better, sometimes not better. And why the hell should I not feel the way I want to feel? The shrink thought among my many other problems that I was oversexed. Well, maybe he's right if there is such a goddamn thing." Mike grew sober. "And yes, I get to restrooms all over the campus every once in a while. And you know what, doc? This isn't the first time I have run into Todd. He seems to get around to all of them too." He grew even more intense. "Sometimes he's in places when the action is going on. I've no clue whether he's ever gotten in on any action or not, because usually I'm involved with one damn thing or another." A wide grin reappeared on his face. "But I kind of suspect that old Todd just kind of fades into the background, wanting to get in on the action but scared shitless that he will. And that's one hell of a goddamn bad feeling. I know. I've been there." His eyes fairly beamed, matching the intensity of his voice. "It's a hell of a thing to have feelings that you're scared of death of having. That's what I want to say, and that's why I'm telling you all this. Believe me, I know Todd has these feelings."

"Todd?" Denton asked. "What do you think?"

Todd made no response to the invitation, so Mike continued. "I've been watching for Todd lately, although I didn't know his name. So when I saw him go into the restroom this afternoon, I simply followed and sat in the stall next to him."

Todd looked up. "You were waiting for me? Oh, God," he cried.

"Oh, hell, Todd. It's not that bad. And I wasn't waiting for you particularly. It's just that when I saw you go in I decided to go in after you."

"But I didn't see you," Todd protested.

"Perhaps you didn't, but that's just part of the game. You know, to see but not to be seen. And then there's the difference between you and me. I know my way around. You don't."

"I don't want to know my way around," he mumbled.

"That's what you say," Mike admitted. "But actions speak louder than words. You go where the action is. If you don't want any, you shouldn't go around. Only I think that you want action."

"You're putting words in his mouth again, Mike."

"Yes, I know I am. But I'm trying so hard to get him to see that this is really a great opportunity for him to develop some insight into the way he thinks and feels."

"Maybe he doesn't want insight, Mike," Denton admonished the youth. "Or maybe he's not ready to go into any of it. Is that how you feel, Todd?"

Todd looked up. "I really don't know how I feel, Doctor White."

"But you don't really feel like talking, do you? Or, maybe, you don't feel like talking in front of Mike?"

"No, that's not it."

"Well, would you like to talk?" Denton asked.

"I don't know how to begin," Todd replied simply.

"How can I help?" Denton prodded.

"I don't know that you can," he said.

"For Christ's sake, Todd," Mike argued, "let him try."

"I'd like to talk to you later, Doctor White. Not now. And I'd like Mike to be here when I come back. Is that okay? I just don't feel like I can go on right now. Is that okay?"

"Perfectly okay, Todd. When do you want to come back?"

"Tomorrow?"

"We'll make you an appointment on the way out. And Mike?"

"I'll make it," he said. "Even if I have to cut a class. I like coming out parties."

"I would make a judgment that that was a very unkind thing to say, Mike," Denton scolded him.

But Mike only smiled broadly in return.

"That's okay, Doctor White. And Mike." Todd turned to face the psychologist. "It's like he said: I owe him." He stuck out his hand to Mike, and the young men shook each other's hands firmly and with obvious feeling. "But it's going to be quite difficult. And that's why I want Mike here. I have a feeling he'll be able to help me out over the rough spots."

The prologue introduced two members of the group; the other five members were extended an invitation to join by Denton White, who also became a member by virtue of his role as trainer. The psychologist plays the role of the intervener in group design. He is the axis on the wheel while the members are the spokes which emanate from the centre. The interrelationships of the membership are circuitous, the axis not being a diffusion point but rather the core which welds and holds. The expertise and skill of the intervener is evident in group coalescence, but in other ways he is completely removed. Although a group does move towards some hazy and undefined goal, even this would be unattainable without the skill of the intervener. Deliberations without a leader are fraught with danger, because he is alert to the need for a re-direction when one becomes necessary.

Todd agreed to join the group only after being strongly encouraged to do so by Denton White. Mike Stewart welcomed the opportunity to join, telling Denton that it was an experience he had long sought. The other five members responsed to a personal invitation from Denton White, and there was initially varying degrees of enthusiasm vis-a-vis membership.

Although he might have wished for better physical facilities, Denton White had to settle for the space which the College made available. As a matter of fact, he had held groups in less desirable and less comfortable surroundings; yet he recognized that additional facilities such as a coffee bar remained a desirable addition. Yet the space was great. The room was long, almost rectangular in shape. For soundproofing the psychologist had begged and borrowed hundreds of cardboard egg cartons which he and students had stapled to the sides and walls of the room. The ceiling egg cartons were spray painted in a light yellow color while the wall egg cartons on all sides were treated to a dark blue spray. The one item on which he had splurged the college's funds was carpeting. Although the light blue carpeting was most assuredly not the finest that money could buy, it was of high quality. The placement of thick foam underlay made walking on the carpet a pleasure, much like walking through a heavily grassed pasture. Additionally, the carpeting and its underlay aided the soundproofing of the room.

Furniture in the room was deliberately sparse. One end of the room boasted a leather chaise lounge, placed at the end of a large comfortable sofa done in a paisley design of blue and green. End tables with huge table lamps boxed in the sofa. Placed facing the sofa were identical overstuffed chairs, one in solid red material and the other in yellow. In the middle of the room marking the spot at which the group would normally convene, eight wooden captain-style dining tables were spotted in a circle. An additional straight chair was placed in the circle, bringing the total of chairs in the circle to nine.

There was not a stick of furniture at the other end of the room, but a door was set dead centre. This door provided the only entry into the room, and opened into a hallway that was a continuation of the corridor running down the centre of the Counselling Service Office. The corridor passed Denton White's office and led eventually to the outer office where the receptionist's desk was placed.

The first meeting of the group was a chance for it to coalesce. Billed as an encounter group, it was that and nothing more. The young men sparred with one another, and the beginnings of freedom to express deep-seated convictions were made. It was a meeting where eight people encountered each other on the most veneer of psychological levels, but a base was laid for later gut-level work. The psychologist was the leader and the intervener, but he had as much to learn from the struggles of the group as they moved towards self-understanding and self-realization as any one member had. It was the collective experience that mattered.

Denton White had suggested to the men that the group be considered open-ended, in that it would continue to function for as long a time as the majority cared about each other and wanted to continue. A consensual agreement would suffice to discontinue meetings at any time, and, of course, each individual must feel the freedom to exit if and when his desires to leave emerged. The sole charge that Denton placed upon individual withdrawal was a statement to the effect that any member should, by allegiance to the group, give indication of his intent to leave and possibly his reason. In other words, he should feel required to discuss with the group his feelings.

The psychologist also suggested that the group meet once a week for a period not to exceed two hours.

Dr. White introduced a word to the group and defined it as an absolute. The word was "structure", and he spelled out very plainly that no defense against its use by him was to be tolerated. When the word was used, it meant that whatever was going on had to come to an immediate halt. The term could be inserted to stop dialogue or it could be used to force a discontinuance of a game. The most relevant thing, he told them in the most serious manner that he could muster, was that the word commanded immediate compliance. "You may never hear me use it," he concluded, "but if and when I do, remember that it is the one control that I have."

After the young men had been seated in the captain's chairs which were placed in a wide circle, Denton White explained his function as leader of the group. He enumerated five special duties and responsibilities which were uniquely his, and he suggested that the group make note of his comments. "I will not repeat them again," he smiled. "Not because there will be complete understanding, but because a responsibility which I particularly feel is not injecting myself in any way. Therefore, don't count on me for much of anything. Nevertheless, these are the five responsibilities which I feel are particularly mine. Okay?" He first stated that one of his duties had been partially fulfilled by the simple convening of the group. This came under the general heading of initiating procedure and membership, but a certain amount of continuance of this function would be necessary especially were he to be asked to suggest action steps or propose procedure. A second area of responsibility he delineated by the term regulating. This included summarizing discussion, when advisable, enforcing time limits and restating goals, if any were ever established. Another area of responsibility he termed informing, and clarified this by stating that this area indicated that he was the resource person upon whom the group could depend for any information it might require. A fourth area was designated as supporting, but he purposely avoided detailing the limits of this function. No one questioned him regarding the omission. A final area was noted as evaluation, and he suggested that this function would include testing for consensus within the group.

The work of the group began when Denton White noted the empty straight backed chair to his left. During the period in which the group was forming there had been a sort of contrived gaiety as to the purpose of the chair. Each individual had been told of the composition of the group. The consternation of the group members increased as it became obvious that Denton had taken the trouble to reserve it.

In detailing the role which he would play in the group and the limits which he set for his personal involvement, Denton White saved the explanation of the chair until the last. "You have all noted, with due concern I might add, that I've reserved a chair. It's on my left hand side, so we get away from the right hand business." There was general laughter at his somewhat sacrilegious remark. "Well, I want to give to this chair the name of the hot seat. It is a special place. It's a place where any one of you might want to be at any given time. It's the place to be when you have something you want to say that you think is of great significance. It puts you in a special position; if nothing else, it makes you the centre of attraction. You are free to go to it of your own choice. I might add that others in the group can call upon you to occupy it." He laughed heartily. "I guess it's somewhat ominous. But just let me say that you can develop a 'feel' for it."

Again, his words were greeted with a round of laughter.
"I think probably the best way for us to get started is for each of you to tell us something about yourself. It really doesn't matter what. Just something that you consider important about yourself in addition to your name. Okay?" Heads were nodded in response. "Let's begin with Frank."

Frank: (self-consciously) Well, my name is Frank Westcott. I'm a senior, majoring in psychology. I want to do graduate work, and I hope I can get a doctorate in counselling psychology. Let's see. What else? (looks quizically to Denton) Well, I'm twenty-three years old. I've been in the Air Force, and that's where I got married. I guess that's it.

Denton: Any questions? Anybody want to ask Frank anything. Stand up, Frank, and let us all see you. Anyone want to touch him, feel him, smell him? (Laughter) Frank is a real live human being, you know. And we all have senses other than sight. One of the things we want to learn to do in these sessions is to bring these other senses to bear. Don't be afraid to touch him. Any others? No? Well, okay, Frank. Be seated for now. (Surveying the group.) Mike, you're next since you're seated beside Frank. How about telling us something about you?

Mike: (stands in centre of circle) Well, my name is Mike Stewart. I'm a year older than Frank. I was in the Navy, and now I'm back in school. I was kind of wondering when Frank told us he was a senior how he moved along so quickly. I think I'm a sophomore but I really don't know how many course credits I've picked up. I kind of just move along. I guess. And I don't have a major picked out. Maybe something will occur to me one of these days. Okay?

Denton: Anybody want to ask Mike anything?

Mike: (sitting down) I guess they are afraid to ask me anything since all of them have a turn coming and don't know what I'll ask them if they have a prior go at me.

Denton: Could be, Mike, could be. But all in good time. These things take a while to get moving. We don't want to push. There's too much pushing in life as it is. That's one of the reasons we sometimes get alienated from each other. We are so much in the habit of defending ourselves from other people that we take on overtones of aggressiveness for ourselves. Anyway, let's move on to Carlos.

Carlos: I'm a Mexican-American, and I'm one hell of a long way from home. I'm originally from Brownsville, Texas. In case you never heard of it, it's a city on the border across from Matamoros, Mexico. I'm eighteen years old, and I'm in my first year. Probably I'll major in social work or sociology. Mike Stewart is my roommate.

Denton: I noticed you didn't stand up, Carlos. Anyone else notice that?

Frank: I didn't stand until you told me to. Maybe he was waiting to be asked.

Denton: Well, there's two things I would have to say to that, Frank. First, another one of the things we want to break down very quickly is any kind of ceremony or ritual. Forget being asked or not being asked. You can consider this group as a kind of laboratory experience where you try new forms of behaviour. Do what you want to do.

Frank: That's exactly what I am saying. Maybe Carlos didn't feel like standing.

Denton: Fair enough. I was just curious as to why he didn't. But my second point does have more validity. When I asked if anyone else noticed that he didn't stand, you responded, Frank, by replying directly to me. Why are we talking around Carlos?

Frank: (in an annoyed tone of voice) Dr. White, I think we are playing re-games with words. You were the one who asked if anyone noticed, so I replied directly to you. What was I supposed to say?

Denton: It's a legitimate point you are making, Frank. But if you remember, I said to Carlos that I noticed that he didn't stand. Then I asked if anyone else noticed, and then you replied. I think you might have added after your statement that you had noticed a question to Carlos as to why he didn't stand.

Frank: (shrugging) I still can't see it.

Denton: Okay, we'll leave it at that. But my point is that we don't want to perpetuate this thing - especially in this group - of talking around people.

We want to talk to them, and we want honesty of feeling. (Denton turns to Carlos) You have anything to add?

Carlos: No, I guess not. Only that I see what Frank means. I can't agree that he was talking around me.

Denton: But was he talking to you?

Carlos: No.

Denton: Well, then that gives us all something to think about. We can be with people and be the topic of conversation and still not realize that we are being excluded from the conversation. Perhaps that's an indication of how insensitive we can allow ourselves to become.

Frank: (laughs) I'll take your word, Denton. Right now I don't understand.

Denton: Okay, we'll leave it. But anyway think about it. Next on the list is Todd.

Todd: (stands in centre of group) I'm standing in the centre of the group because I feel I should stand in the centre of the group after that last exchange between Frank and Dr. White. (laughs) My name is Todd Callahan. I'm in my third year of studies at the University and I want to become an architect. I'm twenty-one years of age and I sometimes wonder if I'll make it through the University. I'm not a very bright student, I don't think at least; my studies are hard for me. I played hockey in high school and I guess what I'd really like to be is a professional hockey player. Only I'm not good enough and never could be. (stops to think) Oh, yes. I live at home. My dad's an attorney, and he and mother seem to be happy. I've got a younger brother and a younger sister, both in high school.

Denton: Good, Todd. You like living at home?

Todd: Not particularly. I'm anxious to get out.

Mike: (laughs) Haven't I seen you somewhere before?

Todd: You know bloody well you have, you bastard. (Denton waited to see if anyone picked up on the last exchange. When no one did, he motioned Todd to sit down.)

SESSION I

Joe: (taking Todd's place in the centre of the group) I'm with Todd. I'm standing here like a silly fool because I think its expected.

Denton: Would you rather not be there, Joe?

Joe: It's a bit uncomfortable, but I don't mind.

Frank: We seem to be geared to a format.

Denton: Right! And unconsciously so, wouldn't you think? It's almost like playing follow the leader.

Mike: Yes, I get that impression.

Frank: Well, as the one who started I guess I'm the leader. Only I don't feel like one.

Joe: Maybe not in that sense, Frank. But I feel I have to say the same things about myself that everybody else said.

Todd: That's exactly what I thought.

Denton: Well, maybe you can vary the main theme.

Joe: Right. (shrugs his shoulders) Only I don't know how. Anyway, I'm Joe Chambers. And I'm twenty years old. I live at home also. I'm thinking about law school someday; but if I don't get my grades up I'll never make it. I went to the same high school that Todd did, and I also played hockey. I never did have a thing about being a professional hockey player mainly because it didn't grab my interest all that much. It was a way of being noticed by the girls. They all love a hockey player and I decided I'd have to go that route if I wanted to make out. But I was good enough for high school, I guess.

Todd: Yeah, you made all-city.

Joe: So did you.

Mike: My God, we've got a mutual admiration society going.

Joe: (laughs easily) Looks like it, eh? Well, that's all I've got to say, so I'll go sit down.

A STRANGE BREED OF CAT

Denton: The next man in line is Rick Fischer.

Rick: (remains seated) Well, that's my name. Richard Fischer. Only I like to be called Rick. My thing in high school was swimming. I'm twenty years old, and I guess I'll go to law school too. But what I'd really like to do is to coach a swim team. Maybe I'll end up doing both.

Frank: Rick, why didn't you stand?

Rick: I didn't want to.

Frank: That's a good reason.

Denton: I would wonder, Rick, if the reason you didn't stand was because you felt that if you did you would simply be doing what was expected of you.

Rick: I didn't want to stand.

Denton: Yes, but the reason you didn't is what I'm after. And I am suggesting that the reason you didn't is because you felt that because it was something you should be doing, you simply wouldn't do it.

Mike: That seems to me to be a possible reason, Rick. I know that very often when I know something is expected of me, I do the opposite.

Rick: Okay. Big deal. So I'll stand now. (stands) Satisfied?

Denton: You shouldn't have stood up if you didn't want to, Rick.

Rick: It seems to me I'm dammed if I do and I'm dammed if I don't.

Denton: That's how it goes sometimes. And now, last but not least, Jim Harris.

Jim: (moves eaily into centre of room). The name is Jim Harris. I'm second year. This is my last year here. I'm going to Toronto next year to study fashion design. I know I'm good at sketching, and I want to get out of here anyway. It's inevitable I should leave, one way or another. I'm nineteen, and will be twenty next month. Let me add that I live at home with my mother and father and a younger sister. I don't like living at home. It's too restrictive to suit me. I want to get out just as soon as I can. (almost as if rehearsed) And my father is anxious for me to leave. He doesn't think I'm a proper son.

Todd: Why not proper?

Jim: Oh you know. I'm not a hockey player and I don't like a lot of things that he thinks I should like.

Mike: Girls, for instance.

Jim: (visibly caught off guard by Mike's abruptness, a large measure of poise drained from him. His reply was defensive to the point of belligerence.) Yes, girls for instance.

Denton: Good, Jim. How about taking your seat now and let me give some ground rules. Okay? Everyone has said something about himself, so you all know a little more about each other than before you came in. I guess. Anyway, it leaves me to say something about myself. I guess what I have to say is that I'm on the staff of the College. But let me say right away that for all practical purposes these sessions are not a college function. I have to say that and make sure you understand it, for this type of group activity is still relatively new on college campuses. I'm not saying that it shouldn't be done; all of you being here kind of tells you how I feel. But what I am saying is that this is neither a college-sponsored nor college-authorized activity. And each of you have to understand that. We're here for a purpose. That purpose is to get to know ourselves better by getting to know other guys one hell of a lot better. As we learn what makes other guys tick, we're bound to get a better picture of our own thinking. Now what this type of thing is called, like I told you, is a t-group. Others call these sessions sensitivity groups, but the term I like is encounter group. It all means pretty much the same thing. Basically, we are meeting as a group in order that we can tear into each other and learn more about ourselves in the process. We can learn to recognize signs and feelings, and become sensitive as a result of having a dynamic interplay one with the other. In this room there is freedom to say or do anything you want. Your feelings and emotions are on trial just like everyone else's. There is no way that I could spell it out any clearer, so I won't even try. You'll get the picture without all the spelling. Now, as I suggested a minute ago, this group is not a college function. It's each of us individually and all of us collectively. I should make clear that what goes on in this room is the exclusive property of the group, and must not ever be a subject for discussion away from the group. It's not a secret society in most senses, but in that one sense it is. Each person in this room owes every other person in this room a chunk of his life. An encounter group is not designed to be a mutual admiration society in which every one likes every one else; nor is it to be a back-slapping kind of thing. You can go to any party or any bar and join in a mutual admiration kick. But here you can have something else, so unique that the same sort of experience can never be yours again. The thing I'd like to stress to each of you is that participation in a group like this is somewhat akin to a good cook following a special recipe. You're only going to get out of it what you put in it, so you make damn sure you use special ingredients. You must not be afraid to bruise the other guy, and on the other hand you can't allow yourself the luxury of not being bruised yourself. And if you let it happen naturally, you will be bruised. And you'll learn something from it. And if you can get over the natural reluctance to bruise the other guy, you'll be able to do that too. And you'll learn from that also. And you'll wake up one day more aware, more sensitive, more in harmony with your fellow human beings. Okay? That's the name of the game as a matter of fact. Yet one very important thing to remember is that what you dish out in the group and what is dished out to you in the group is the exclusive property of the group. What happens here, happens here. Not outside. Remember that. Although it's a difficult trick, one of the first things to learn is how to compartmentalize your feelings. What you say to anybody else and what anybody else says to you in this room is a happening (or something) that has taken place here. It didn't take place outside the room. Okay. Therefore only experiences go out of the group, and the learning that has taken place as a result of those experiences. Got me? I guess finally what I'm saying is that in here you have the freedom as well as the responsibility to lay it on the line. But that goes for in here only. One last thing. I've tried to spell out that I'm not a real member of the group, but yet I'm here anyway. So in a way that makes me some kind of a member. Anyway, my name is Denton. Okay?

Frank: I've called you Dr. White for so long now that I'm conditioned to it. It's going to be hard to switch to Denton.

Denton: Don't count on it, and don't force it. Here we're all for one and one for all, and the name will come easy as soon as the group gets moving. In the meantime, don't call me anything if you feel better about it.

Frank: Yeah, sure. Well, anyway, Denton, what's the special significance of the hot seat?

Denton: I guess you could term it a special significance. Anyway, it's a gimmick used that insures that whoever is occupying it is recognized by all members of the group as being in a special position in reference to the group. Literally, the guy occupying it is facing up to a hot spot.

Frank: Oh.

Denton: What does the "Oh" mean, Frank? Does it mean you understand?

Frank: I guess so. (an afterthought) No! not really.

Denton: That's okay. There's a lot of things in life people don't really understand but they live with it nonetheless. Shall we put it down that you'll live with this? And hopefully eventually understand.

Frank: Sure, Lord knows, there's plenty I don't understand. What's one more thing?

Denton: Well, I suspect one way of explaining it is to show you how it works. Frank, how about you being the first occupant of the hot seat?

Frank: (shrugs, but laughs) It figures. I should have remained quiet.

Denton: You'll see. It's not that bad. It's show-and-tell time, Frank. You just sit there, and the guys will tell you what they pick up from you. You can keep still or you can argue. Okay? Whatever you want to do.

(Frank nodded his head, but he wasn't really sure why he was nodding.)

Denton: We'll go in turn, starting with Mike.

Mike: I don't know what to say.

Denton: What would you like to say?

Mike: Well, he looks scared as hell.

Denton: Tell Frank, not me.

Mike: You look scared as hell, Frank.

Frank: Okay, I'll accept that. To be truthful, Mike, it feels pretty damn strange sitting here not knowing what any of you guys are going to say.

Denton: What's the worst thing any one could say, Frank?

Frank: I don't know, Denton. None of them know me.

31

Denton: Does that mean that if they did they would have bad things to say about you?

Frank: No one is perfect; everyone's got good and bad about him.

Denton: Want to tell us all about your bad side?

Frank: (laughs) No.

Denton: Okay, Mike. Go on.

Mike: Can I pass?

Denton: Sure. Any time. Jim?

Jim: Not knowing anything about Frank yet, I'd say he has a friendly look about him. He looks smart and he dresses sharp. Okay? (Denton recognized that Jim was "stroking" Frank. Stroking is a form of support. In this case, Denton reasoned that Jim was laying the groundwork for Frank to say good things to him in turn. It was all an expression of Jim's anxiety.)

Denton: Carlos?

Carlos: I'd like to pass. Can I?

Denton: Sure. Todd?

Todd: Frank, are you sure you don't want to tell us something bad about you? That way I'd have something to latch on to.

Frank: (becoming more comfortable) That's for me to know and for you to find out.

Todd: You're making it difficult.

Frank: Being on the hot seat is hard enough. You've got an easy job. All you have to do is say something. I've got to anticipate what you say.

Todd: Why?

Frank: Well, keep one jump ahead is a good motto.

Todd: Oh. Well, in that case, I pass.

Denton: Joe?

Joe: Damn, I hardly know the guy.

Denton: What difference does that make? You'll know him sooner or later. Sooner, if you guys will get on with it. You're treating Frank like something that will fall to pieces if you don't handle it delicately.

Frank: Thanks, I think.

Denton: Joe, you were going to say something but what you did say was something in the form of an apology. In advance, huh? But what were you going to say?

Joe: Well, okay. I was going to say that Frank doesn't look as scared to me as he looks like he's awfully pleased with himself. And I just wonder why he is pleased with himself.

Denton: Ask him.

Joe: Okay. Frank, why are you pleased with yourself?

Frank: Maybe it's because I'm nearing the end of school.

Joe: Maybe. But you're doing graduate work. That doesn't necessarily mean you're near the end.

Frank: True. But that's another story.

Joe: Okay. That does it for me. I will have to pass.

Rick: I was getting ready to say the same thing as Joe. I think you look pretty damn smug, Frank.

(Frank laughed, but it was hollow. Rick was smiling in a fashion that can best be described as a leer. His tone was conciliatory. Denton thought it sounded as if he were almost begging Rick to lay off.)

Rick: You look okay physically, Frank. It's that damn smugness. You know. Like the cat that swallowed the canary. And hell, I think I know why. You got things going for you. You've got a wife to put you through school. That's it, isn't it? That's why you think you're so much better than everybody else.

Frank: What the hell is the difference between having a wife put you through school or having your parents do it? (He was very defensive.) It seems to me to be six of one and a half-dozen of another.

Rick: Oh, hell, there's a difference. I don't go to bed with my parents.

Mike: Maybe Frank doesn't go to bed with his wife.

Frank: (ignores Mike) Maybe what you say is true about going to bed with my mealticket. But she knew that this would be the way we'd get through before she married me. Hell, we were in love and didn't want to wait. If she were here, she'd tell you the same thing. She wanted to work while I finished school. Besides, I'll be supporting her once I get through.

Jim: A Ph.D. is a long way off.

Frank: We'll make it.

Rick: I'm sure you will.

Denton: Okay, Frank. Go back to your seat. It's Mike's turn. (Mike moved eagerly to the hot seat. If he had any reticence about occupying the position, it didn't get broadcast in his movement. He projected an air of great confidence.)

Frank: The only thing that bothers me about you, Mike, is that you said you haven't made any plans for the future.

Mike: I'm a free soul, Frank baby. Something will occur to me. Don't worry about it.

Frank: Personal growth requires planning. There's an old Chinese proverb that says the seeds of tomorrow are planted today.

Mike: Great God! What else did Confucius say?

Frank: I'm not even sure Confucius said it, Mike. But okay, if you want to be a man of mystery, we can leave it at that.

Mike: Hell, I'm no man of mystery. Ask me anything. It won't faze me. I guarantee it. But as for as what I'm going to do, I just sure as hell don't know anything positive about that. What's the big deal in knowing in advance what you're going to wind up doing anyway? Like I said, something will occur to me. When it does, I'll know if I think it's right or not. If it continues to be right for me, I'll keep swinging with it. If it's not, I'll move along. Hell, there's no mystery there. At least, not for me there isn't.

Frank: But you're only half-right. I contend that you still have to plan for change. And you're not planning. All I'm saying is, you've got to plan in order to meet the challenges of the Future. If you plan, problems won't come as a big surprise.

Mike: Ah, bug off, Frank. Or are you trying to tell us that you planned getting married so that your wife could put you through school? What the hell are you? A professional student?

Frank: Damn. What's this preoccupation with my wife? You guys! First Joe, then Rick, then you. And again you. Gee! Is it a problem that you guys aren't married?

(All three began to respond at once. But the cacaphony produced nothing. Frank listened to the trio of voices coming his way, and half-heartedly threw back comments.)

Mike: You're too structured, Frank. You like everything in a nice box. Maybe even with a ribbon marking that the whole bit is a gift. I don't. Okay?

Frank: Okay, it's your life. If you don't want to plan for the future, it's up to you.

Mike: You're damn right.

Jim: I know Mike. He's a great guy.

Mike: Thanks, Jim.

Carlos: (mocking) Thanks, Jim. You didn't expect him to say anything else, did you, Mike? Oh, God!

Mike: What in hell is that supposed to mean?

35

Carlos: Let's keep it private.

Mike: Why the hell for? The trouble with you, Carlos. is that you don't give Jim a break. He wants to be friends with you.

Carlos: Friends? With me?

Mike: Hang a label on it. Anything you want.

Jim: Hell, I want to be friends with everybody.

Carlos: I bet you do. But especially with Mike. Right?

Jim: Why not? But also with you. So have your turn, eh?

Carlos: Shit, I pass.

Todd: All I want to say to Mike is that I'm sorry. You're right. I did make a damn fool of myself.

Mike That's okay, Todd. I make an ass of myself every once in a while. It's par for the course when you're human.

Todd: That's all I have to say.

Joe: It's a difficult act to follow. First, Mike and Carlos have a round. Then Todd apologizes to Mike. I don't get it. So I pass.

Rick: In spades. I pass too.

Denton: Okay. I guess Mike can move out of the hot seat now unless somebody has something else to say.

Joe: Like I said, I'm so damned confused at this point that I couldn't even ask a sensible question.

Rick: Agreed. There's a lot going on that I don't know about.

Denton: Would you like to?

Rick: I suppose.

Denton: You suppose you would? But you don't know for sure, eh?

Rick: (laughs) At this point I think I would have to say I'd like to know.

Denton: Are you thinking that if you wait awhile the different pieces will fall in place?

Rick: Something like that.

Denton: Fair enough. Okay, let's move on and let Jim have his place in the hot seat.

(Jim stole a glance at the door leading out of the room. He appeared to be indecisive as to whether to take the path to the door or the few steps to the straight backed chair. Courage won out over cowardice as he lowered himself into the chair. He looked at Mike who in the meantime had moved back into his chair in the circle. They returned friendly smiles to each other. It had the effect of bolstering Jim's courage.)

Frank: Jim, what's between you and Carlos? Did you know each other before today?

Jim: Oh, sure.

Frank: Then what gives?

Jim: Ask him when he gets up here.

Frank: But you must have some kind of an idea?

Jim: I do.

Frank: Then?

Jim: Well honestly I'm not sure. But I think it's because he thinks I'm trying to get Mike to move in with me.

Frank: Oh?

Jim: Well, I think that's it. Like I said, I've been wanting to move away from home. I don't dig it there. I met Mike. We hit it off okay. I need a roommate if I'm going to be able to swing leaving the house. So, there you have it.

Frank: And this is why Carlos has it in for you?

Jim: Mainly I think.

Frank: Well, have you tried to get Mike to move in with you?

Jim: Sure, I know we'd get along great.

Frank: But wouldn't that leave Carlos without a roommate?

Jim: Sure would. But I don't think that's my problem.

Frank: True enough. The guy is old enough to make up his own mind.

Jim: That's how I see it.

Frank: And Mike agreed to move in with you. Away from Carlos, I mean?

Jim: No, he said that he'd try to talk Carlos into letting me move in with them.

Carlos: (interrupting) Mike never told me anything like that.

Mike: Only because you wouldn't even listen to me when I started to talk to you.

Frank: Hell, I pass.

Mike: What the hell is there for me to say? I guess I'll have to pass.

Carlos: (angrily) I will too. I'm not going to waste my breath with that one.

Todd: Well, I guess I should wait for Carlos to move up there. But maybe you can answer me. I'd like to know why you and Carlos can't be friends.

Jim: I don't see any reason. Carlos makes me mad as hell because he won't even give me a chance to be friends with him.

Carlos: Maybe we could be friends, Jim, if you hadn't tried such a high-handed deal.

Todd: (to Denton) Can I pass this back to Carlos? He's already passed but it looks like he might want to change his mind.

Denton: If it's okay with everyone for Carlos to move back into line, it's all right. Do you, Carlos?

Carlos: Might as well.

Denton: Any objections from anybody? Okay, Carlos. Go right ahead.

Carlos: (angrily) You tried to get Mike to move in with you and you weren't even going to talk with me about it.

Jim: First, Carlos, you don't own Mike. Second, you don't know what the hell either Mike or I was going to say to you. All you did was overhear Mike and me talking about sharing a pad. Mike had already said that he wasn't going to move out on you, but that maybe we could all share a place together.

Carlos: I didn't hear that.

Jim: No, you didn't hear it. You just heard a little bit, and then you jumped to all kinds of conclusions.

Carlos: Well, I had trouble enough before Mike and I moved in together. I mean, there was just no money. Then you showed up Friday night, and you can't tell me that it was the first time you and Mike had ever met each other.

Jim: I'm not trying to tell you that. Hell, I'd tell you anything if you'd just listen.

Carlos: I listen.

Jim: Like you're doing now?

Carlos: Well, I didn't know about the other part.

Jim: And you didn't seem to want to hear it Friday night. All you were doing was yelling at me to get the hell out of your god-damn apartment.

Carlos: Okay, I admit it. But it's all water under the bridge now as far as I'm concerned. What's done is done. I pass.

Todd: I still don't know if the bitch between you guys is resolved. Is it?

Jim: Hell, you'll have to ask Carlos.

Todd: I will, when he gets up there. I pass.

Denton: I'd like to ask it now if I may, Carlos?

Carlos: I get mad, but I get over it.

Denton: That doesn't tell me anything.

Carlos: (shrugging his shoulders) Time will tell.

Denton: That's not good enough. Are you two guys willing to try something that might get these feelings out of the way sooner?

Jim: Why not?

Carlos: It's okay with me.

Denton: Okay. Both you guys stand in the middle of the circle.

(Jim moved to a position opposite Carlos, both facing one another.)

Denton: All right. Carlos. Jim. Close your eyes. Now, move closer in to one another. That's right. Now, reach out with your hands and let your fingertips run over temples first; then move your fingertips along the face. What you're doing is "seeing" each other through tactile perception. You can pick up maybe some different ideas about one another by "feeling"; in other words, get all these words out of the way.

(Neither of the young men had yet moved.) Okay, get moving now. Think of someone you've known in the past and have some pleasant association with. Try to relate the perceptions you're getting now with those other ones. Keep your eyes closed.

(Carlos' hands moved away from his sides. What had been clenched fists were now open hands, fingertips outstretched. The tips of his fingers came to rest on Jim's face. Then they glided up and found his temples. Jim followed suit. The two young men stood facing each other. Each had his eyes closed. A communication was made between them via fingertips.)

Rub, using a gentle clockwise motion.
(Without a moment's hesitation, both began the movements with their fingers. Almost immediately a harmony of movement was reached. The upturned faces of the other members of the group watched the unfolding action with great attention.)

Denton: What are you thinking, Jim?

Jim: It's a good feeling.

Denton: Carlos?

Carlos: I like it. I think he's trying to tell me that I'm okay.

Denton: Oh? And what are you telling him?

Carlos: Same thing.

Denton: Good. You see, with words out of the way you can get down to the gut level of feelings. It makes a bit of difference, a large bit. Words are what get most of us in trouble. A lot of times it's a lot better if we back off from a situation and try to feel it rather than think it through. (He checked out the expressions on the faces of the other members of the group to see if anyone wanted to take issue with his words. There appeared to be total cognition and understanding.) Well, now. Carlos. Jim. You can stop now if you want, or you can go on. Makes no difference.

(Carlos hands dropped to Jim's shoulders. He gave several firm squeezes which Jim accepted with obvious relish. Jim rubbed his hand in a friendly fashion over Carlos' head. Carlos opened his eyes first. Without- comment he moved back to his seat in the circle.)

Jim: And I go back to the hot seat?

Denton: Yeah. You go back. You have a comment, Todd?

Todd: Gee, I have nothing to say. I just don't have a thing to say.

A STRANGE BREED OF CAT

Denton: Okay.

Joe: I've got a question for you, Carlos. When Denton asked you what you were thinking, you told him "it feels good." Right? First, what felt good?

Carlos: Well, I guess the pressure on my head.

Joe: Okay, I can buy that. I've had that done in the barber's chair, and I agree it feels good. But I guess my next question covers it a little better. I don't know how to say it anyway but to just come out with it. So here it is. Didn't you feel a bit silly letting him do that to you?

Carlos: It didn't even occur to me that it was silly. Denton said to do it, so I did it.

Joe: Okay, Denton told you to. But you mean to sit there and tell me that you didn't think the whole damn thing was silly as hell?

Carlos: No, I didn't. Like I said, Denton said to do it.

Joe: Let me put it this way. You said you don't like the guy, and it may be that you had reason. Hell, I don't even know what I think about that. But anyway, you don't like the guy. Yet you get up, let him put his hands all over your face and damn if you don't do the same thing to him. Okay, it's because Denton told you to do it and we're supposed to do what he tells us to do if we're going to profit from this. Now I buy that. But I still want to know, didn't you feel silly as hell?

Carlos: The answer is that I didn't even think about it.

Joe: Now that you think about it! Now don't you feel silly as hell?

Carlos: I don't know. But I don't think so. Like I said it was a good warm feeling. It was like someone was telling me that he liked me and that he cared for me. And it was a nice warm feeling.

Frank: Jim, how did you feel?

Jim: I guess, maybe the same way Carlos said he felt.

Joe: Christ. It doesn't seem that two grown men could massage each other's temples and get good feeling from doing it. Hell, here's two guys who

42

were raising hell just a few minutes ago. But they get out in the middle of the goddamn floor and rub each other's face and then they discover that they are good friends. I don't get it.

Denton: I don't think they've discovered they're good friends, Joe. But I think they have discovered that there are different ways that an individual can learn to handle his hostility. This is one of them.

Joe: I'm sure I'd feel better if I had just hauled off and let my fist feel a solid jaw.

Denton: That's you, Joe. That's most people. That's what we've learned to do with hostility. Strike out. Hurt if possible. Get hurt if we're not careful. And what does it prove?

Joe: What do you mean what does it prove? What's to prove? If a guy pisses me off, I just want to slug him good.

Denton: Rather than trying to understand why he pisses you off?

Joe: Oh, I guess I could say sometimes I try to understand, but my main thing is to slug him.

Denton: But I again ask you, what does it prove? After all the slugging is over, do you make friends?

Joe: Most of the time guys shake hands.

Denton: And each goes away nursing a grudge of some kind.

Joe: Well, the winner doesn't. At least I don't think he does.

Denton: How about the loser, Joe?

Joe: Maybe he does. I don't know.

Denton: You've never lost a fight?

Joe: I've got good sense. I never get in a slugfest unless I feel I've got it made.

Denton: That's good honesty, Joe. But you're evading my point. I'm asking if the loser doesn't bear a grudge.

Joe: Oh, I suppose he does.

Denton: So, what does it prove? Right here we have neither fellow bearing a grudge. And we've got both of them thinking that maybe there's a way out of their argument after all. At least there's a much greater statistical probability of honest settlement. Don't you see?

Joe: Well, it does make a little more sense now than before you explained it. I can see where maybe it works.

Denton: It does work, Joe.

Joe: Okay. But at the time, it kind of turned me off. You know what I mean?

Mike: Xenophobia. Fear of the new, the strange, and the different.

Rick: Well, I say what Joe said. It turned me off too.

Joe: Let me say just one more thing, Rick. (to Denton) Okay, I buy what you say. You know, about maybe there being a better way to express hostility than with fists.

Denton: Or curse words.

Joe: Or curse words. But the part that bothers me is that they were rubbing each other's heads, Doctor. For Christ's sake. What I mean is, okay, here in the group we can try it out and see if it works. In this case I might even say it did. Although I don't know how I would react. Probably not in the same way. Knowing me. Anyway, for Christ's sake. Can't you see a man doing this out on the street somewhere when he has a tiff with someone? Hell, he'd be packed off to the looney farm. Wouldn't he?

Denton: But a lot of things come out of laboratory experiments, Joe.

Joe: You consider this a laboratory experiment then?

Denton: Not as you are thinking I mean it, Joe. It's a laboratory in that each of us has something to learn about how to relate to other people. What you can come up with in here there's a chance you can modify for use out of the group. Do you understand?

Joe: I guess so.

Denton: Well, trying is all a man can do. And there's another thing. Everybody's a different breed of cat. Right? Your understandings and perceptions are not going to be the same as anybody else's. After perceptions filter through what you've gotten through learned experiences, it becomes a sure thing that the distortion that results is going to cause you to have a different outlook from someone else who has a different kind of a filter. Right?

Joe: I guess so, doc. But you'll have to face the fact that I'm what you guys call a slow learner. (He grinned widely.) But I'm going to try to learn.

Denton: Good boy, Joe. Just stay with us.

Rick: Okay, I'll start again. Like I said, I kind of thought like Joe. It seems strange to me too.

Frank: But hell, Rick, it's like Denton said. It doesn't have to be strange. He pointed out that words get in the way. Sometimes it's a hell of a lot better to show than it is to tell. At least that's the way I get it.

Rick: Maybe, but how in the hell do you go about rubbing people's heads trying to show you want to be friends with them? (After he finished the sentence, he became convulsed with laughter; and the laughing was contagious.)

Denton: Well, of course we all see what you mean. And I tried to explain it once. But let me try it again. You probably can't do it with the vast majority of people. Here we are a special group of people working at a very special project. There is more understanding, huh? But even so, the most important thing to learn is that there are different ways in which feelings can be expressed, and some are better than others. This is one of them. When you get real angry at someone, maybe it's true that you can't reach over and rub their head to try to soothe away the hostility. But maybe, just maybe, you can imagine yourself doing this to the other person. Who knows? Some of your own venom might get lost in the shuffle. Huh? Wouldn't this be great?

Joe: It might be. But suppose while you have your eyes closed thinking about how you're rubbing the hostility away from the other guy, he reaches out and slugs you. (Joe's question was greeted with laughter, but he himself was very serious.) No, I think it's a good question, I really want to know.

Denton: Trusting is the answer. You have to trust before like or love can come in the picture. Now, some people aren't used to being the recipient of trust. These are the kind who will strike out at you if they get half the chance.

Joe: So what do you do about them? Provided, of course, that you can tell them?

Denton: Pure and simple, Joe. You trust everybody. Being open and trusting has disadvantages in that it really leaves the door wide open for somebody to get to you. If they want to, that is. The only thing I can tell you is that if somebody does take advantage of a trusting nature once you have been committed to the concept itself, then you are aware that this one person needs help in overcoming fears that he has which causes him to strike out.

Frank: And then it's your duty to help him?

Denton: Not necessarily. It's up to you then what you want to do with it. You can help or you can become wary. It's one of the decisions that comes along with the whole ball of wax.

Joe: I think I'm beginning to see.

Rick: I wish I could say the same.

Frank: The entire message, Rick, is that man can transcend the physical.

Rick: What does transcend mean?

Joe: Oh, come on, Rick. You know what transcend means. It means to go above. You're just being difficult. (Rick muttered something, but it was obvious no one understood him. Yet no one thought it important enough to ask what he had said. Denton observed this, but spoke not a word.)

Rick: (in a voice loud enough for everyone to hear) I pass.

SESSION I

Jim: A hell of a lot of good it did for me to go back to the hot seat.

Frank: What does that mean?

Jim: Well, it means that everybody talked around me. I wasn't even in the conversation, let alone being in the centre spot.

Frank: Oho! So you're telling us you like to be the centre of attention.

Jim: Oh, go screw yourself. That's not what I meant, and you know it; you keep thinking that you're some kind of latter-day Sigmund Freud. (Jim moves back into his chair, but appears to be very sullen.)

Mike: (smiles) So it's Todd's turn then.

Todd: A game of musical chairs, this. (Sits in hot seat.)

Frank: Looks to me as if you think the chair really is hot.

Todd: What's this you said about not knowing what to expect? Why should I be different from you?

Frank: You know, Todd. The way you come across to me is that you try to be the strong silent type. That's the role you try to play, eh?

Todd: I don't know if I'd agree to that.

Frank: It doesn't matter to me whether you agree or not. That's the way you come across to me.

Carlos: He just doesn't come across to me at all.

Mike: Yeah, Carlos. You've said that.

Frank: But I haven't finished yet. I've said that you try to come across as the strong silent type, Todd. Only you don't quite make it. I bet that right now your gut is acting up on you.

Todd: (defensively) If it is, I don't know about it.

Frank: Oh, hell, Todd. You're scared all the time. You're scared right now. That's what I mean.

Todd: Comes out the same way. Anyway, I'm sure as hell not scared of you, Frank.

Frank: So you reduce it to a personal level. Which means you are scared of something. I pass. (Disgustedly.)

Mike: (to Frank) How come all of a sudden you got a hard on for Todd?

Frank: Who says I got a hard on for him? I asked him a question, and he was evasive as hell.

Mike: You know, Frank, for a budding psychologist, you're stupid as hell. How many people do you think are running around who are able to objectively analyze their own fears? (Having made his point, he turned back to Todd) I pass.

Carlos: So do I.

Joe: I don't, Todd. I want to know what in hell you meant awhile ago when Mike was on the hot seat and you told him that you were sorry. What were you sorry about?

Todd: It's between Mike and me, Joe. Sorry. It's none of your business.

Joe: The hell it isn't. Dammit, you're on the hot seat and that gives you a special obligation to answer my question. And by God, I asked you a question.

Todd: And I said it was none of your goddamned business, Joe. Go fuck yourself.

(Joe was set back for a second, but then his face flushed and he got a stunned look on his features.)

Joe: You said what?

Todd: I said it was none of your goddamned business, and that you should go fuck yourself.

Joe: You son of a bitch. And we've known each other for such a goddamn long time. (Joe turned to Denton) Hey, if he's on the hot seat how can he get off not answering one of my questions?

Denton: I don't know, Joe. Why don't you ask him?

Joe: Hell, I did. And everybody heard what the mother told me.

Todd: Wise up, Joe. Don't press it too far.

Joe: (sneers) Big man!

Frank: I personally think he has to answer.

Mike: Oh, clam up, Frank.

Joe: Look, buddy. Are you going to answer me or not?

Todd: Nothing personal, Joe. But I'm not going to answer you.

Joe: All I can say is that you are one sorry-assed bastard.

Todd: If that's the way you feel, I'll repeat what I said a minute ago. Go fuck yourself.

Joe: (To Denton) Hell, man. That's not right. I thought the hot seat guaranteed honesty.

Denton: No such thing, Joe. It guarantees that the guy sitting in it is made to feel a hell of a lot of pressure. I know it's hard to accept, Joe. But maybe Todd doesn't feel he can be that open with you yet. He gave you an answer. even if it was an indirect one.

Joe: Well, you're right. It was an answer. A shitty one, but an answer nonetheless. So I'm going to pass. (Joe narrowed his eyes at Todd) I guess it's okay for you to tell me that in here, buddy, so there'll be no hard feelings on my part. But I lay you odds that if you ever say a thing to me like that outside this room, I'll wipe up the goddamn floor with your ass. Get me? (Joe was tall, dark and muscular. And now his muscles were rippling with rage. His eyes were like slits, but fire gleamed from them.)

Rick: Well, it seems to me that when you start reading between the lines you find that Mike is in the middle of a lot of things.

Mike: (laughs) Seems that way, doesn't it? But let me tell you something, baby. You want to know something? You just ask.

Rick: Him? Or you?

Mike: I'm a little guy, remember? It's probably safer with me.

Joe: Hell, Rick. You're not going to get anywhere. Just go on and pass.

Rick: Sure, why not. But even so, I'd like to ask Todd the same question as Joe.

Mike: That figures.

Todd: (laughs) You'll get the same goddamn answer.

Rick: I ask the same question and I get the same answer. Right?

Todd: Right.

Rick: Seems to me I'm getting screwed.

Mike: Again, that figures.

Joe: What in hell does all these "it figures" mean?

Mike: Look, Joe. Work it out for yourself. You're going to have to learn that I don't explain things as good as Denton does.

Rick: Let it alone, Joe. I've got it all figured out anyway.

Frank: Well, why don't you let all of us in on it?

Rick: Do you think that Todd and Mike are the only ones who can play the secrets game?

Jim: (sweetly) Oh no, we don't think that at all. I for one bet you and Joe have all kinds of delicious little secrets.

Joe: Oh, Christ. Listen to him.

Todd: (To Denton) Well, it looks as if I've gone the full circle. Can I go back to my regular chair?

Denton: (nods) That seems to be the end of it, Todd. (Todd moves back to his chair)

Denton: Joe?

(For a minute it looked like Joe wouldn't get up. He looked around at the members of the group, and he had anger written around his eyes. Finally, he got up and moved to the chair. His movement combined with a fierce countenance to spell out that he was in no mood for any crap.)

Frank: You're displaying a lot of hostility, Joe.

Joe: Shit, Rick told the bunch of you. Now I tell you. Those four guys are like a bunch of girls with their goddamn secrets.

Frank: And this bothers you?

Joe: (exploded) Bothers me? Hell, yes, it bothers me. And it would bother you too if you had any balls. Christ! They're going around playing like a bunch of silly virgins.

(Mike roared, and Jim joined in the laughter at Joe's expense. Carlos broke his reverie to give a thin smile, but Todd glowered at Joe.)

Frank: So what? Even if they've got secrets from us, what difference does it make? Maybe none of us trusts each other enough yet to start baring our souls, so to speak. But to call them 'girls' and 'silly virgins' is pretty stupid in my opinion.

Joe: What? You calling me stupid?

Frank: No, I'm not calling you stupid. I said your words were stupid. There's a difference.

Joe: Same thing, buddy. And I'm telling you the same as I told Todd. Watch your fucking step.

Frank: Joe, I don't want to argue with you. Be reasonable. Okay? All I'm asking is why you used the term foolish virgins?

Joe: Yeah, but you made me mad asking it.

Frank: Okay, but what about me? Hell, you even said I had no balls.

Joe: I said that it would bother you if you had balls.

Frank: Same difference.

Joe: Okay. But I'm bigger than you are. (Joe laughed through perfectly even teeth.) Okay, Frank. I get your message. I'm sorry.

Frank: Accepted. Now will you answer?

Joe: Sure. They remind me of silly-assed girls who go around letting guys lay them but only after they put out a lot of crap about how you're the first one and how you're never to tell anybody. All that kind of shit. You know.

Frank: (laughing) Fuck them and leave them, Joe. Eh? Is that your motto?

Joe: It'll do until a better one comes along. Believe me, I make out okay.

Frank: Okay. You make out okay.

Rick: Right, and I can vouch for that. (sneers at Frank) You see, he didn't have to get married to get tail.

Frank: What the hell?

Rick: It makes me vomit to see Joe apologizing to you. As far as I'm concerned you're a smart aleck son of a bitch.

Frank: What the hell did I do to you?

Rick: Like I said, it hits me in the gut to see Joe apologize to a know-it-all bastard like you.

Frank: I think all of this is crazy as hell.

Todd: Everybody's got his feeling on his sleeve.

Joe: You're a hell of a one to talk.

Todd: But what did Frank do?

Rick: Well, look at his parting shot. (mimics) Fuck them and leave them, eh? Is that your motto, Joe?

Joe: (Laughs) Like I said, I make out okay.

Rick: And what's more, I know what he says is true.

Mike: What the hell? You follow your buddy around from bed to bed counting the number of pieces he gets. What in hell is your trouble?

Frank: (Laughs very loudly) With that I pass.

Mike: And so it's my turn. (Sarcastically) So you're one of those hot studs we read all about in those plain wrapped books on the newsstand. You know, tall, dark, and handsome. Lots of muscles all over. Suave and sophisticated. A broad chest buried beneath black virile hair. Hot balls and hot lips. Not a single member of the female sex safe from your charms. Poor Joe. Balling from one bed to another, and only his buddy Rick knows how overworked the poor stud is.

Joe: Who flipped your switch, wise-ass? Last I heard these two guys over here were fighting about who was going to live with you. Tell me that that action doesn't stink to high heaven.

Mike: It looks like we have a lot in common, Joe. Like you said, these two guys are fighting over me and you've got a buddy dragging ass behind you wiping up and keeping score.

(Rick jumped up from his chair. But he had second thoughts about taking on Mike by himself, and Joe hadn't moved. So he sat quietly back down.)

Joe: For a little man, you talk plenty big.

Mike: Like you, Joe baby, I find I can always back it up.

Joe: You know what, Mike. I'll tell you what I think. I think it's damned funny how Callahan apologizes to you and won't tell us why; and I think it's damned peculiar that both Vaca and Harris want to live with you. Just what have you got, buddy?

(Mike deliberately rubbed the fly on his pants. His hand movement was slow and deliberate, so that Joe could not in any way miss the message.)

Mike: Just about anything you want, baby. You pin a label on it, and you can have all you want.

Joe: Shit, buddy, I think you're queer as hell.

Mike: Now, that's a happy and friendly note.

Joe: Alright then. Suppose you tell me where in hell you get off making all those bad jokes about my being such a stud. Can you give me chapter and verse about how you make out with the chicks?

Mike: Vicarious living is no fun, Joe. That's what I was trying to tell your buddy Rick. Nonetheless, I do things. Not talk about them. (He again let his face be wreathed in a broad smile.) There is a difference, you know.

Joe: Only it's not with girls that you make out, buddy. Otherwise you wouldn't be so damned reluctant to talk about them.

Mike: It's a commitment, Joe baby. You owe it to your fellow human being not to kiss and tell.

Joe: Kiss and blow, you mean.

Mike: (shrugging his shoulders) Okay. Go on thinking you're superior. You sure as hell believe that man is superior to woman. You sure as hell believe that a guy can kiss and tell his buddies, but that the goddamned broad better keep her mouth shut.

Joe: I don't give a good goddam what the broad does.

Mike: Yeah, it shows. Joe, you've got a goddamn superiority complex.

Joe: In your terms, buddy, maybe I do. I sure as hell know when I am in a superior position to a woman. And in case you don't know, that's when I'm laying on top of her and pumping a hard cock into her. I'm giving her something that she wants and doesn't have, and she's giving me something I want and haven't got. I don't see where that makes me come off as superior to a bird, though.

Mike: It shouldn't, but somehow that's how you feel about it. You like that warm moist hole just as much as she digs your body, man; and don't you forget it.

Joe: (laughs) Her warm moist hole is something I can't forget, buddy. And, just for the record, I know I want it. But I'm wondering about you. I'm not even sure I can be convinced that you give one shit in hell for that warm moist hole you so neatly describe.

Mike: Tough shit what you think. Okay?

(The dialogue had reached an impasse. Denton allowed several minutes to go by. He was letting bottom pressure apply itself, so that the group could become revitalized after the battle which had raged between Joe and Mike. Two powerful rams had locked horns, and sides had been chosen by most of the sheep. The followers looked to the leaders to determine if the battle was to continue, or if anyone of them should even intervene. The process was fascinating to Denton, and he mused whether anyone else was in on his secret.)

Frank: (breaking the silence) Where do we go from here?

Mike: It's probably up to me, Frank. (turns to Joe. Mike wears a big smile on his face.) Joe baby, let's cool it. Okay? Look. Let me concede that you are the best looking stud in the room. Let me also say that I think you can probably make it with any girl you want to. Okay? Hell, you are goddamn good looking. It doesn't take a girl to see that. You've got broad shoulders, narrow hips; and to be truthful, you look virile as hell. Even to me. And these are big items with the birds. No one is denying that. And you can go on thinking I'm queer as hell because I do think you're damn good looking and the whole bloody bit. I say it where other guys may think it. So what? But my big message for you, Joe, is that I don't give a good goddamn at this particular place in time what the hell you think of me. Or anybody else for that matter. I kind of wish I did care for you, because I like to care for everybody. But the truth of the matter is that I don't care. Maybe in time I will, but right now I don't give a damn. Okay? So we've got no bones to pick on that score, eh? And my even bigger message to you is that you don't give a damn about people. Not even about anybody. And that's the damned thing about you that I don't like.

Joe: I don't know what to say, Mike. I'd like to argue the point with you, but I truly don't know how to go about doing it.

Denton: Well, why don't you ask him how he reasons the way he does? That's a beginning.

Joe: Okay, just how in the hell have you got it figured out so neatly that I don't give a damn about anybody?

Mike: Damn, there's so much. But for the record, things like virgins having round heels. And like how you had to sit around and listen to a lot from most of them about the little secrets you'd have to keep before they'd let you get inside of them.

Joe: Hell, yes. I said that. And it's true, by the way. But that doesn't really mean any thing. Just because I recognize that certain games have to be played with the chicks doesn't mean that I don't give a damn about anybody. Hell, everybody plays games.

Mike: I'm not denying that I could be misjudging you, Joe. Time will tell, especially if we keep at this particular game. Still it seems to me that an attitude like you say you have goes far beyond the girls you take to bed with you. The way I see it is that you will take anything anybody will let you take. One thing leads to another. Taking advantage of a lay from a bird or anything else.

Joe: A lay is a lay.

Mike: You really don't find my reasoning logical, do you?

Joe: I can't think of a thing to say.

Mike: Well, will you think about it?

Joe: I'll think about it.

Mike: You're showing some improvement, you know. Earlier this afternoon you would have reacted in a more violent manner.

Joe: (smiles) So I might have. But, Mike, I'm getting used to you too, you know.

Mike: Thank God for little favours, and I pass at this point.

Jim: (sarcastically) What Mike was trying to get across for you was really very simple.

Joe: Well, maybe a simpleton like you could explain it to me.

Jim: What Mike was trying to tell you was that if you use some people you use all people.

Joe: And I say crap. I don't go around using people.

SESSION I

Jim: You do. It's the same thing as if you'd rob from a bank you'd rob from a church. Same thing.

Joe: Shit. Is that supposed to mean something?

Jim: I give up! I just can't get it across to you that if you screw one guy, you screw them all.

Joe: (angry) That's what I mean, friend. I screw chicks, not guys.

Jim: I was using that as a figure of speech.

Joe: I bet you were.

Jim: Okay, I get your message. Try it this way then. If you are willing to take advantage of just one person if you get the chance, then it stands to reason that you'll take advantage of anybody. That is, if you get the chance.

Joe: It doesn't figure, buddy. Like I said. I see a lay as something a guy's gonna want to get. (contemptuously) You probably don't know much about the subject. But for your information you've got to give them a line. Snow them. Make them think that they are the one and only. It's a game, that's all.

Jim: You miss the point completely.

Joe: Aw shit. You wouldn't know what I was talking about when it gets down to girls anyway.

Jim: It's a free country. Think what you want.

Joe: I can, and I do. And I think you're full of shit. How does that grab you?

Jim: Doesn't make a damn bit of difference to me. You can't be rational with an irrational. And you're irrational as hell. And I pass.

Joe: Proper thing! If I were you I wouldn't have said anything in the first place.

Carlos: Well, all I can say is that I think you feel it's easier to tell somebody he's full of shit rather than try to discuss the matter with him.

57

Joe: Hell yeah, I expected you to say something like that. It figures. (laughs) The gays are ganging up on me. (To Denton) Man, is it some kind of a stupid joke that this bloody room is full of queers?

Mike: Paranoia, Joe. Watch it.

Joe: You know, Mike. It's a funny thing. You don't bug me as much as these other guys. And yet I know you're queer as hell, too.

Mike: You know that, eh?

Joe: Well, I think it.

Mike: Nobody's ganging up on you, Joe. All of us are trying to make the same point with you. And you just don't even try to understand that we might be right.

Joe: (defensively) I can understand something when there's something to understand.

Carlos: For the moment I'm going to pass. I don't see any future in it.

Joe: Good. No guts.

Mike: Spoiling for a fight, are you?

Joe: (laughs derisively) I'm trying to be the rational man that Jim wants me to be.

(Todd didn't speak at first. He was looking at the floor. Finally Joe coaxed him.)

Joe: Todd, how about you? Do you pass?

Todd: No, I was just thinking. Tell me, Joe, are you sorry you came?

Joe: That's a hell of a question, Todd.

Todd: No, it isn't. At least I didn't mean for it to be. I was really interested in how you felt.

Joe: I get mad, Todd. That's all. But I'm not sorry I came. I think it's a real interesting thing ... this group meeting.

Todd: And you're going to keep coming?

Joe: (looking surprised) Sure. We're supposed to.

Todd: Well, good. I hope you don't change your mind.

Joe: I won't. Are you trying to tell me something?

Todd: No, I don't think so. I was just being curious. You got so pissed off with Mike and then Jim. And then with Carlos.

Joe: That don't mean a thing. Like I said, I get hot easy. And Denton told all of us that we'd learn something from all this. No lie! I wish I knew more right now about all that is going on, but it's okay.

Todd: I pass.

Rick: There's nothing I want to say, Joe. You might as well get down. My turn in the hot seat. (Joe gets up from the chair and Rick seats himself very quickly.) Okay Frank, have at me.

Frank: There's nothing like being eager.

Rick: Hell, might as well do it in the grand manner. (forces a laugh.) I don't see any other way out of it.

Frank: Right. Well, tell me, Rick. You identify very strongly with Joe, don't you?

Rick: Well, we're good friends.

Frank: But I didn't ask that. I asked if you didn't identify with him. There's a broad difference.

Rick: Back to differences, huh? Okay. What's the difference?

Frank: The difference is that you think Joe is the greatest guy in the world, and you try to ape everything he does.

Rick: We're good friends, but he's not the greatest guy in the world.

Frank: Oh, no? Who is? You?

Rick: I didn't say that. (Laughs again.) Got anything else you can try to get me mad with? I might as well warn you. Joe's the one with the hot temper. Not me.

Frank: There you go with the you-and-Joe comparison again. (Rick smiles, contemptuously framing no reply.)

Frank: (Throws up his hands.) What else can I do? I pass.

Mike: Frank's right, Rick. You're well steeled for the occasion.

Rick: Thank you.

Mike: I think you're a snob, Rick.

Rick: For the record, Mike, it doesn't bother me in the slightest what you think right now.

Mike: Oh. Well, that means in the future you're going to let me get to you, eh?

Rick: Like I said. Or do I need to repeat?

Mike: You don't need to, Rick. I recognize the problem.

Rick: You do, eh? (His tone was ultra superior.) Well, bully for you.

Mike: But I don't think you do. You don't really know that you're one of those people Joe uses all the time, do you? (He paused for the effect.) It's like I thought. (To Carlos) Joe keeps this one around to make him feel superior. (To Rick) You're so inferior that you could make anybody look good, baby.

Rick: Probably even you. By the way, Mike, was that supposed to get to me?

Mike: You silly ass. You really don't see. (He threw up his hands in dismay.) I pass. (Carlos and Jim passed in quick succession.)

SESSION I

Todd: Gee, you guys didn't even give me time to come up with something.

Rick: Just ask or pass, Todd.

Todd: (Appears stunned by the vehemence in Rick's voice.) Hell, you put it that way, I pass.

Joe: (He looked at Rick for a moment. It appeared he might say something, but at the last minute he seemed to have thought the better of it.) I pass, Rick.

(Rick got up from the hot seat and moved back to his chair, a smirk drawn across his face. It was the "cat ate the canary" type look, and seemed to shout out the fact that nobody could rile him.)

Denton: (To the group.) It occurs to me that this is a good stopping point. We've gone over our time limit, but not too much.

Frank: Is it important to have a time limit, Denton?

Denton: I think I'd have to answer that with both a yes and a no, Frank. Certainly it's important that we start on time. As for winding up a session, it's not essential that we break in the middle of a sentence in order to keep to the time limit. You see, what we're trying to do over "x" number of weeks is what most groups attempt to fit into 3 or 5 or even 10 days.

Rick: Christ, I can't see sitting around shooting the shit for ten days.

Denton: Are you saying you're sorry you came, Rick?

Rick: (sullenly) I'll live.

Frank: You're evading the question.

Denton: Okay. Maybe he doesn't want to answer it right now. He's got that right, doesn't he? More important is whether he'll be back next week.

Rick: I said I'd be here for all the sessions. And I will be!

Denton: Good. And I hope everyone sticks to his commitment as well. (There was a universal nodding of heads in agreement.) But as I was explaining, we're trying to have an experience which usually can come about only through a more intense immersion. So we've got to face the battle of time as well. And I think that if we're under a time pressure, we'll invariably get more things done. My reasoning is just that simple. Okay?

Frank: I see your point. (Rising.) One of these times you'll have to tell us how groups work, Denton.

Mike: Hell, better than that! Let's live it up in this one. Let's learn by doing.

Frank: I can't argue with that. (The group left quietly, and, seemingly, without remorse. Predictably Jim left with Carlos and Mike, and Rick went with Joe. Also predictably, Frank remained for a chat with Denton. Todd simply disappeared.)

SESSION II

The group assembled for Session II. Denton noted the unstated anxieties as the young men came into the room. All were on time for the session, and this pleased him almost as much as the fact that all showed up. He would have been greatly disappointed if any of the members had dropped, and would have been surprised as well. Denton had not actually expected that any of the fellows would drop from the group, for he had spent an almost inordinate amount of time with each one of them preparing them for group membership. But the fact that they were on time suggested eagerness to get on with it at the best; or, at the worst, a determination to see the experience through.

Groups invariably experience long periods of silence. At the beginnings of involvement, periods of silence weigh heavy on each of the members. It is something to struggle with, much a problem as getting to know the other members of the group. And a group has to experience the pressures of silence in order to grow. Too little of anxiety-provoking silence inhibits the growth of the group; if the trainer allows for no silence the group will never transcend the social barriers, and the group accomplishes nothing. Antithetically, silence if allowed to go on for too long a period becomes destructive. The trainer needs to continuously evaluate what is going on, whether it be during periods of silence or in times of animated discussion.

Session II began with an uncomfortable silence. Foot shufflings, clearing of throats, movements that were intended to be quiet but didn't remain so ... all were manifestations of the anxiety provoking silence.

Carlos: Gee, I can't stand this. Isn't somebody supposed to say something?

Frank: You just did!

Carlos: Well, you know what I mean.

Frank: No, what do you mean?

Mike: Oh, for Christ's sake. Here's the psychologist again.

Frank: What's the matter, Mike. Your hostility level off today?

Mike: (laughs) Knock it off, Frank. Carlos was just saying that somebody ought to be saying something.

Rick: The thing I would say is that you two guys are still living together. Look how one stands up for the other.

Mike: Sure, we still live together. We told you we were roommates.

Rick: That you did. (Drily) So what else is new?

Joe: Maybe he's right, Rick. Surely somebody is going to have to say or do something. We're not going to sit around here for hours on end just looking at each other, are we?

Rick: God, I would hope not.

Todd: Why doesn't Denton say something?

Frank: Maybe he doesn't want to say anything.

Todd: Well, I think he should.

Frank: Why?

Todd: But sure there's some plan to all of this. Why doesn't he tell us what it is?

Joe: That makes sense to me.

Mike: I'm glad something is beginning to make sense to you.

Rick: Christ, are you going to start that crap again?

Mike: You know, Rick. It might come as a surprise to you, but I think Joe is big enough to take care of himself. What in hell do you think you are? His alter ego?

Rick: (defensively) I'm not going to get drawn into any kind of a hassle with you, Mike.

Mike: Oh, you've decided that, have you?

Rick: Yes, I've decided that.

Jim: (echoes the words, but very sarcastically) Yes, I've decided that.

Rick: That goes for you too, fellow.

Mike: Simon Pure doesn't want to dirty his hands with us, boys.

Joe: You three are real bitches, you know. Now why in the hell are you ganging up on Rick?

Carlos: It figures. If Rick isn't coming to Joe's defense, Joe is coming to his defense. What I want to know is what are they defending?

Joe: Oh, butt out. There's not a goddamn thing either of us have to defend.

Rick: And I can't say the same about you three.

Mike: What's there to defend? You know, Rick. You keep saying all these goddamn things about queers; both you and Joe. But when it comes right down to it, you don't know one goddamn thing about any one of us. Now isn't that right?

Rick: A man's got a right to think what he likes.

Mike: Man! You sure are hung up on that word "man".

Frank: (Interrupting before Rick could respond.) Denton, what do you make of all of this? Is it helpful to the process to let them fight all the time?

Denton: Do you call it fighting, Frank?

Frank: Well, not in so many words maybe. But they're sure doing a hell of a lot of arguing.

Denton: Maybe they are just getting to know each other. Isn't it possible to grow closer together after all the words are out of the way?

Rick: No chance. I don't want to get to know any of them better than I do right at this very minute.

Todd: Well, if that's the case you might as well get up and leave, Rick. Don't you think? (He looked surprised that he had put words to his thoughts, but having once done so he continued.) What I mean, Rick, is that I don't want to get into any kind of argument with you, but isn't the point of this whole experience getting to know each other to the point where we will feel completely comfortable with each other?

Rick: Yeah, that's true. But a man's got a right to pick who he wants to get close to. Right?

Mike: There goes that word again.

Todd: (Ignoring Mike, and continuing to speak to Rick.) Okay, that's true. But do you really think you know either Mike or Carlos or Jim?

Rick: I know enough about them already.

Todd: You've got your mind made up, eh?

Rick: Yes, I have.

Frank: Well, why don't you leave?

Denton: Todd and Frank have a good point. Why don't you leave?

Rick: Well, I promised you that I'd stay with it the whole time. That's why.

Denton: And your promise to me is important?

Rick: Don't you think it is?

Denton: Well, like you said, a man has a right to change his mind.

Rick: And even break a commitment?

Denton: Sure, people do it all the time. You've gone back on your word before, haven't you?

Rick: (mildly defensive) Yes, but I guess we all have.

Denton: So what's so wrong about going back on your word this time?

Rick: You seem like you want me to leave.

Denton: Far from it, Rick. I want you to stay. I want you to stay very badly. (addresses the group) I want all of you to stay very badly. But I'm just trying to help you put into words those things which you may be feeling.

Rick: Well, I promised you I would stay. And I will.

Denton: But that's not good enough, Rick. You have to stay because you want to stay. Not because you've given me or anybody else a promise.

Rick: Well, I swear to God I don't understand. First these guys suggest that I should leave. (to Denton) Then you agree with them that I should. And just when I get ready to leave, you try to talk me out of it because you say you want me to stay very badly.

Denton: I didn't agree that you should leave, Rick. I said that if you felt you wanted to leave, then your commitment to me or to anyone else should not stand in your way.

Rick: But I owe you, Denton. (very earnestly) And I want to do what you think I should do.

Denton: And I'm telling you, Rick, that even if you feel you do owe me something that nothing should stand in the way of your doing or saying exactly what you want to do or say. And if you are willing to suffer the consequences.

Rick: What consequences?

Denton: For leaving this group? None in particular. Except an opportunity to get to know a group of fellows much better than you've ever known anybody before in your life. You might miss out on that. But if you never become aware of something, how can you miss it? Do you see what I am saying?

Joe: I think I do, Denton. You know, I'm really with Rick on this one. And I know that Mike thinks this is how it's always going to be. So don't lay that one on me, buddy. But I think what you are saying is that if any one of us should leave the group at this time we will never really know what might have happened had we stayed.

Denton: That's about the size of it, all right.

Rick: Well, I can't see where any of this is leading us.

67

Denton: And you think I can?

Rick: I would hope to God you could. Otherwise, what's the point?

Denton: The point is that I'm a member of this group, just like any one of you. And I don't know where we're going, or what we're going to do.

Rick: Well, I'd say that's a pretty damn sorry state of affairs. You're supposed to be the trainer. You're supposed to be the one who tells us what to do.

Denton: I don't agree, Rick. No one can ever tell you what you're supposed to do.

Rick: Oh, hell.

Joe: Yeah, we're like a bunch of silly-assed bastards sitting around playing games.

Frank: Maybe that's the way it's supposed to be.

Joe: Hell, I can't buy that. I can go down to any corner in town and pick a fight.

Frank: But can you pick a fight with the certainty that you're not going to get beaten up?

Joe: (smiles) I think I said before that I am usually very sure of that.

Frank: That's not exactly what I mean. You know, like I told you before, I've had quite a few courses in Psychology.

Mike: (drily) You've made that abundantly clear.

Frank: No, Mike. Let me finish, please. I don't really mean to come across like a latter day Sigmund Freud.

Mike: Sorry, Frank, but you do.

Frank: Well, don't you see? That's exactly what I mean! To you guys I come across like some kind of a know-it-all. But I don't really mean to be like that at all. What I'm saying is that having the course work in Psychology is not enough.

Mike: You mean nobody has ever told you that before?

Frank: Oh, if you want to include all the kidding . . . sure. I've been told that before. But you know, I never really believed it until you guys laid it on the line for me last time. It really got me to thinking. Now, I'm still not convinced that I act like I know everything; but the possibility is there. Yet, it wasn't possible for me to think about me like that before. Do you see what I mean?

Mike: Yes, I do. It comes down to the point that you respect our judgment.

Frank: No, Mike. That's not true at all. I don't know whether I respect any of your judgments yet. And I'm not talking just to you. I mean all of you. I'm not even sure I like any of you yet.

Carlos: That's telling it like it is!

Frank: No. I don't mean it like that. All I'm saying is that for the first time in my life I'm wondering if I don't project to other people the fact that I'm a know-it-all. And if I'm going to be a psychologist, I think that would be a fatal flaw. A psychologist has to come across to people as a warm human being; not somebody who pretends to know all the answers. And you see I've learned from you guys that what I certainly don't want to be is what I might be unconsciously doing. Does any of that make sense?

Joe: In a way, Frank. Basically what you are saying is that you learned last week that you're a know-it-all.

Frank: Not really. I said I learned that I might be a know-it-all. And I don't want to be. Now if that's the way I'm coming across to you guys, it's very possible that I'm coming across the same way to other people as well.

Todd: But I don't understand why you think that is such a big deal.

Frank: Well, hell. I don't even know that I can explain it.

Denton: Let me try to capture what Frank is saying. What I hear him saying is that through you guys the message came across to him that he is pretending to be a know-it-all. And he doesn't want to be that way at all. But there's something basic to his personality which allows him to project something about himself which he doesn't really want to project. In fact, what he hopes to project is almost the opposite. Is that about it, Frank?

Frank: Right! That's exactly it.

Todd: But you admitted that this is not the first time you've heard it.

Frank: That's right. But the difference is that I know you guys mean it when you say it. You said it with a vengeance, and I know you meant it. When I've heard it before, there was always the possibility somebody was kidding around or was just trying to see if he could hurt my feelings.

Joe: And you don't think anybody was trying to hurt your feelings?

Frank: Well, in all honesty, I'd have to answer that I don't know whether that was the purpose or not. But the word honest is what I'd like to get across. I felt you guys were really being honest with me.

Denton: And are you saying that if somebody is really being honest with you that you can take criticism from them?

Frank: No, I don't know that I can generalize that much. But I do know that if I feel someone cares for me, I will respect their judgments a hell of a lot more.

Joe: Oh, come on now, Frank. Do you mean to tell me that you think somebody in this group cares for you?

Frank: Maybe not cares in the sense that they have feelings of like or dislike for me. But cares from the point of view that they are levelling with me.

Joe: It's beyond me. You know, I took a lot last week too. But I sure as hell don't think anybody who took out after me cares about me.

Frank: Well, maybe that's something that will come in time. I don't know. All I do know is that I felt last week's session was extremely beneficial to me. And I'm anxious to learn a hell of a lot more about myself.

Todd: Are you saying that you can learn from us?

Frank: Hell, yes, I am saying I can learn from you. Maybe I can't learn the same things from you guys that I might learn from listening to a lecture or reading a textbook, but I can learn something about myself from you. I can listen to you guys say how you think I come across to you . . . what kind of an impression I make, so to speak . . . and then I can do something about it.

Rick: Are you saying that if I told you that you were a lousy creep that you'd believe me?

Frank: Not necessarily. But I might, and if I thought you were right I'd try to find out how I could quit being a lousy creep. But, really, I think it has to be more definite than that. You know, like suppose you criticize the way I talk. Now that doesn't mean that I'm going to go home and start learning to talk in a different way. But what I will do is to try to listen to myself a little more to see if your criticism has validity. If it does, I sure as hell would try to do something about it. If it doesn't have validity, I'd leave it alone. But the important thing is that I would think about it.

Carlos: Gee, you know this is almost creepy.

Todd: What do you mean by that?

Carlos: It's like getting outside your body and looking back at you. Real objective like.

Frank: Well, I don't think it's creepy, Carlos. I think it's a damned good thing.

Todd: Rick, do you still want to leave?

Rick: I don't know.

Joe: Oh, come on. Admit it, Rick. You know you don't want to leave. You're as hung up on this as I am. (To Denton) All week long he's been driving me up a tree wondering if I knew what we were going to be doing.

Todd: Do you guys talk about what goes on here outside the group?

Joe: We might have said a few things. But don't try to tell me the rest of the guys keep quiet.

71

Todd: Don't you think we should?

Joe: Well, Christ, Todd. It's not as if we got time on the radio. It's just something between us. That's all. Why? What have you got to be afraid of?

Todd: I'm going to be honest with you, Joe. A hell of a lot is what I have to lose.

Joe: I don't understand.

Todd: Well, let me spell it out for you. Frank used the word honest a while ago. I didn't feel one way or the other to the group until Frank said what he did. That kind of turned me on. I'd like to honestly know what you guys think about me.

Joe: Fair enough. Hell, we'll tell you.

Todd: No, Joe, you don't understand.

Joe: Everybody's always telling me I don't understand. Does this mean that I should do what Frank did? Should I go home and decide that I'm stupid or something just because you guys say to me over and over that I don't understand?

Mike: Joe, baby, pardon the interruption. But it might be an idea, you know. Not that you're stupid. But maybe because you don't listen.

Todd: (interrupting) Damn it, I've got something to say. Would you please listen? (His words, aimed like missiles, hit the target. Both Mike and Joe sat back to listen.) I want to feel comfortable with you guys. I want you to tell me how you think I come across, and if there's something wrong with me. But how in the hell are you going to make any kind of a judgment about me unless you sit back and listen to me? You can't tell me anything much simply by looking at me. Hell, I know plenty of people who tell me things because they think they know me. My parents do that all the time. And they don't know me! Nobody knows me. But Denton told me that this would be an opportunity for me in that I could tell other people how I feel and what I think and how I want to be. And he told me they'd respect me for it. And that they would listen. And that they would help. But I don't see this happening. And then Frank said it was beginning to happen to him. Oh, he didn't say that exactly. But that's what I understood him to say. Then I started getting courage, which I didn't have before. And then you,

Joe, tell me that you and Rick talk about what goes on in this group outside this room. How in the hell do I know that if you talk about it between yourselves you won't talk about it someplace else?

Denton: The name of the game is trust.

Joe: Well, let me ask you, Mike. Did you and Carlos talk about it this week?

Mike: Yeah, we did. A little. But we didn't say anything to anybody else.

Joe: (to Todd) You see?

Todd: (sadly) Yes, I see all right.

Denton: Somebody tell us what Todd is saying.

Rick: I think he is saying that he wants all of us to keep secrets.

Mike: The way you sneer that out, Rick, makes me think that you feel there is something inherently wrong in keeping secrets.

Rick: Like a bunch of silly girls.

Mike: Christ, you're hung up on not wanting anybody to think you could possibly be a girl.

Frank: Castration complex?

Mike: My god, there he goes again.

Frank: (laughs) Sorry. I've got to do some more practicing on that.

Denton: Does anyone else see it as keeping secrets?

Joe: I do.

Carlos: That figures.

Joe: No, Carlos. God damn it. It doesn't figure. Now shut up or I'm going to belt you one.

Denton: (in a stern voice) Joe!

Joe: I'm sorry. I got carried away. Figuratively speaking is all I was doing.

Carlos: You didn't come across like that.

Joe: Okay. Maybe I'm like Frank in that I'll have to learn how I come across to people. And maybe even dumb old Joe can change if he sees the need. But what I was trying to say was that in a way it's kind of like keeping a secret. But I like the word that Frank used also. I like the word honest. I wish to God I could be more honest with people. And Todd's right. You can't even be honest with your own parents.

Todd: Did I say that?

Joe: In a way. You said that they don't understand you. And the way you go about understanding people is by getting to know them. And in order to get to know them you have to listen. Right? (to Mike) See, I can get things right once in a while.

Mike: So what you're saying is . . .

Joe: What I'm saying is that I'm willing to go on record as promising to let nothing that goes on in this room outside this room. No ifs, ands, or buts. Who else feels like that?

Denton: I think you stated that very well, Joe.

Mike: I agree. And I also agree that what goes on in here stays in here. Anybody disagree?

Denton: So how do we know that everyone will stick to that promise?

Todd: Oh, Christ. I was just getting to feel good again when you laid that one on me.

Frank: Like you said, Denton, the name of the game is trust. Does that make you feel any better, Todd?

Todd: (unconvincingly) Yeah.

Frank: Well, I'll tell you something else that bothers me. Am I the only one to realize that one member of the group hasn't said one bloody thing this entire session?

(Slowly, as his words penetrated into the awareness of the group members, all heads were turned to look at Jim.)

Mike: No, I knew it. But lay off him, Frank.

Joe: Why?

Mike: Because I asked you to.

Joe: There's something going on that we don't know about.

Mike: Probably is. But I don't think Jim wants to talk about it right now. Is that right, buddy?

Jim: (sadly) What's there to talk about?

Joe: But maybe we could help.

Jim: (staring at Joe) You help me? What a laugh!

Joe: I'd like to if I could.

Rick: Jesus Christ, Joe! What's getting into you?

Frank: Maybe the milk of human kindness? (To Rick) You ought to try some of it yourself, you lousy creep.

Mike: God, you can come on strong after all.

Frank: Well, anybody can see that Jim has something bothering him. I noticed and wanted to help. You said you noticed, and you also suggested that you already knew what it was. And then Joe said, whether he noticed or not, that he wanted to be of help if he could. And then you told Joe to leave it alone. I can understand that. Maybe we haven't gotten involved with each other enough yet that we can be of much help. But at least it seemed that people wanted to try. All except for Rick, who for some reason or other doesn't want to even try to be kind.

Carlos: Maybe it's because he's jealous that Joe wants to help Jim.

Rick: (direct to Carlos) I rather doubt that we have the same kind of emotions.

Carlos: You sure as hell think you're something else, don't you?

Mike: Aw, lay off him, Carlos. He's got some kind of problem that he's not about to let come out into the open.

Denton: Maybe Jim and Todd and Rick are all saying the same thing?

Joe: What do you mean? This confidentiality bit?

Denton: I'm suggesting it.

Joe: I know Rick pretty well. I don't think he has anything to hide.

Denton: I'm not suggesting he has anything to hide, Joe. Yet I wonder if there aren't things about him that he simply is unwilling to share yet.

Joe: Well, how about you? Do you have things you're not willing to share?

Denton: At this moment, yes. We all do. But if we all work at it, we'll be able to get to the level where we are completely comfortable with each other.

Joe: Well, Christ! How long is it going to take?

Denton: That's completely up to us.

Joe: My God! You ask a stupid question and you get a stupid answer.

Frank: Well, I'd say that's progress, Joe. A couple of weeks ago would you have talked to Denton like that?

Joe: Probably not. Although not because he's a professor. Although come to think of it I don't think I'd get smartassed with any of my professors. But especially Denton. You know, Rick said something a while ago about owing Denton. Well, I owe him something too. And I'm beginning to suspect that we all do. But it isn't on the basis of my owing him something that I wouldn't have smartassed him; not because he represents anything. I really like the guy.

Mike: Congratulations. You're human.

Joe: (smiling) You note I didn't use the word love.

Mike: Like and love aren't all that far apart, Joe baby.

Joe: (staring at him) An interesting point.

Frank: In any event, it seems we're making progress. What do you think, Denton?

Denton: Oh, sure. We're making progress.

Frank: You don't sound convincing.

Denton: What would you have me do? Go around and pat everybody on the back?

Frank: I asked for that.

Denton: No, you didn't, Frank. I threw it, and not because you asked for it. I threw it because I don't think any of us need to be congratulated because we're beginning to act like warm human beings.

Frank: I see your point.

Joe: I guess then that what we're all trying to learn is how to come across like warm human beings?

Denton: I'd say something like that.

Carlos: But how do we learn that? Hell, I think I come across that way anyway.

Rick: I don't think you do. You whine too much.

Carlos: Now what the hell is that supposed to mean?

Rick: Forget it.

Mike: I don't think you can forget something like that, Rick. Hell, you made a statement that was derogatory to Carlos. I took it that way, and obviously he did as well. Now what's the sense in telling him to forget it? Why say it in the first place if you're not prepared to explain why you feel the way you do?

Rick: It's a hassle, man. Every time I open my mouth in here somebody sees the chance to twist my words around and make me come out as the villain of the piece.

Joe: Maybe that's what we're supposed to do.

Rick: Well, I can't understand how it's going to do any good.

Frank: I told you how I felt.

Rick: Yes, Frank, I know you did. But it seems to me that whether or not you come across as a know-it-all is no big awakening. You should have known that all along.

Frank: How should I have known it?

Rick: Because by your own admission people have told you that before.

Frank: But the point is that I didn't listen.

Rick: Yeah, that's what you said. But I don't dig how you will pay attention to what guys in this group will tell you when you don't pay attention to what other people tell you.

Frank: It probably means something like you have to trust the people before you listen.

Rick: Hell, I don't buy that. I'd listen to a hell of a lot of people before paying any attention to anybody in this group.

Mike: Except for Joe, eh?

Rick: All right. Except for Joe. We've been friends a hell of a long time.

Frank: And you think he's always honest with you?

Rick: Sure. Why shouldn't he be?

Frank: Are you always honest with him?

Rick: Of course.

Frank: Crap. You're not always honest with him. You're a bloody liar. Do you mean in your whole period of being friends with Joe that you have always leveled with him one hundred percent?

Rick: That's exactly what I'm saying.

Frank: And I repeat that you are a bloody liar. (To Joe) Have you always been honest with Rick?

Joe: I think so.

Frank: You mean you've told him things about himself that you don't like? You've told him everything about how you feel, and so on?

Joe: Well, hell, Frank. I really and truly doubt that anyone tells anybody else what he really and truly thinks all of the time. Do you tell your wife?

Frank: I know very well that I don't.

Joe: Why not?

Frank: Frankly, there are things about her that I don't like!

Joe: So why don't you tell her? You're so big on this honesty thing.

Frank: The reason I don't tell her is that sometimes I don't want to hurt her feelings. I don't know how to say it exactly, but I kind of weigh the alternatives. Now that I think of it, I believe what I do is to determine how much of an aggravation certain things she does cause me. If it doesn't cause me a lot of aggravation, I say nothing.

Denton: But do I hear you also saying that you burn up inside sometimes in order to keep from hurting her feelings?

Frank: I sure as hell am saying exactly that.

Joe: I don't get it. Why don't you say something about whatever it is that's bugging you?

Frank: Like I said, sometimes I do. A lot of times I don't.

Denton: I think he's also saying that he loves her and thus is prepared to put up with a certain amount of crap from her.

Frank: Exactly. You know, this is a small thing. But she leaves her stockings and pantyhose and God knows what else hanging all over the shower curtain rod. It bugs the hell out of me that before I can take a shower I have to move all that stuff. When I get finished with my shower I have to put it all back.

Joe: Man, I'd tell her I wouldn't put up with it.

Frank: I told her once that I wished she wouldn't do it. But we got into a hassle about where she was going to hang them. I don't know why, but it turned into one of the worst goddamn arguments we've ever had. She told me she had to pick up for me all over the place. Man, she got mad as hell about it. So, since that time I haven't said a word. I just go on and move the stuff.

Denton: But it still makes you mad.

Frank: I seethe inwardly.

Denton: So would it be safe to say that you put up with this even though it tears away at your gut because you don't want to get into a hassle with her?

Frank: I've thought about it a hell of a number of times. And that's exactly what I'm doing.

Denton: Does talking about it make you feel any better?

Frank: It sure as hell does.

Joe: But the point is, what are you going to do about it?

Frank: Nothing, probably.

Rick: Talk, just talk. Just like I said.

Mike: Yeah, but maybe if he gets the steam off his chest here he can go home and be less uptight about it next time it happens.

Denton: I kind of think it works that way. (The conversation ended abruptly. There seemed to be nothing left to say.)

Mike: We're back to the silence again.

Denton: It seems that way. However, it's just as well. I'd like for us to try playing a game.

Joe: Before we do that, Denton. I'd like to ask Jim a question.

Denton: Okay.

Joe: (to Jim) Is there anything anyone of us can do?

Jim: Thanks, Joe. I know you mean it, but not right now.

Carlos: That goes for me too, Jim.

Jim: (long pause before answering) Thanks, Carlos.

Mike: (admiringly) It took a lot of guts for you to say that, Carlos. I thank you, too.

Rick: See. There they go again. Frank talks about this honesty bit, but there's something going on between those three that the rest of us know nothing about. (To Frank) Now, in the name of honesty, don't you think they should tell us what the hell is going on?

Frank: Maybe they're not ready to tell us yet.

Rick: Why not, for Christ's sake?

Frank: You heard what Todd said.

Rick: Well, we all promised to keep what goes on in here just in here. So what's the big deal?

Frank: It's just possible that Jim doesn't believe us. Or, it's just as possible that whatever is bothering him is something he just doesn't want to get into at this time.

Rick: I don't know what else to say, but I wish to God he'd get on with it.

Denton: Maybe if you told him you also were interested in helping?

Rick: So I'm interested.

Joe: You don't come across to me as being sincere, Rick.

Rick: (taken aback) My God!

Joe: Now you're taking it personally that I said that to you, Rick. I wish you wouldn't, because I didn't mean it that way.

Rick: How in the hell else did you mean it?

Joe: A simple statement of fact! You didn't sound to me as if you cared whether Jim had a problem or not.

Rick: And you do?

Joe: Yes, I do.

Rick: Damn, I don't dig what's happening.

Joe: I don't know if it will help you or not, Rick, but I don't dig what's happening either. I don't understand. But all of a sudden it does seem to make a big difference to me whether Jim has a problem or not. And I'd like to help.

Todd: So would I.

Rick: So I'm the oddball, eh?

Mike: No one said that, Rick. You know, way in back of that shell you carry around with you you are probably one hell of a nice guy.

Rick: Thank you. I think.

Joe: I'll swear that Rick is a great guy. But I'll tell you that it sure is one hard goddamn thing to get him to admit he's ever wrong about anything.

Mike: Have you ever told him that before?

Joe: No, I haven't. I don't think. Why?

Frank: And yet you said you were honest with him. Hell, it's just like me and my wife.

Joe: Only he's not my wife.

Frank: Yeah, but he is your best friend.

Joe: There's that bloody difference again.

Frank: Not so much as you would make it to be, Joe. You know, it's like being pregnant. You can't be just a little bit pregnant, nor can you be just a little bit honest.

Denton: I'm going to break in right now. I think what we've all said today gives us plenty to think about before next week. And it would be great to carry on further if Jim wanted to say anything. But he doesn't seem ready to do so today. So let's spend the rest of the session playing that game I was suggesting earlier. Okay?

Mike: That strikes me as being a good idea.

Joe: Me too.

Carlos: Why not?

Rick: Depends on what the game is, I'd say.

Joe: Oh, hell, Rick. You remember what Frank said. It's like being a little bit pregnant. Either you play the game or you don't. Which is it?

Rick: I didn't say I wouldn't play. I just want to know what it is.

Frank: What difference does it make? Denton is our fearless leader. If he suggests we play a game, there's probably some purpose behind it. So I say let's get with it.

Rick: (Shrugs his shoulders.) Why not?

Denton: Well, the first thing we'll all do is to get up from our chairs and move off to various parts of the room. Don't bother moving the chairs or anything. Just get up and go stand in different parts of the room. Okay?

Frank: We go off by ourselves?

Denton: Right. Find yourself a spot in the room and try to be as far away from the next guy as possible.

(The directions were heeded. The only one not seeming to be interested in following directions was Rick, but he eventually moved into a place where he was off by himself.)

Denton: Okay. Now that we've all spotted around the room, the thing that we're going to do is very simple. We'll keep it up for ten minutes. I've got the alarm clock set. When the bell rings, everyone will leave this room. Got it?

Joe: Sure. But what do we do in the meantime?

Denton: What we're about to do is an exercise in nonverbal communication. There's to be no talking at all. No laughing. In other words, no sound. Not even when the bell rings. If you do it right, it'll be one of the good experiences you'll long remember. If you don't follow instructions, you'll be cheating yourself. Nobody else. Is that understood?

Joe: Right. But what is it we're supposed to do?

Denton: When I say begin, I want you to close your eyes. And keep your eyes closed. You are not to open them until the bell rings. You will remain silent even when the bell rings, and then you'll get your things and leave this room as silently as you can. Now between the time when I give a signal and the bell rings, I want you to walk around the room with your eyes closed.

Joe: Christ! We'll be bumping into people and into chairs.

Denton: Right. The chairs we can do without. So you'll have to be careful. You can pretend you're blind and walk very cautiously. But it's the people I want you to bump into. You'll be moving around the room very carefully and with your eyes closed. When you find yourself coming into contact with someone else, I want you to try to communicate some kind of inner feeling to them. Remember, no words! I'm not going to tell you what you're supposed to do, because I can't tell you how to express your feelings on a nonverbal level. Only you can learn to do that through practice. And that's what this game is! It's practice to allow you to try to communicate nonverbally with somebody else. Okay?

Rick: You mean we're supposed to shake each other's hands?

Denton: Well, that's one way. But you might want to give some kind of an embrace, or you might want to let your hands run across the other guy's face. Anything at all that you feel like doing. Anything that will enable you to communicate that you would like to know this other fellow better, or that you would like to communicate some feeling to him. Okay? Any questions?

(There were none, so Denton told them to begin. At first he didn't take part in the exercise, because he wanted to gauge how it was going. The movements of the young men were at first slow and cautious, and the first encounters ended in formal handshakes. But then the handshakes turned into something a little more than mere formalities. Denton observed as several experimented with reaching out and touching faces. When he was certain that things were moving along as they should be, Denton closed his eyes and began moving around the room.)

SESSION III

Denton: (after everyone had assembled) I'd like to begin today's session by getting some feedback from last week.

Frank: It was most helpful to me.

Todd: How?

Frank: I already said. I felt I got a lot of help. Believe me, this week I have really been doing some introspection. What I'm trying to do is to modify the way I talk so that my words don't sound so dogmatic.

Denton: You feel you're making any progress?

Frank: (laughs) You can't change overnight of course. But I'm counting on you guys to help me shape up. As trite as it sounds, I really want to help people. The message I got last week was that my technique as of this moment would tend to drive people away, rather than pull them to me.

Denton: Good. Well, what else happened last week?

Joe: I decided that I might have been a little hasty in some of my judgments. It came as a shock to me to learn that I have begun to like Mike a lot and am beginning to wish I knew Carlos better. The biggest surprise of all was that I told Jim I wanted to help him.

Frank: You've changed your mind about wanting to help him?

Joe: On the contrary, I'm more eager than ever.

Denton: This was a big surprise to you then?

Joe: I've got to admit that Jim turned me off more than anybody else in the group.

Frank: Even Mike?

Joe: Even Mike. Whether I can explain it or not, Mike came across to me as somebody I didn't like. But he's forceful, and I can understand that.

Carlos: How about me?

Joe: To be honest, Carlos, I still don't like you. But even at that, you didn't turn me off the way that Jim did.

Denton: But you feel differently about Jim now, eh?

Joe: I think so! It's hard to say, but I guess I'm trying to understand him. In fact, I guess he has become the one in whom I'm most interested.

Rick: (entere the discussion) I guess I'm more interested in what's happening to Joe than I am anything else.

Frank: What the hell does that mean?

Rick: Well, I think Joe is showing me a lot of things that I wouldn't have expected. You know, Joe was always predictable; I could count on him always.

Frank: And you don't think you can now?

Rick: Well, I suppose so. But I'm kind of shook up right now.

Denton: It's a good thing to have friendships shook up now and again, Rick. What usually happens is that two people go on year after year in a state of mutual dependency. Time simply does not pass without effecting some kind of a change on people. So there you have people in a flux, changing subtly and almost imperceptibly but those who may be closest to them are unaware of the changes. Then some kind of exigency arises when reactions become typical in the relative sense, and a blow-up may ensue. You often hear people say "I don't know what got into him!" Of course the truth of the matter is that they don't know simply because they hadn't bothered to keep up with the changes.

Joe: In other words, they kind of grow apart.

Denton: Unless they continue to keep their interpersonal relations alert and alive.

Todd: That makes sense, because even children and parents grow apart.

Denton: True, but that's rather simplistic. A more dramatic way of illustrating the same point is to think about the fellow who leaves his high school buddies and goes off to college by himself for a period of years. He'll find it to be pretty damn difficult to pick up with them again.

Frank: Yeah, but there's a physical distance separating them.

Denton: There's also a psychological distance, Frank. Why do you think so many marriages fall apart?

Frank: Oh hell! There are any number of reasons given.

Denton: True enough; but don't you think that in the majority of instances it's simply because the two people have grown apart and have very little left in common?

Frank: I guess that's another thing I'll have to watch.

Todd: You know, that's really heavy.

Mike: The best part of last week as far as I am concerned was the last ten minutes. You know I've never done anything like that before, and it was one of the greatest things that ever happened to me.

Rick: (sarcastically) I bet!

Joe: For Christ's sake, Rick. Will you knock it off?

Rick: (appears stunned) What's this? Get Rick day?

Joe: No, it isn't. I'm just getting fed up with all your crap, that's all. Now for Christ's sake, if you don't have something positive to add, why don't you keep your goddamned mouth shut?

Carlos: Is the worm really beginning to turn?

Joe: That goes for you too, smartass.

Frank: It's like I said. Something's going on. I don't understand it, but it seems to me all kinds of feelings are showing up.

Rick: As far as I can see, friend is turning against friend.

Joe: Well, Rick. I'm sorry you see it that way, because I don't feel like that at all. You and I are very good friends, but I'm trying to be honest with you. And I don't think you're trying to be honest with anybody.

Rick: If you mean by being honest that you should go around hurting your buddy's feelings, then I'd say you were being honest.

Todd: (to Rick) Has it occurred to you that your friendship with Joe is phony through and through?

Rick: (mimics) No, it has not occurred to me that my friendship with Joe is phony through and through.

Todd: Gee, I'm sorry I said anything.

Frank: Never mind, Todd. Rick's touchy is all. He'll get over it. (to Mike) But go on, Mike. Tell us about how you felt last week.

Mike: Well, first off it was very hard to keep my eyes closed. The first guy I bumped into was Todd. I knew it was Todd because I peeked.

Frank: How about you, Todd? Were you aware it was Mike?

Todd: No. I was keeping my eyes closed. Really!

Joe: So what happened, Mike?

Mike: Well, we shook hands. That's all.

Denton: Did you feel any warmth or anything? In other words, was he trying to communicate something to you? Were you trying to tell him something?

Mike: I guess I was trying to tell him "Let's be friends."

Denton: Did Mike succeed, Todd?

Todd: No. As far as I was concerned, it was just a handshake.

Denton: Mike?

Mike: Like I said, I knew who he was. That may have diluted the experience for me somewhat. But I kind of felt he wanted to shake my hand and get the hell away from me.

Denton: Rick, how about you?

Rick: I shook a couple of guy's hands. That's about all I remember.

Frank: Somebody sure had wet hands. I can remember that.

Denton: Anyone remember sweating?

(No answers)

Todd: I remember somebody putting his hands on my shoulders and kind of pressing hard.

Frank: That was me, Todd. That's what I tried to do to everybody.

Denton: How did that feel to you, Todd?

Todd: Oh, Jesus. It was great. I was just sorry when he patted me on the shoulder and moved away.

Joe: Frank did that to me too. At least I know it was Frank now. But he gave me an idea. And the next guy I bumped into I did the same thing.

Denton: Why?

Joe: Well, it's like Todd said. It felt so damn good. And I remember thinking that if somebody can make me feel this good, I'll just pass it along.

Denton: And what kind of reaction do you think you got from the fellows you tried it on?

Joe: (struggles for words) The next fellow I moved up against followed my lead. I shook hands with him, and then I put my hand on his shoulders. I kind of pressed my hands on his shoulders, and then he did the same to me.

Denton: What were you thinking?

Joe: It's hard to put into words, but I know I was experiencing a good feeling.

Frank: Euphoria?

Joe: Oh, I don't know. That may be a bit strong. But it was a good feeling. And you know, the next thing I knew I had my arms around him. And he had his arms around me. Christ! I've never held a guy like that before.

Mike: Joe, did it scare you?

Joe: No, it didn't. Not then anyway. But I've thought about it since.

Frank: Who was he?

Joe: I don't know.

Frank: You don't know? Or you don't want to say?

Joe: I don't know.

Denton: Knowing who it was doesn't really matter. Experiencing the feeling is what's important.

Joe: You know, I'd like to say one more thing about it. And believe me, its embarrassing to me even to talk about it. But there was simply no sex to it. Can you believe it? There was simply no sex to it.

Denton: You find that difficult to believe, Joe?

Joe: Well, yes. Usually when I hold a girl I get a sexual feeling; sometimes it's stronger than others. But this hug had no sexual overtones at all.

Frank: Would you like to go through it again, Joe?

Joe: I'm not sure.

Frank: What do you mean by that?

Joe: Well, what happened was so damned spontaneous. I think if it were to happen again I might try to contrive the same situation. And I don't think it would be the same if I tried to fake it.

Mike: Were you still holding each other when the alarm sounded?

Joe: You know, that's another funny thing. It dawned on me that the bell would be ringing. I remember thinking I didn't want anybody to see me holding on to this other guy. So it must have been a minute before the bell rang that I broke it off ...

Todd: You broke it off?

Joe: Yeah, I backed off. When the alarm rang I was clear on the opposite side of the room and away from everybody.

Denton: How would you describe your feelings, Joe?

Joe: I don't know if I could, Denton. I felt good, but then I felt I had done something wrong.

Denton: You're saying you had ambivalent feelings about what had happened.

Joe: Right.

Todd: Gee, nothing like that happened to me.

Mike: Maybe because you didn't let it happen. (laughs) You were probably the guy with the sweating palms.

Todd: Was my hand sweating when we shook hands?

Mike: No, Todd. I'm just kidding around.

Denton: (to Mike) You think the reason Todd didn't get involved was because he kept himself back? He wouldn't give of himself?

Mike: I think so, because at first I went around shaking hands too. (looks at Joe) But then this one guy comes up to me and puts his hands on my shoulders. At the time I didn't know for sure who it was, although the strength in his hands gave me a clue. But his hands felt great on me, so I responded by putting my hands on his shoulders. I started massaging him like he was working on me. The first thing I knew my arms were around him and his were around me. It was a strong hold, and I felt very good about it. We held each other for a long while, and I thought the break came naturally. I did not sense that he had planned it that way. But there was no sexual excitement in it for me; and in a way that's strange for me. Laugh if you want to, but I'm always pretty close to a turned-on feeling. Only this didn't turn me on. I can't remember, of course; but it must be like being a baby and having your mother hold you. At least that's what it seemed like to me.

Joe: Christ, it was you, Mike.

Mike: (smiles) You're right, Joe. It was me.

Joe: Did you know it was me?

Mike: I had an idea.

Joe: And it made no difference?

Mike: (simply) No difference.

Denton: Do you feel you could relieve the experience, Mike?

Mike: It's probably like Joe said, Denton. The whole damn thing was spontaneous. It just seemed natural at the time that we were drawn together. But I guess maybe I could. I just don't know. I don't know even if it would be worth the effort. Joe and I have very little in common. It's going to take one hell of a long time for us to get to know each other well enough that we could be in communion.

Denton: And yet you were!

Mike: (throwing up his hands) I tried to explain.

Denton: Both of you tried to explain all right. But the only thing I hear you saying is that because you had your eyes closed and because spontaneity seemed involved, you were able to transcend the effective obstacle that basically you neither like nor appreciate each other. Now what does that suggest to you?

Frank: It suggests to me that because of an artificial situation created by you, Denton, that Mike and Joe were able to have a worthwhile experience.

Rick: Was it really worthwhile?

Joe: For what it's worth, I think it was, Rick.

A STRANGE BREED OF CAT

Rick: And you'd like to do it again?

Joe: I really can't say. Maybe I would, maybe I wouldn't.

Rick: How do you feel about it, Mike?

Mike: At the time I thought, you know, Joe's not such a bad guy after all! If he can communicate his feelings like this, maybe the problem that I think he has is bound up in the fact that we can't give words to his feelings.

Denton: In other words you think Joe's vocabulary lacks warmth.

Mike: Something like that. I think society robs a hell of a lot of people of their ability to communicate effectively. I think we all find a role we think we should play, and then we play it. Anyway, though I'd like to, I doubt we could relieve the experience.

Denton: It's possible to relive experiences, Mike. Sometimes we feel cheated when the repeat performance doesn't live up to the premiere one. I wonder if you've ever reasoned why this may be true.

Mike: But it can work the reverse as well. Sometimes the second go-around is better than the first.

Denton: True, but I wonder why.

Frank: I would suspect expectations have something to do with it. If something beautiful happens to you, you just naturally believe it's going to be as beautiful the next time. If it doesn't work out that way, you become disenchanted.

Denton: I suspect that's the biggest part of it, Frank. I think I'd state it another way though.

Frank: How?

Denton: Simply that we preconceive experiences and situations, and when we learn that our preconceptions are not an accurate reflection of the experience or situation, we become disillusioned. And maybe the disillusionment isn't a resultant of anything other than disappointment with the preconception, per se, rather than with the situation or experience.

Frank: Well, why wouldn't it work the reverse as well? In other words, if we expect a lousy situation but it turns out to be a good one, why wouldn't the negative aspect of ill-reasoned preconception hold true as well?

Denton: Because I think that within all of us we have a capacity for being pleasantly surprised and therefore can handle a shift for the better. But I think this capacity does not extend to discomfort or being negatively stimulated. This would explain disappointment.

Joe: So what you're saying is that it is possible to be able to experience the same thing over and over, and be able to continually derive pleasure despite the lack of newness.

Denton: Right. Oh, there'll be variations on the main theme of course. But normally it's our attitude about coming events that determines the degree of enjoyment.

Todd: But this does away with the sponataneity that Joe was talking about.

Denton: No. At least I don't think that is a logical continuing point. Spontaneity simply allows you to let yourself go in the spirit of the moment. Preconceptions may or may not have one damn thing to do with it.

Carlos: I was scared last week.

Rick: Scared? You? Why?

Carlos: Well, for one thing I'm scared of you, Rick. Also of Joe. And maybe Frank, too.

Frank: Gee, I see no reason to be scared.

Carlos: I'll lay it on the line. Suppose I would have accidentally brushed Rick on the ass, don't you think he would have slugged me?

Jim: (laughs) And I thought I was the only one who had that idea! You know what I did to solve that problem, Carlos?

Carlos: No.

Jim: (laughs even louder) I kept my hands very high.

Frank: (to Denton) Will we ever get over being scared of one another?

Denton: You can, if you work at it. You can learn to place ultimate trust in other human beings in this type of lab experience and then maybe you can get out from here and try 'trusting' in the larger society.

Frank: But surely you can't give ultimate trust to everybody.

Denton: Granted. You must be cautious in the larger society. You have to teach others how to trust; and you're going to fail sometimes. It's risk-taking, but I've learned that you have to take risks. If you keep yourself like a clam to other people, there's no chance that they can learn to relate to you. Or you to them. It's only when you have the guts to take risks -- when you have the guts to expose yourself -- that other people are going to feel free to open up to you. And not a minute before! The onus is on you. Now, take it from me. You guys have a great opportunity going for you, and I hope all of you take advantage of it. (He looked at the seated youths.) I hope I'm getting across to you as being real serious, because that's what I'm trying to be. Because no matter what one of you says to the other, you have a golden opportunity to learn to grow in character. You know, this is one of the real gains an individual derives from participation in a group such as this. Most of the people in the world operate on partial perception of cues that are thrown around, and then form closure around a half-truth. For most people, not to understand fully is no big problem. They throw closure around what they do think they know, and from that point on proceed as if they really knew what the hell they were doing. That's probably one rea-son there is such of a hell of a communications gap between people. Closure is formed on imperfect and inadequate perception, and then it's full speed ahead like everybody knew what the hell they were doing. So, one of the beauties of a group like this is that you get a chance to test reality on a real life basis. Sure, the numbers are small; but cues you can pick up here will be readymade for all the generalization you want and can give to them. Anything goes on in here you don't understand, you ask. If you still don't understand, you ask again. And you watch yourself too. You can learn about yourself from the way you operate. Somebody asks you a sticky question ... watch out for the way in which you find your ego defending itself. And as you begin to recognize the ways in which you defend your ego structure, recall that others are using ploys of their own. What are those ploys? Why are they using them? Then you can start getting beyond the nitty-gritties of defending your every action by determing if all this de-fense is necessary, or if you're not really basically a pretty good guy without all this crap of appearing like something that you are not. You might decide you are, but there are things you can improve on. Why not? Or, you might decide you don't like yourself at all, and give with the big change. It's all done. But what you do with all the gut level feelings you come up with is your bag. The important thing to do is dig. After the dig comes the acceptance or the rejection, but with full knowledge. You'll learn that as you become very free in your relationships with other people that they'll become freer in their relationships to you. It's just that complex and just that simple. You learn that you can give and you can love, that's all.

Joe: So it's a matter of learning in here and then taking it outside?

Denton: In a way. But remember the head-tapping. You don't just go out and do that. (He laughed.) Remember? You pointed that out. What you do is modify to some workable extent what you have tried and found to work. You're never going to have the same degree of freedom with everyone you know.

Frank: But it is possible to have more freedom somewhere else, isn't it?

Denton: Well, I'm not sure what you mean, Frank, but I think I have to say that if you do have more freedom outside the group than what you find inside it, then I think I have to add that you're holding back from membership. Even with your wife or parents or closest girl friend, it's dangerous to assume that the relationship is the same as in here. For one thing, this business of ground rules needs to be spelled out.

Frank: And if they were?

Denton: Maybe. But I'd be very careful.

Joe: I'm going to slip in here. Much of what Denton is saying is something that's been of concern to me since the last session. In fact, to be honest about it, I went by his office early this afternoon to see if he could give me some answers. I don't think I need to tell anybody that I didn't get to first base.

Mike: Denton has a way of not answering any questions that are put to him. It's the tool of a psychologist, Joe. (He turned to Frank) That's something you're going to have to get under your belt, Frank. Never answer a question if there's anyway at all to get out from under it.

Frank: (Laughs) I'll try to remember, Mike.

Joe: The thing I went by to see Denton about, fellows, was to find out if he could tell me why I seemed to be jumped on the hardest.

A STRANGE BREED OF CAT

Mike: Well, speaking only for myself, Joe, I felt you had it coming.

Frank: We've all seemed to be catching it, Joe. How about me and Mike?

Joe: (ignoring Frank) Why did you feel I had it coming, Mike?

Mike: Well, I tried to tell you then. You were hearing my words, but you weren't really listening.

Joe: Mind if I try to listen now?

Mike: Okay, I can try again. And believe me, Joe, I mean to be very sincere. As far as I can see, and nothing Denton has said today has changed that, the purpose of our meeting together in a group has to do with each of us looking at ourselves by looking at each other and trying to figure out the how's and why's of what we do and say. Trying to grab meaning all over the place is how I see it. And whenever I get into any situation I try to do as good a job as I can. So if our purpose here is picking out parts about others that we don't like in order that we might get a better picture of their behaviour in order that we can understand our own selves a lot better, then it was my job to get after you for your smugness. If I'm going to relate better to you, I've got to get out all that crap about you that I don't like and can't accept. At least as much as I possibly can. And it seemed to me, Joe, that when you were talking about girls, you were saying about pushing other people around too. And I just happen to think that one of the things everybody ought to do a lot less of is pushing other people around.

Joe: You really think I push people around?

Mike: My real feeling is that you push people around only if you don't have to exert yourself too much to do it, Joe. Your main problem is that you use people. You exploit them. Or, at least, I think you do. That's how you come across to me.

Denton: Words are getting in the way, Mike. Do you understand what Mike is saying, Joe?

Joe: Yes, I guess I understand. But I don't agree.

Frank: Naturally you wouldn't. You're defending.

Joe: Isn't it natural to defend?

Denton: Sure, it is. But how much of a defense is necessary before you're willing to accept?

Joe: One hell of a lot if you don't happen to agree.

Denton: But agreement and acceptance are two different things, Joe.

Joe: Huh?

Denton: You can accept without having to agree.

Joe: You can?

Denton: Sure. Accept that Mike thinks that you project an image of exploiting people. That's his perception.

Joe: But he's wrong.

Denton: Nonetheless, that's his perception. That's how he sees it. You don't have to agree with it.

Joe: Well I don't, and that's for sure.

Denton: But more important than what Mike thinks, Joe, is for you to decide if you really give a damn that Mike does feel that way. In other words, accept it or reject it. If you accept it and want to live with it, that's fine. Then you've got nothing to do at all. However, if you accept what he says but decide to reject it on the basis that it's not comfortable for you to live knowing that he feels that way about you, then you've got to do things that will change his perception.

Joe: You say "things", Denton. What kind of things?

Denton: Well, it's just like relating to anybody. It's all a matter of acceptance or rejection, these interrelationships of ours. Sometimes it's a clearcut matter of rejection, because the person is not important enough for us to stir ourselves over. But if the person is important, then "things" to do include words but more importantly actions. Show Mike that even if this is the perception that he's currently getting, that you feel he's wrong and do intend moving heaven and hell in order to get him to change his perception.

Joe: Seems impossible.

Frank: To do? Or for you to do it?

Joe: Both.

Denton: That's an honest admission, Joe. Say, I've got an idea. Would you want to attempt to relate better with Mike, Joe?

Joe: (surprised) Do you mean like the other day?

Denton: Yes, Joe. Do you think it would help?

Joe: God, I don't know. I really don't think I could.

Frank: Why not?

Joe: Well, I've never done anything like that before.

Rick: It's all right for Carlos and Jim to get up like that; they're a couple of fairies. (He snickered) A man like Joe doesn't relate to another guy like that.

Jim: You're a stupid son-of-a-bitch. You know that.

Rick: (Rick gave a superior smile) Careful, sonny. I'm liable to step on you like the vermin you are.

Mike: (He took Rick's measure. There was no hint of humour in his voice nor was there any suggestion of a threat. It was a statement.) To get to Jim, you have to go through me first. Remember that.

Rick: That figures.

Joe: Oh, hell, lay off, Rick.

(Rick took Joe's admonition with mixed emotions. He looked like he wanted to continue the verbal battle with Mike, but on the other hand he couldn't risk fighting with Joe. He would truly be isolated without his buddy in the group, for he had already decided that he had alienated everybody else but Frank and possibly Todd. Neither of those two would ever

come to his defense if he really needed help, so he decided to remain
still.)

Denton: It's only a suggestion, Joe. Again, accept or reject. But it might
help both you and Mike. Get some feel of each other. (Rick snorted.)

Joe: That's enough, Rick. (He turned to Denton) Hell, yes. Why not? Tell
me what to do.

Denton: Mike?

(Mike shrugged his shoulders in a noncommital fashion. He got up from his
seat and moved to the centre of the circle of chairs.) ·

Denton: Move in on him, Joe. Come together so that your arms can com-
fortably reach each other's heads. (Joe inched slowly forward, obviously
fearing this intrusion of his psychological space. But Mike took up the slack,
and the two were standing inches apart.) Close your eyes.

(Joe was by far the taller of the two students, possibly a half a head taller.
And objectively, Joe was the more handsome of the two. Dark and very
muscular, he was broad of shoulder and narrow of hip. Mike was neither as
handsome nor boasted as good a physique as Joe, but a certain animal mag-
netism about him that seemingly was summed up by long unkempt side-
burns made him the equal in physical appearance. Mike's hands went up and
found a position on Joe's face. He rubbed in upward movement on each
side, appearing to check out if his morning shave had lasted. Joe's eyes came
open; but with forceful inner movement, he shut them again. His hands remained at his sides, still as he could make them. Mike's fingertips brushed
against Joe's eyes, and he passed his hands back to Joe's ears and slowly
rubbed them. Joe tentatively reached out and grabbed Mike by the
shoulders. He allowed his hands to rest there for a minute, but then dropped
them. They remained motionless at his sides. Mike's left hand moved a-
round to the back of Joe's neck. With firm movements he kneaded the
tense neck muscles. His right hand dropped to Joe's back. Almost in a defensive reaction, Joe's hands came up and again rested on Mike's shoulders. In
something of a movement to push Mike away, Joe began pressing against the
shoulder muscles. Mike continued kneading the muscles in Joe's neck and
his other hand began a massaging pattern in the small of the back. Minutes
raced by as the game progressed. The other members of the group watched
the action as it unfolded with varying amounts of interest and commitment.
Rick alone appeared completely removed in either interest or commitment.

Mike moved his left hand away from Joe's neck. He allowed the arm to slide slowly down the other boy's back, coming to rest when his hand touched his other hand at the waist. He moved arm over arm, pulling Joe firmly up against him. Joe acquiesced in the pull, and allowed himself to be pressed up to Mike. The colour which had initially flushed his facial features and had subsequently been drained by the first contact by Mike's fingers went back to normal. Both Mike and Joe seemed oblivious of the presence of the other group members. Joe's strong hands began a rhythmic massage pattern on Mike's back, his lower body seeming to be driven by an urgent need for contact. Mike returned the push, heightening it by allowing his hands to curve around Joe's buttocks. Mike pulled Joe even closer to him, the while resting his head in the cavity formed by Joe's arched neck. Mike rested his face sideways. Joe moved his hand up and forced Mike's face gently down to his chest. Both Mike and Joe had expressions of contentment on their faces.)

Rick: (in a very agitated manner) For God's sake, how long does this go on?

Denton: (finger to his lip, asking for silence) Just a couple more seconds, Rick.

Rick: (persisting) I don't like it one goddam bit. Joe doesn't know what the hell he's doing.

Todd: Leave 'em alone, Rick.

Rick: Stuff it, Todd.

Denton: (mindful of the tension building in the group) Keep the racket down, fellows ... Please.

(Joe and Mike had not moved. Instead, they were as immobile as statues; holding each other steady as if each was hypnotized.)

Todd: (quietly) Denton:

Denton: Shh. Yeah, Todd?

Todd: Do you think they know we're still in the room?

Denton: (looks puzzled) Sure they do.

Rick: Shit. I hope to God Joe remembers.

Todd: Why? What in hell do you think he'd do if he didn't remember?

Denton: Okay, not much longer now, guys. Keep it quiet, eh?

(Todd threw Rick a look which was meant as an attempt to reinforce Denton's plea for quiet. But the almost hypnotized youths in the middle of the circle of chairs remained oblivious to their surroundings.

Joe ceased the massaging of Mike's shoulders, and allowed his hands to cup over Mike's buttocks. He pulled Mike closer to him, and Mike yielded by increasing the pressure beneath his hands. A pushing movement began that symbolically enacted the traditional expression of love.

Todd quietly rose from his chair. Denton, who had been surveying the actions of both Joe and Mike, shot him a quizzical glance. By sign language, Todd indicated he wanted to join the two youths in the centre. Denton nodded his okay, not bothering to verbally communicate to Todd that such permission was unnecessary. Yet acceptance of himself as an authority figure when such acceptance was neither desirable nor necessary was something he recognized he had to live with. People have been conditioned to accept authority figures from their early years, and the remission of these acceptances rarely is an overnight thing. Todd moved in on Joe and Mike. Although certainly Todd had the strength in his arms to have forced his way into the game, he nonetheless exerted no pull; but was content to let his arms rest around the young men's waists. His communication was that he rejoiced in their togetherness; expressed not in words, but by a tender embracement of their bodies. Frank seemed to want to also join in. Yet any movement on his part was inhibited by his own inadequacies, and he recognized that he was yet not free enough to communicate as Todd had. But when Jim and Carlos rose, he became emboldened and rose to his feet also. Signalling Todd, Frank joined hands with him; and together with Jim and Carlos, the four youths formed a circle around the drama. Rick was alone. Despite an encouraging look from Todd that asked him to join in the circle, Rick stayed out. He slumped in his chair and stared at the floor. His line of vision was obstructed by Frank's back, and it came at a time that he was just experiencing interest in the game. He wished that he had risen to join the circle earlier, but pride kept him from being the last to give acceptance to the game. Denton White noticed the extent to which Rick was shutting himself out of group participation, and he resolved quickly to have Rick reenter before his cognitions stabilized. He moved quickly to the group. With minimum confusion, he motioned all the youths away from Mike and Joe.)

A STRANGE BREED OF CAT

Denton: Let's all go back and sit down now.

(During the exercise Denton, like Rick, had remained separated from the group. He had moved back to the far end of the room to sit in the black leather contour chair. It would be an admission that he was something less than human to deny that the air of sexuality, incipient or otherwise, was not contagious even to him. It was contagious and he was mildly affected. Yet group members have a way of working these things out, and he was better placed away from the members than being with them. The inhibitory effect was one determinant, but another and more compelling one was the degree of involvement which he could allow himself. He was well aware of the possible sexual overtones of the exercise between Joe and Mike, but his concern included the other group members as well. He knew definitely from any number of past experiences that even the unlikeliest group member can rise to the occasion of order maintenance if and when the need arises. He was barely concerned with the sexual overtones, even though on an affective level he had to admit they were somewhat disturbing. But what often passes for passion and sexuality is actually espressions of hostility and feelings of anxiety. Taking feelings from a cognitive level and placing them on the affective more often than not places them in a higher perspective.)

Frank: Christ, that was really beautiful.

Rick: Beautiful? Hell, I think it's sick.

Denton: Why do you think it was sick, Rick? Could you explain?

Rick: That's not the kind of thing men do for one thing.

Jim: Christ, are you ever hung up on proving yourself to be a man.

Todd; It strikes me the same way, Rick. It's almost as if you're afraid someone won't think you're a man unless you bullshit all over the place.

Rick: (to Todd) You think I'm not a man?

Todd: There's no question in my mind, Rick. I think you're a man, but the important thing is what you think. You act like you're scared that unless you are rough and tough somebody is going to question your masculinity.

Rick: Well, you can bet your goddamn bottom dollar I am a man.

Jim: With a box like that you'd have to be. Or a reasonable facsimile anyway.

(Rick sneered at Jim)

Denton: Anybody else want to ventilate?

(Joe looked sheepishly at Mike. Mike yawned.)

Jim: Damn, did you sleep through the whole thing?

Mike: No, baby. I sure as hell did not sleep. I lived up every minute of it.

Joe: (He placed his hands against his face and rubbed.) I'm getting sleepy.

Frank: Well, tell us how you feel?

Mike: Some things can't be put into words, baby.

Joe: I guess I'd say the same thing. I tell you one thing. I've never felt more relaxed in all my life.

Denton: Okay, let's look at this thing for a minute. Mike's telling us it was a great experience and Joe is saying basically the same thing. Todd was the first to join in. Why did you do it, Todd?

Todd: (embarrassed) Shouldn't I have? Was it meant to be something special for Mike and Joe?

Denton: But I asked you why you joined them, Todd. I didn't mean to suggest that you shouldn't have.

Todd: It's that spontaneity thing, I suppose. But those two guys looked like they were so damned happy I just thought if I even touched them some of it might rub off on me.

Denton: Did it?

Todd: I feel for Joe and Mike like I've felt for nobody in my whole life.

Frank: I'd say that was putting it very strong, Todd. I didn't feel that way at all.

A STRANGE BREED OF CAT

Todd: How did you feel?

Frank: Now don't get me wrong. I enjoyed it, but it's like I wasn't even there. You know? I had good feelings about what was going on, I guess, because it seemed to me that a lot of the hostility crap that's been going on between Mike and Joe was being dissipated. But I can't say I felt I was really part of it. It was kind of like I was sitting back somewhere watching what was going on. I knew I was in on it, but yet I didn't really feel like I was. To be really truthful, I can't share your feelings, Todd, that Mike and Joe have become any more important to me.

Denton: What about you, Jim?

Jim: I'd like to have been more a part of it. I felt like Frank. I was an outsider, only I didn't want to be. You know, those guys really looked at peace with themselves. (soberly) I've never known that feeling.

Denton: Okay. Another exercise. Everybody get up, and come over here and form a circle. Jim, you get in the middle. (Jim moved into the middle of the group.) Now, Jim, what I want you to do is close your eyes. Allow yourself to fall. Don't worry. One of us will catch you. We'll all move in a bit closer. Now, Jim, close your eyes. Don't force yourself to fall, but just kind of glide into it. Okay?

(Jim closed his eyes and performed a slow rocking from heel to toe. Finally he fell forward into Denton's outstretched hands. Denton had a firm hold on him.)

Denton: Now relax, Jim, you're too tense. Just relax. What I'm going to do now is to push you away from me so that someone else can catch you. Okay.

(Denton gently shoved Jim backwards. The youth fell into Mike's hands. Mike held him briefly, and then pushed him to Frank. At first the gentle shoving movements propelled Jim back and forth within the circle, but as the seconds ticked by a natural pattern evolved in which he was passed slowly around the circle. Tense at the outset, Jim gradually relaxed until his body became as resilient as a water bag. His eyes were closed and for all practical purposes he could have been asleep.

Denton: (Whispering to Joe who was next to him.) Next time he falls your way, hold him steady and don't let go.

106

Joe: (appears puzzled, but answers in a whisper.) Okay.

(Denton left his place and walked quickly around to the opposite side of the circle, easing in between Frank and Mike.)

Denton: (softly to Mike) When Jim falls back onto Joe, Joe is going to hold him steady. You reach down and grab his right foot and I'll grab his left. We're going to pick him up.

(Mike nodded. Because the other young men in the circle had observed Denton first whispering to Joe and then to Mike, all were looking at the trainer in an attempt to determine what was going on. Jim was still very relaxed, still being moved gently from one set of hands to another. Denton motioned with hand signals that the next task would be to pick Jim up and hold him in a horizontal position. He motioned to everyone that they would have to get a hold on Jim in order that the group could support him. When Jim fell back against Joe, Joe adroitly stepped back and grabbed him under the armpits. Denton and Mike picked Jim up by the ankles, Carlos held his head while Todd and Rick gave support to the trunk. Jim's eyelids fluttered briefly, but he continued to remain relaxed. Upon Denton's hushed urgings, the men lifted Jim's body high above their heads. Then Denton indicated he wanted them to move the inert form backwards and forwards in a gentle rocking position. They followed his lead, and Jim's body was gently moved backwards and forwards. Denton allowed this movement to continue for a period of time that must have been close to five minutes. Catching Joe's eye, Denton indicated he and Mike were going to lower the youth's feet. On silent cue everyone did his part and Jim was going on his feet. Denton moved inside the circle and put his arm around Jim to steady him.)

Denton: Okay, Jim. We've stopped now. Open your eyes.

(Jim opened his eyes slowly. There was a mist in his eyes, and he appeared dazed.)

Todd: (concerned) Are you all right, Jim?

Jim: (slow in replying) It's the most beautiful thing that ever happened to me.

Mike: What did it feel like?

Jim: I can't say. No, really I can't. I know I was floating, and at first I felt people holding me. But after a while it was like I was unsupported. I was floating. It was really beautiful. It was so great I'd like to do it again.

Denton: Another time, Jim. I promise. But how about someone else now?

Joe: Rick, how about you?

Rick: No, I don't want to.

Todd: Please, Rick.

Joe: Yes, Rick. Come on now.

(Rick weakly protested as he entered the circle.)

Denton: 'Attaboy, Rick. Come on, fellows. Crowd in closer.

(The circle became smaller.)

Denton: Now just relax, Rick. Try to relax as much as you can. No one is going to let you fall. We're all here to support you. Now close your eyes and keep them closed. And relax. And don't try to think of anything. Just let your body swing and fall from side to side.

(Rick fell forwards into Joe, and Joe shoved him sideways to Todd. Todd pushed him gently on the shoulders backwards to Denton. Denton could sense the youth's rigidity, and he held onto him.)

Denton: Relax, Rick. Just relax. You're too tense. Remember, we're all here to support you. No one is going to let you fall.

(Denton gently shoved the youth sideways to Mike. Mike passed him to Jim. And so it went. After a while of being passed from hand to hand, Denton could sense Rick's relaxation. Knowing the scenario, the boys all seemed eager to lift Rick; but Denton made no sign that he was ready. He allowed Rick to be passed from hand to hand for a much longer period of time than Jim was passed. Even though he could sense the youth's increased limpness, there was danger in haste. Frank and Mike appeared to be bordering on impatience, but the other four members of the group were intent on what they were doing. Rick fell back into Denton, and he moved quickly to get a firm hold on the boy's shoulders.)

Denton: (loud whisper) Now.

(Carlos and Todd grabbed Rick's feet, and Jim held his head. Frank and Mike and Joe supported his trunk. Denton could sense the youth becoming tense.)

Denton: Easy does it. Relax, Rick. Don't think about what's going on, just relax.

Joe: Play it cool.

(Having had the benefit of experience, the group members knew their task. It seemed as if only the smallest of effort was being expended in lifting Rick's body above their heads. And with a common purpose to give the youth a new and unique experience the atmosphere became one akin to a holy communion. Denton searched the eyes of the youths in an attempt to detect tiredness, but there seemed to be none. It was almost mystical. Finally, and after an even longer period than Jim had experienced, Denton signaled that Rick should be let down. Carlos and Todd lowered his feet to the floor and the others lowered in rhythm. Rick stood alone in the centre of the group. His eyes remained closed, but there was no movement to his body.)

Joe: (moving inside the group and putting his arm around Rick's shoulders) You all right, buddy?

Rick: I don't know what to say.

Denton: Then don't say anything. Let's go back and sit down.

Mike: It's always the same, isn't it?

Frank: What do you mean by that?

Mike: Well, neither Joe nor I could put into words what we felt. And now neither Jim nor Rick can say what they felt.

Todd: There are a lot of times I can't say the way I really feel. Hasn't that ever happened to you?

Frank: Oh, I guess it has. It's just that I haven't thought about it too much.

Mike: Well, I have. And I know there are a lot of times that I can't really describe how I feel about something.

Denton: Are you saying that words are inadequate?

Mike: Something like that.

Frank: Yes, but isn't it also true that sometimes you don't really want to say how you feel?

Todd: Oh, that's true. And that happens to me all of the time. Only thing is, sometimes I just don't really know how I feel.

Frank: You're out of touch with reality, buddy.

Jim: No, I don't think so. I know what he's talking about. Like right now. I feel very good about what happened to me this afternoon. And believe it or not I feel very close to all of you guys. Maybe some of the feelings I have towards several of you as individuals I'm not prepared to put into words; especially not here. Not yet. But I think I can own up to all of you right now what Rick has said about me earlier. For what it's worth, I am a homosexual. But there's more to it than that. The part I was just talking about is something like keeping a secret. But this other thing about how I felt when I was up there in the air is something I just can't describe. Words are simply inadequate. All I can say is that you'd have to experience it to know what it was like.

Denton: But isn't that true of just about everything, Jim. Before you really know the experience personally, you have to live through it yourself. You can read books, you can be lectured to, and you can have a high degree of understanding. Even empathy and sympathy. But until it happens to you, you just can't appreciate the experience. And then you find you're really unable to pass it along in the way you'd like to.

Jim: That's exactly it.

Rick: I've got to say it. (To Jim) I'm sorry as hell.

Jim: For what? That I'm gay?

Rick: I was pretty damned obnoxious about it.

Joe: So was I.

Jim: Forget it. The way I look at, I was giving as much as I was taking.

Frank: Jim, why did you say that you consider yourself a homosexual?

Mike: Knock it off, Frank. You can't be that naive.

Denton: Does that bother you, Frank?

Frank: I'm going to be as sincere as I can. When I wondered, it was one thing. Now that I know, it's another.

Mike: Well, hell! Just pull it together and let it all hang out, Frank. If you have some beef, we ought to hear it.

Denton: Well, I hate to break this up, fellows, but now may not be the right time for us to go into it any further. We've gone overtime again, and this time I've got a meeting I've got to go to. But before we go, I'd like to say that we've had a damned good session today; and I'm very proud of each and every one of you. I think we got a lot done.

(The fourth session began very well in that, without exception, the members of the group were early. As a matter of fact, Denton White was the last to arrive. The youths were involved in an animated discussion when Denton entered the room.)

Denton: Hey, aren't you guys even going to wait for me?

Mike: We have to! You're our fearless leader.

Rick: What we're doing now is listening to Frank's bullshit.

Jim: Bullshit it is, too.

Frank: You see, that's exactly what I'm saying. Now we've got Rick and Jim agreeing, where before it was Rick and Joe. Joe couldn't stand Mike's guts, but they loved it up last week like they were getting ready to jump in the sack together at any minute.

Mike: Is that what love is for you, Frank? Jumping in the sack?

Jim: You're a goddamn male chauvinist, Frank. You know that?

Frank: And what are you? A castrati, like your rival Carlos?

Joe: Gee, I thought after last week we were making progress. I felt pretty damn good about everything, and now we've gone back to recriminations and name-calling.

Carlos: You're a sorry son-of-a-bitch, Frank. You're screwing up the mood.

Frank: What kind of a mood, baby boy? Answer me that. What kind of a mood?

Todd: Well, I don't know about you; but last week meant a hell of a lot to me.

Frank: Define a hell of a lot.

Todd: Oh you know! I just felt great about Mike and Joe hitting it off.

Frank: (sarcastically) There's that, all right. And what else?

Todd: And I wonder what Jim and Rick felt about their experiences.

Frank: (continues in a sarcastic vein) They told you that last week; only they couldn't tell you.

Rick: What in the hell are you after, buddy? For someone who is trying to get over being such a goddamned know-it-all, I'd have to give you a mark of zero for effort.

Mike: Or is it Frank against the world?

Frank: You know, Mike, I think you hit it. Only it's not Frank against the world. It's more like Frank against this group.

Jim: Oh shit! Who's paranoid now?

Denton: It sounds to me that Frank has something to say.

Frank: I know I do. Only nobody's going to like hearing me say it.

Mike: Who are you? Jesus Christ? Man, lay it on! If we don't like it you sure as hell are going to hear about it.

Frank: And that's just it. I don't know whether or not I want to take any more of this verbal abuse.

Denton: Oh, come on, Frank! Verbal abuse isn't the word for it.

Frank: (to Denton) What in Christ's name do you call it when a group of guys sit around and shout at each other?

Mike: You learn, Frank. You learn. Just like you told us you learned something about yourself.

Frank: I admit that. But I wonder if I wouldn't have learned it sooner or later anyway.

Joe: You might have. But the point is you learned it here.

Frank: Okay. But maybe there are some things about yourself you should never learn. Did you ever think of that?

Mike: My God! Here's our budding psychologist pleading for a continued repression of the unconscious.

Jim: I think I'm going to vomit.

Denton: Just a minute, fellows. Maybe Frank's got a point to make. We ought to give him a chance to make it.

Todd: Right. Let's hear him out.

Frank: Like I said, I'm going to be opening a whole can of worms.

Mike: And you're afraid if the worms get out we can't get them back in the can?

Frank: Right on.

Joe: Shit. Put your money where your mouth is.

Denton: In all fairness, guys, we're not giving him much of a chance. (to Frank) I think I hear you saying you want to question the games we played last week.

Frank: (very seriously) Were they games?

Carlos: Christ Almighty, Frank. What the hell do you think they were?

Denton: (to Carlos) Let's give him a chance, eh?

Frank: That's just it. I don't know whether they were games or not. I've thought about it, and the part about Rick and Jim I can accept. That between Mike and Joe was something else.

Denton: Well, you must be saying that you can't see any purpose for Mike and Joe embracing.

Frank: Right. That's exactly what I'm saying.

Denton: You're saying in essence that the fact that they embraced brought up some sexual feelings in them.

Frank: Yes, that's right. They might have talked out their hostility in time.

Denton: That they might have.

Frank: And yet you brought them together like that?

Denton: I hear you saying something else, Frank.

Frank: I hadn't planned to go into it.

Denton: But that's the point, Frank. You should want to go into it. There's not a one of us here you can't trust.

Joe: Would sitting in the hot seat help, Frank?

Frank: (shaking his head) No. I can do it without moving over there.

Carlos: You don't seem to be able to.

Joe: Shit or get off the pot, Frank.

Rick: I think he'd phrase it more delicately, Joe.

Frank: Look! I know you guys are trying to make me mad.

Todd: That's not true, Frank. At least I'm not.

Frank: And it doesn't make a damn to me whether you get mad or not. I could care less.

Rick: Same for me, but only in spades.

Denton: I don't really believe you guys mean that. When you say things like that, it kind of suggests you don't care; and yet last week there were positive signs that we were beginning to care about each other. (To Frank) Now, Frank, how about giving us a chance to at least know what you're thinking.

Frank: Well, I've given a lot of thought to something I want to say. And I must confess I have all kinds of self-doubts and tortures, but here's the place to deal with them. Or so I've been told. So even though I walk with fear and trepidation and maybe even on thin ice, here goes.

Mike: Sounds ominous.

Todd: Sure does.

Frank: Mike, you first. How do you feel about the little therapeutic massage you got from Joe the other day?

Mike: Like I said at the time, baby. The greatest. If you're asking me if I've got regrets, forget it. (grinning) I was kind of angling for the same kind of adventure today. And if that's therapy, boy, well hell, I'm all for it.

Frank: Precisely what I thought you'd say. (Smugly, but there was a hint of a laugh in his voice.) And now, Joe. You? What about you?

Joe: You mean how did it feel?

Frank: Of course.

Joe: Well, let me put it this way. It's a damn good thing I had a date the other night. Cause if I hadn't had one, I would have been too bright eyed to go to sleep.

Todd: You could have pulled on it. That's what we shy fellows do.

(There was no denying it. Todd was developing a sense of humour, or a sense of freedom. Freedom in that he could come out with his humour, that is. Riotous laughter greeted his words. Joe looked strangely at him for a minute. He was trying to decide if Todd was making a joke or making fun of him. He decided that it was the former. He laughed too.)

Frank: (chuckling) Todd's solution to the contrary, you did have a date the other night. And you did work out your feelings of heightened sensation on her?

Jim: Wow! He is going to be a psychologist. Listen to the jargon.

Joe: Answering your question, Frank. You better believe it. Want details?

Frank: No, no details. Just answers to questions.

Joe: Shoot.

Frank: So you were sexually stimulated by Mike?

Joe: Now, hold on Frank. Damn it. I don't know about that question.

Frank: Well, no offense, Joe. Let me rephrase it. Because I'm not trying to get you hot under the collar. I've come up with an idea and, damn it, I want to explore it.

Joe: Okay. Try it another way.

Frank: Whatever happened in here the other day or whatever caused it, you got a high need for some kind of sexual expression. Okay?

Joe: Yeah, I follow you now. Right. I did need to go out and sexually express myself. (Grinning) I wouldn't have phrased it just like that, but it expresses the idea all right.

Frank: And you had a date with a girl?

Joe: Sure.

Frank: And you're telling us you had intercourse with the girl.

Joe: (smiles) Like I said, you want the details?

Frank: No, thanks. (turns to Mike) And you?

Mike: I'm ready for the inquisition. What do you want to know?

Frank: The exercise with Joe brought about later sexual activity?

Mike: Christ! What a phrase to use. But yeah in answer. Somewhat.

Frank: But not as much as Joe?

Mike: Jesus, Man. How do you measure such a thing? But if you're asking if I ran out to find a girl to lay, the answer is no.

Frank: You're sure of that?

Mike: (smiles) Hell, yes, I'm sure. What's to forget?

Frank: Then you didn't go off and have sex that night?

Mike: I didn't say that.

Frank: But you did have some kind of sexual expression as a result of the activity?

Mike: My God, Frank. Why don't you just come out and ask without all this goddamn beating around the bush? (He narrowed his eyes at Frank) I doubt it was a result of the activity as you so quaintly put it. But yes, I did have sex with another human being.

Frank: That very night! Indeed. But not with a girl.

Mike: If you expect me to either lie or bury my head, Frank baby, you've got another think coming.

Frank: I know you would do neither one, Mike. Believe me, I have great respect for you. At first I didn't like you very much. But I'm changing my mind. And one reason for my change of mind is that we can always count on you for the unvarnished truth.

Mike: Thanks, Frank. I know you're sincere.

Frank: But I have a point I want to make, and I think you probably are already two jumps ahead of me. Do you mind?

Mike: Hell, no. If you've got a bitch, say it. As for my being two jumps ahead, I don't know.

Frank: Okay, then. My big question.

(Denton was alert. He was not only two jumps ahead of Frank, but three. Yet, of course, it was his job to be several jumps ahead, not only in words said but in reactions anticipated.)

Joe: You got a question, Frank? Ask it. Don't leave us hanging in suspense.

Frank: All right. (He cleared his throat.) How many of you guys are homosexuals? (He breathed easier, having blurted it out.)

Mike: If you want an answer from me, Frank baby, you've got to phrase it another way.

Frank: All right. Can do. Let's try it this way. How many of you guys have had homosexual experiences?

Todd: What kind of homosexual experiences do you mean?

Frank: As far as I know, there's only one kind of homosexual experience. It's when you have an orgasm provoked by a member of your same sex.

Denton: I wonder if that's not an oversimplification, Frank.

Frank: How can it be defined in any other way?

Denton: Well, I think paramount objection to such an operational definition would come from the nature of its all-inclusiveness.

Todd: You're going to have to translate that for me, Denton.

Denton: All I'm saying is that if you use the label homosexual for anyone who has ever played around with a member of his own sex you're going to have to include about just everyone walking around on two legs.

Frank: You can exclude me.

Denton: Okay. Maybe we can.

Rick: I've never had any homosexual experiences.

Mike: Rick, maybe you've repressed them?

Rick: I've done no such goddamn thing.

Todd: (to Denton) What do you mean you'd have to include just about everybody?

Denton: Sex play is rather common among young boys. And I'd even go so far as to state categorically that it's normal.

Frank: Okay. Among young boys, maybe. The textbooks are full of statistics about voyeurism, mutual masturbation and other kinds of sex play. I'll admit that.

Carlos: And when you were younger, Frank? Did you get involved in what you call sex play?

Frank: There you go backing me in a corner again.

Denton: Maybe you're not being fair, Frank. It seemed to me that Carlos' question was legitimate.

Frank: Okay, I'll answer it. Yes, a buddy of mine and I used to fool around.

Joe: (interested) What did you do?

Frank: Well, you know. Mutual masturbation.

Mike: To the point of orgasm then?

Frank: Yes, to the point of orgasm. But let me tell you two other things: (1) it happened when I was about twelve or thirteen; and (2) it only happened two or three times.

Joe: What made you stop?

Frank: (laughs) I think we were afraid of getting caught.

Denton: But yet, Frank, should we label you a homosexual? What you've told us fits your definition of homosexuality.

Frank: (angrily) That's twisting my words, Denton.

Denton: I'm only repeating what I hear you saying.

Frank: (defensively) But I told you how old I was.

Denton: Well, but does that mean that if you're a teenager you can't be a homosexual?

Frank: As you said, Denton. It's a stage people go through.

Denton: But at what age do you draw the line? Ten, eleven, twelve, thirteen, fifteen, twenty, forty?

Frank: I think you're baiting me, Denton.

Denton: And you don't like it one goddamn bit?

Frank: I don't like being made fun of.

Denton: Frank, believe me. Making fun of you is the last thing in my mind. I'm just trying to get you to be precise in your definition of a homosexual.

Todd: (interrupting) Frank, are you saying a homosexual experience is one when girls aren't around?

Frank: That's one way of putting it.

Todd: Well, what about wet dreams?

Frank: Oh, damn, Todd. I said a member of the same sex has to provoke it. There's no one around when you have a wet dream, is there?

Todd: Well, what about mutual masturbation?

Frank: (caught off guard) Well, yes, I guess so. Depending on their ages.

Mike: (to Frank) But what about the age? Denton has been trying to get you to give out with a figure.

Frank: Well, I think that's an impossible question. It depends on simply too many factors.

Mike: Such as?

Frank: I've said age. That's obvious. You've got to remember that kids naturally fool around. Frequency would certainly be among the criteria. (clears his throat) I could suggest others, you know.

Mike: Sure you could, Frank. But it strikes me that the criteria you are now suggesting are a hell of a far cry from your original definition.

Frank: Well, if you're telling me that a sweeping generalization is always wrong, forget it. I know that. Things simply aren't black and white. You've got to think in terms of shades of grey.

Mike: Shit! On two counts! First, you're coming across as Mr. God himself all over again. Second, when you thought about your original definition of what a homosexual is and then discovered you'd fit neatly into a category, you backed off. Now isn't that a fact?

Frank: Hell, no, it's no fact. Look at me. I'm the only married guy here.

Jim: Big bloody deal. That makes you something special? Look, you silly bastard. I've been out with guys who are married.

Mike: Sure, Jim's right. You'll find closet queens who are married and you'll find closet queens who aren't married. Makes no difference a lot of the time. So what does it all prove?

Frank: (sneers) What is it supposed to prove?

Mike: Not a goddamn thing, I don't guess. Anyway, it's attitudes like yours that really bug me.

Denton: I think we're getting off the track. It seems to me that I heard Frank trying to make a point. (To Frank) And he hasn't made it yet. Have you, Frank?

Frank: You've got to admit they're not giving me much of a chance.

Todd: Well, let him go on with it. (To Frank) You were talking about mutual masturbation.

Frank: There was more to it than that.

Todd: I've never done it, but I've heard about it.

Frank: Good for you, Todd. Now will you get serious?

Todd: Well, but I've masturbated a lot.

Joe: (laughing) Todd, tell us about your masturbations.

Todd: Hell, I've jacked off in the shower so much that I even get a hard on when it rains.

Frank: (annoyed) Very funny. But you're keeping me from making a point I wanted to make.

Mike: (laughing) Oh, yes, Frank. Back to your point.

Frank: (ignoring Mike) The point I want to make is very simple. I would like for those who have had homosexual experiences in the last year to raise their hands.

(Mike raised his hand immediately. Carlos followed suit. Jim, noticing Mike and Carlos with hands raised, elevated his.)

Frank: Todd?

Todd: God damn it, I didn't raise my hand, did I?

Frank: Rick?

Rick: You've got to be kidding.

Frank: Obviously I didn't think so. So, Joe, that leaves you and me and maybe Rick.

Rick: What the hell?

Frank: I said I didn't think so. But Mike's right. You do identify very strongly with a masculine figure. And at your age, that's definitely not good.

Rick: Shit. Joe and I are buddies. What the hell am I supposed to do? Quit being friends with him in order to show that I'm not hot for him? You're crazy as hell!

Frank: I'll let that pass. And Todd. Well, he's another story.

Todd: I tell you I never had an orgasm around no other guy.

Frank: But I'd be willing to lay odds you've given thought to the matter, Todd. There are just too many cues emanating from you.

Todd: You and your goddamn cues.

Mike: Todd's right, Frank. You got something to say? Hell, say it. This is not an inquisition, you know.

Todd: Well, no. Frank's right. I've played around a lot with thinking. But no action. Get me. Just thinking.

Frank: (sarcastically) Good for you, Todd.

Joe: (to Frank) And Denton? You haven't said anything about him.

Frank: Denton is not in on this.

Rick: But he should be. You're afraid of him! Right?

Frank: Wrong. He shouldn't be. He told us before he wasn't in the group membership as such, even though he said he'd like to be.

Joe: Frank's right. I agree that Denton shouldn't be put on the spot.

Frank: It's not a spot. Denton is just not in the group. Period. Okay?

(Joe and Rick nodded agreement with Frank's words)

Frank: So, Joe. Where does that leave you?

Joe: I don't follow you, Frank.

Frank: So what do you think you and I and maybe Rick have gotten ourselves into?

Joe: What are you driving at? You'll have to spell it out, Frank.

Frank: Christ! What has to be spelled out? The truth of the matter is that you are not a homosexual. Right?

Joe: You're goddamned right.

Frank: Then doesn't it strike you very odd that we're surrounded by faggots?

Mike: (calmly) Frank baby, if you think you're going to get by with calling me that, you've got another think coming. Encounter group or no encounter group, I'll wipe up this bloody goddamn floor with your crazy ass if you lay that word on me again.

Todd: (stands) And what Mike leaves, I'll sure as hell finish. As a matter of fact, I want an apology out of you this goddamn minute.

Carlos: Sit down, Todd. Cool it. That stupid stud's not worth it.

Todd: (sits down, but shakes his fist at Frank) What a goddamned nerve. You better get ready to apologize, dummy.

Mike: Carlos is right, Todd. Forget it. Who wants an apology from a clown like him?

Todd: It's been said before, but I'll say it again. In here, I'll take it. Outside it's a different story. (To Frank) I still want that apology.

Jim: Carlos is right, Todd. The trouble is you're not really making the scene. If you were really gay, a dumb ass like that bloody bastard wouldn't get under your skin.

Todd: You mean you don't mind being called a faggot?

Jim: Sure I do. And I must admit I'm not too fond of words like queer either. But what you've got to remember is that a creep like him defends his own precious masculinity by calling guys like me a faggot or a queer.

Frank: Now who's practicing psychology?

Todd: You better keep your goddamn mouth shut, buddy.

Mike: (lisping) Hey, fellows. Any of you gays hot for Frank's body?

Joe: Look, Mike. Maybe this has gone far enough? What do you think?

Mike: I'm cool now, Joe. It's just that I don't dig such a heavy approach.

Carlos: As far as I'm concerned, Frank's a shithead.

Jim: In spades, baby, in spades!

Rick: As far as that's concerned, Frank owes me an apology too. He wasn't quite sure where he should group me, for Christ's sake.

Mike: But you're not as mad as Todd, Rick. And you know why? It's because he gave you the benefit of the doubt. So you are only mildly annoyed because in the final analysis he didn't pin the label on you. Do you see that?

Rick: Sure, I see it. And you're right of course.

Mike: And you understand why Todd's mad?

Rick: Hell yes, I do. If it's not the truth he has every reason to be angry.

Mike: And what if it's the truth?

Rick: I'm sorry, Mike. I see now where you were leading me; and I know what you must be thinking about me.

Frank: Jesus Christ! Are you apologizing?

Rick: Yes, I am, Frank. I think I've learned something about name-calling this afternoon.

Frank: (sarcastically) You've done your share of name-calling.

Rick: Right. And I go on record right now before you guys that I'm sorry as hell that I've been guilty of it.

Frank: I don't get it. You must have developed some fantastic insight these last few minutes.

Rick: Call it what you want.

Frank: Okay. So I'm the odd guy out. I mention homosexuality; a couple of you want to fight me, the others want to ignore me. (To Rick) And you end up being maudlin.

Carlos: You did more than mention it!

Rick: (ignoring Carlos) Like I said, call it what you want.

Frank: Okay, have it your way. Anyway, Joe, there you have it. Now, how in the hell did you get into this goddamn mess?

Joe: Shit, Frank. This is group involvement. Denton said so.

Frank: I know. And Denton told me the same thing. But does group involvement mean letting some guy rub all up against you?

Joe: (smiling) I wouldn't have phrased it that way, Frank. My feeling remains that it was a great experience.

Frank: Which you could have any day of the week in any restroom in any park in town.

Jim: How do you happen to know so much about the trade, Frank baby? You been nosing around?

Carlos: You forget, Jim. He reads a lot.

Frank: (drily) We've established who is queer. (Mike starts out of his chair. Thinking better of it, he relaxed, and let the battle continue to rage around his head.)

Joe: You know, Frank. I agree with Rick. You're carrying this name calling a bit too far.

Jim: At least that's a switch. (To Joe) Usually it's Rick who's agreeing with you.

Joe: You dumb bastard! I'm arguing the point for you in case you didn't get the message.

Jim: What in Christ's name do you expect me to do? Do you really expect I'd be grateful to you for your mild objection to some bastard calling me a faggot and a queer? Forget it, baby. If you're in the Civil Rights battle, I must say you're bringing up the fuckin' rear.

Joe: Look, you silly bastard. I don't want to argue with you. Okay?

Jim: Sure. Why not? You're straight and I'm fucked up.

Joe: Look, I didn't say that!

Jim: Right! You didn't. But I've been crapped on by so many straights and so may jerks who are trying to prove to themselves that they're straight that you'll have to forgive me if I appear not to be overwhelmed by your kindness.

Joe: (laughing) Jim, you're a dumb shithead. You know that? (Jim laughs, and is joined by everyone but Frank.)

Frank: Well, as far as I am personally concerned, I'm still wondering how all of us got together. And for what purpose?

Joe: Well, Denton asked me.

Rick: And he asked me too.

Frank: And, of course, me too. But my question is, is it all part and parcel of an ordinary encounter group for this to be going on?

Joe: God, I don't know.

Rick: Well, it's a fair quesion. Mike, were you invited by Denton?

Mike: Yes, and so was Carlos.

Rick: And you, Jim?

Jim: I received my invitation all right.

Rick: Todd?

Todd: Denton asked me if I'd like to join a group.

Frank: Did he say what kind of a group?

Todd: He said it would be a group of fellows getting together to discuss things in an open and honest manner and that the result of it would be that I might get to know myself better and at the same time learn how to get on better with other people.

Rick: He put it to me the same way.

Joe: I guess Denton told everybody just about the same thing. Unless maybe it's you, Frank, who is in here for a different reason.

Frank: Not really. God knows I've got a lot to learn about the way I relate to other people. When he mentioned it to me, I was interested for two reasons. First, the way I react to people and the way they react to me is of great importance because I do want to become a good psychologist; but, second, the idea of t—groups and encounter groups is fascinating to me. In this respect I consider it a learning experience because maybe I'd be effective at nurturing groups some day.

Carlos: Fat chance. You can't keep your mouth shut long enough for anybody to say anything.

Frank: I don't notice you talking so much.

Carlos: Exactly my point. Maybe if you'd shut up a while the rest of us would have a chance.

Mike: Aw, quit your bitching, Carlos. Maybe Frank's got a point.

Frank: I do have a point to make.

Carlos: Then, for Christ's sake, make it!

Frank: All right. Have all of you guys been seeing Denton professionally?

Joe: Shit! Have you?

Frank: If by professional you mean that he's my major professor, yes; but I'm not being counselled by him.

Mike: There's where you blew it, Frank. You should have been receiving depth therapy all this time.

Joe: Hell, what's the big deal? Denton's been a great help to me. I'm not ashamed to say it either.

Frank: How has he been of help?

Joe: What difference does it make?

Frank: A hell of a lot. You'll see. (To Rick) How about you?

Rick: I've seen him a couple of times.

Frank: Why?

Rick: Look, man. It's none of your bloody business.

Frank: Mike?

Mike: Sure. Lots of times.

Frank: Want to say why?

Mike: I'm with Rick. It's none of your bloody business until I see what you're up to!

Frank: Carlos?

Carlos: (nods head) Many times.

Frank: And you've seen a lot of him too, haven't you, Jim?

Jim: Right on.

Frank: Todd?

Todd: A couple of times.

Joe: So what does this inquisition prove, Frank? All I can see is that each of us has seen Denton about a problem.

Frank: Yeah, but I don't see anybody telling us what kind of problem.

Rick: Maybe it's because you're the one asking the questions, Frank. For some reason or another I'm finding I like you less and less. The way you asked made me suspicious of you.

Frank: Hell, why be suspicious if you've got nothing to hide?

Rick: I've got nothing to hide.

Mike: (gravely) I don't think any of us have anything to hide.

Frank: The hell you haven't.

Mike: Like what?

Frank: You know!

Mike: Okay, what more do you have to say, Frank?

Frank: I suspect you know.

Mike: Maybe I do. And I don't know if I like the direction you're taking this thing.

Frank: There's a good chance you don't.

Mike: I can assure you, baby, nothing bothers me. But let me help you spell things out a bit since you seem to have a little trouble. Okay?

Frank: It might be a chance for us to see if we're on the same wave length.

Mike: We're not on the same wave length, Frank baby. It's just that I see where you're going. I look at things a different way. (He fixed a stare on Frank.) You're disruptive and I'm not. And that's the big difference.

Frank: How in the hell do you figure I'm disruptive?

Mike: To the group. You started everybody choosing sides. Right?

Frank: I wasn't attempting subgrouping.

Mike: It would have been the end result.

Joe: Suppose somebody tells me what the hell you two guys are talking about.

Mike: (sneering) Frank wants to tell you that Carlos and I not only room together, but we think highly enough of each other that we sleep together.

Joe: (gasps) Is that true, Carlos?

Carlos: (cheerfully) Sure, we're in love.

Rick: Christ, how is it possible for guys to be in love with each other? (He turned to Joe.) I had it figured out all right.

Joe: Christ almighty. I might have thought it, but God! I didn't think you'd admit it.

Mike: Hell, why not? Like I said, it's a matter of attitude in the first place.

Besides, in all of our conversations we've been stressing frankness and honesty. Haven't we? Or is all this just meant to be fun and games?

Joe: But, my God, Mike!

Mike: You look like you've been punched solidly in the stomach, Joe.

Joe: I have, Mike. I was just getting to like you.

Rick: And that hugging you were doing with him last week. Remember?

Joe: Christ, Denton. How did you let this happen?

Denton: Do I hear you saying that you can't like Mike any longer now that you know he and Carlos are more than roommates?

Joe: (shakes his head) I don't know what to think.

Jim: Well, let me give you straights something else to vomit over. The reason Carlos and I have been battling is because he thinks I'm trying to take Mike away from him.

Rick: Jesus! I knew it all along.

Mike: You didn't know one goddamned thing all along, Rick. You've got a dirty mind and you're willing and eager to believe the worst about anybody.

Rick: Could there be anything worse than three guys fighting over each other?

Mike: Threatens your masculinity, does it? Okay. That explains why you're here. Now, how about you Joe?

Joe: I feel bad, Mike. Lay off, will you please.

Mike: Sure, Joe. I can see you've got feelings. And I love you for it. And I hope you don't take that word love in the wrong way.

Frank: How else could he take it coming from you, Mike?

Mike: To guys like you, Frank, love is a dirty four letter word. You don't know what the word means in real fact. You've got a silly idea that love is fucking some girl. And that's the damn truth of it. And I'd bet even money you can't satisfy your wife, let alone yourself. You're the epitome of a filthy-minded, nasty-talking, narrow little prejudiced bigot.

Frank: (taken aback) How in the hell do you have the nerve to say that?

Mike: Because, Frank baby. I've got guts. And I know myself, and I like myself. And because I'm not the same kind of dishonest bastard you are.

Frank: The best defense is a good offense, eh?

Mike: Hell, does anyone see me defending? The reason I'm even talking to you is because I think even the dirtiest, narrow-minded bastard can learn the meaning of love.

Frank: And you think sexual relations between guys are the real meaning of love. You're putting me on.

Mike: Sexual relations between guys as you so quaintly put it can be an expression of love. But so can sexual relations between men and women be an expression of love.

Rick: Crap.

Mike: (To Rick) And I'd like to continue, if you don't mind.

Rick: (resigned) Go on.

Mike: But I think love can be expressed non-sexually as well. Like fathers and sons and mothers and daughters. These are one-sexed love relationships, aren't they?

Frank: (sneers) Fathers and sons don't go to bed with each other.

Mike: So what does that prove?

Frank: To me it proves that you've got a perverted view of love.

Mike: And I tell you that you've got a very dirty and narrow view of love.

Frank: Joe, I don't know what Denton's motives are but I'm telling you that you and I are the only members of this group who aren't queer.

Rick: Now wait just one goddamn minute, Frank. What about Todd and me?

Frank: Yeah, what about you, Rick? Hell, your hero worship of Joe says more about you than all the words that I could possibly use.

Rick: Christ! Mike is right. You've got a goddamn dirty mind.

Frank: Well, Todd. Don't you have anything to say?

Todd: (smiling) You've already settled the matter for me. I've gone through it once and I'm not going to go through it again. You've done all the accusing, and I've done all the denying that I'm going to do. Hell, it doesn't make a good goddamn to me what you think anyway.

Mike: Good for you, Todd. Rick is protesting too much: at least that's what our budding psychologist is thinking. Isn't it, Frank? (turns to Todd) At least you've given up protesting, Todd. But God, I don't know what our self-ordained analyst will think that means. Not that it really matters, of course. It just goes to prove once again that if you really want to believe anything no matter how goddamn foolish it is that all you have to do is con yourself first.

Rick: (interrupts Mike) For Christ's sake, Joe. Are you just going to sit there? (motions to Frank) That bastard has just about come out and said that there is something going on between us.

Joe: Hell, what's there to say?

Jim: Besides, who'll believe you, Rick? Frank? Don't make me laugh. And don't try to get Joe to convince him either. It just can't be done. Mike's right. Frank can believe anything he wants to believe, because he's conned himself into thinking he's so bloody self-righteous. Frank'll call anybody a queer. And why not? It's an easy thing to do. What kind of facts do you have to produce in order to say such a thing? Hell, facts wouldn't get in his way even if there were a ton of them. And there aren't, simply because facts along this line are always hard to come by. Believe me, baby. There's no defense. I've gone the route, and I know goddamn well that there is not one bloody thing you can say to defend yourself that won't make you appear to be in even deeper than before. And there's nothing you can do either. After awhile you become what they say you are simply because you have no place else to go.

Frank: So that's your story, eh? That's sheer rationalization. Nothing else.

Jim: So you see, there's no defense. For my part I no longer even try to make one. But there's a bright side to it as well.

Todd: What's that, Jim?

Jim: Well, in my case I learned to live with myself. To a degree anyway.

Frank: That's a cop-out.

Jim: Maybe it is. But you can do and say the kind of things you were always scared to do or say before. Like, let me say that I admire Rick's taste. Joe may not be all that bright, but he's got a beautiful body.

Rick: (smiles) You're nutty as hell. You know that?

Joe: (laughs self-consciously) And you're liable to get a fist in your mouth besides.

Denton: (interrupting) All you guys are doing is fighting on a level where no sense at all can come of it. You're name-calling; and as long as you're hung up on shouting words at each other, you're going to get no further. Now, may I suggest that all of you calm down to the degree that you're willing to listen to each other?

(Denton had the attention of the group, but Rick continued to mutter under his breath. Joe reached over and touched his arm.)

Joe: Calm down, Denton's right.

Denton: Thanks for the concern, Joe. You'll note that this is the first time I've injected myself into the procedings. I've let you go further in other directions as long as something good was about to come out of it. But no good will come out of just name-calling. No good at all. Now, why don't you all settle back and let Frank get back to what he says he thought about the last session?

Mike: Okay. Get on with it, Frank.

Frank: Well, I've said most of it. Except of course the end conclusion. Right or wrong, and I've got to admit the possibility of error, I have decided that this group of ours is set up for the purpose of working out some homosexual guilt feelings. And I don't know how I feel about it. And thinking that Joe was the only other guy in the group not committed to a homosexual life style, I just wanted him to ventilate how he felt.

Joe: Let me get this right, Frank. You mean to say that what we're doing here is just sitting around arguing with a bunch of queers?

Rick: Now, wait a minute, Joe.

Joe: (to Rick) I'm not saying anything about you. I'm trying to understand what Frank just said.

Frank: I wouldn't put it that way; it's group work that Denton has set up.

Joe: Well, just what else makes it different from the way I said it?

Frank: Let me put it this way, Joe. The way you're saying it makes it sound like Denton is somehow guilty of something. He isn't, and I want to make that much clear at the outset.

Joe: I didn't say he was guilty of anything. I'm just trying to find out what in the hell is going on.

Mike: Like I said before, I'd like to do the explaining for you, Frank. Then you tell me if what I'm saying is right. Okay? You're beating around the goddamn bush so much that you'll never get it out. Do you mind?

(Frank was taken aback, but he agreed with a nod of his head for Mike to spell it out.)

Mike: The thing that Frank is saying is that everyone in the group except him and Joe are homosexual. He is probably trying to say that the whole thing is set up so that homosexual feelings can be explored and ventilated. His feeling is that he and Joe were thrown in so that the occasional straight viewpoint can be given. Right, Frank?

Frank: In essence, yes.

Mike: And in addition to that, Frank thinks that Joe was pretty close to having hands laid on him the last session. The things he was saying add up pretty much to the idea that Joe was being set up for some pretty wild advances. Am I still on target, Frank?

Frank: (relieved) Yes, Mike, you're on target.

Mike: Now, Frank felt that I was in no danger, that I had gone the whole route before. Because of that he has no concern for me.

Frank: But there's where you're wrong, Mike, I do have concern for you.

Mike: Okay, you have concern for me if you say so, but admittedly not in the same way that you have concern for Joe.

Frank: Of course not. You and Joe are a different breed of cat. I have concern for you because in a way I like you and because you are a member of the group. I have the same concern for Carlos and for Jim and for everybody else. It's just that I feel that you and the others have made some kind of commitment to homosexuality. Joe hasn't.

Mike: And you think he might be persuaded into it?

Frank: I think it could happen with enough of that stuff going on like last session.

Joe: For what it's worth, I don't think anybody has to worry about me. (His laugh was hollow.)

Jim: Frank is taking over where Rick left off. Hell, Joe, you're being assaulted from all sides.

(Both Rick and Frank shot dirty looks in his direction. He succeeded in ignoring them. His smile was pure and angelic.)

Rick: You know, Frank, I can't help but get mad as hell the way you've pigeonholed me with those three. (indicates Mike, Carlos, and Jim) I know I'm supposed to remain objective and all that, but shit, man, calling me queer is something else.

Frank: I don't remember using that term.

Todd: What's the difference in terms? He threw me in there too, Rick.

Rick: For you there may be a reason. For me, there isn't.

Todd: Hell, as far as I can see, you're as bad as Frank. You don't mind labelling somebody else, just so long as you're not labelled.

(Rick shrugged.)

Mike: But there's one final question you have to ask, Frank. And that part of it I'm not going to do for you.

Frank: I didn't ask you to do any of it for me.

Mike: Yeah, but you sure seemed unable as hell to follow through once you got the ball rolling.

Frank: Well, I see it this way. We were all told that this was going to be group work. I've read enough about encounter groups that I was real eager to get in on it.

Joe: I haven't done any reading on the subject, but what Denton told me was real interesting. That's why I joined.

Rick: Me, too. Maybe we didn't know what we were getting into. (It was a question, phrased and stated as a sentence.)

Frank: Oh, I knew what I was getting into, pretty much. These things have been known to get pretty wild. They have to be kept within some kind of bounds.

Mike: Go on, Frank. You're about to explode. What you want to say is something to do with the group and its bounds. Hell. Get it out, will you?

Frank: All right, that is my question. Has the group gone beyond bounds?

Mike: Denton's the one to answer that.

Rick: He sure is.

Joe: Ask him, Frank.

Frank: Well, first, I'd like to say that this has absolutely nothing to do with you personally, Denton.

Mike: Oh, hell, Frank, do you think he's going to have you kicked out of the department for telling it like it is? You're so goddamned afraid. Why in the hell do you think this was set up in the first place? Do you really think he wants to hear only the socially acceptable crap we're all so used to giving out with? Man, you've got to learn to take chances with people.

Frank: You've got it all wrong, Mike. (Frank was perspiring.) Like I said, this has nothing to do with Denton personally. But groups have been known to get out of hand.

Mike: Sure they have, when somebody who doesn't know what the hell he's doing tries his hand at it. But what you're saying is that Denton has let this one get out of bounds. In other words, he doesn't know what the hell he's doing.

Frank: (exploding) That's not what I'm saying at all. You're putting words in my mouth. You're making me look like I have no faith in Denton.

Mike: Hell, you're the one doing the bitching, Frank.

Todd: Sure, where is the courage of your convictions? I'm with Mike this time. Hell, if you've got something to say, spit it out. Be a man, Frank. Damn the torpedoes, full speed ahead.

Joe: Frank, all you have to do is ask Denton.

Frank: (He swallowed hard, his adam's apple bouncing up and down.) Okay, Denton, is the group out of bounds?

Denton: First, we'll need an operational definition for when the group moves beyond bounds, Frank. But you're perfectly within your right to ask. It's only natural that you should.

(Denton was making an attempt to positively reinforce Frank, because by this time the young man seemed on the verge of falling apart.)

Denton (continued): But it's a question I'd like to assess for a while before addressing myself to it. Okay? This doesn't mean I'm evading the question. It's a good one, and deserves a good reply from me. What I'd like to do is defer answering it until the next session. Okay?

Frank: Sure, that's okay, Denton. (He turned to nobody in particular and continued) See, I knew he wouldn't mind if I asked.

Jim: Then why in the hell did it take you so long to spit it out, Frank? If the truth were known, you're scared as hell. Hell, and beyond that, you're a stranger to the truth. You just use truth as you see it. You make it work for you, just like stud over here (indicating Joe) uses people.

Denton: (Interrupting, he looked at his watch.) You've got a few more minutes now, group. How about using it for a further discussion as to whether the group is going anywhere, where it's been, and so on. Okay?

(Joe and Rick nodded assent.)

Frank: But you know, Joe, I kind of had it figured out that all these guys were programmed for other guys. Except for you and me. (He looked at Rick.) I could have been wrong about you. Maybe you were thrown in as a ringer. (Having been reinforced positively by Denton's assessment of his question as being a good one, Frank moved right along. He was more confident of his ground than before.) I might have even taken a long shot with Todd.

(Mike looked as if he were about to say something, but the words died on his lips.)

Todd: I'd like to go back to where you said you thought the whole thing was a set-up, Frank. Forget the crap about back-tracking. Just tell us why you think the whole goddamn thing is a set-up.

Frank: Okay, Todd. I guess you've got reason to be hostile with me. But I'll answer about the set-up.

Jim: It's the least you can do.

Frank: (Frank shot him a look of disdain.) Well, the thing is this. It could have been that Denton purposely structured this group as a t-group for the treatment of homosexuality.

Jim: What the hell is this business of the treatment of homosexuality? Who in the hell wants treatment?

Mike: Knock it off, Jim. Frank is unsure of terminology. That's all.

Frank: Anything you want to call it then.

Joe: Now, wait a minute, you're going to have to spell it out a bit better for me.

Rick: Me too.

Jim: That figures.

Todd: (shouting) Knock it off. Frank's got something to say. Let him say it. We spend more time making cracks at one another than anything else.

Frank: Okay, it just occurred to me that Denton could have structured this membership as a t-group for homosexuals. If this is the case, then the several of us are being used as a sub-group to counterbalance the other sub-group.

Joe: Go on.

Frank: There's not much else to say, Joe. The thing is, it seems to me from everything I know and have read about encounter groups that one designed exclusively with a homosexual make-up would get bogged down at the outset. It would be a damn poor design, maybe. Of course it's been done before, but you couldn't hope to get a heterosexual rationale presented to a homosexual group unless several heterosexuals were on hand to present their views. Another way of saying it is that if you only had homosexuals present, the only point of view you would get would be homosexual. And this might serve little purpose.

Joe: I see what you're trying to say.

Frank: And when I backed off, it suddenly hit me that maybe you were an experiment of sorts.

Joe: (His eyes narrowed) What do you mean by that?

Frank: You figure it out. You're not that stupid!

Joe: You mean the experiment was to see how far it would go?

(He looked at Denton, trying to digest the words that were being said. Denton stared back at him)

Frank: That's exactly what I mean.

(Joe slumped in his chair, a study in confused emotions. This was a completely new situation. It was fairly obvious that he was thinking that he should be mad as hell at somebody. And that somebody had to be Denton. But Denton appeared to be so calm that Joe fought the feeling to be mad)

Joe: So what about Mike? What gave you the idea he wasn't part of the set-up? (Looks at Denton) That is, if there really was one.

Frank: Two things. First, since he was your initial physical contact it kind of makes sense to think that Denton believed he was the strongest on the other side of the fence. On our side of the fence, you're the strongest. All this may not be correct, but it's how I'm beginning to see it. And the fact that Mike was on the other side of the fence is my second point. You see, Mike had offered certain cues to his sexual preferences.

Joe: Hell, he's come right out and said it. Not at the time, maybe, but he did later. There's no doubt.

Frank: But at the time, you will recall he had said nothing. But I had picked up a feeling or two.

Joe: Okay, you're right. He had said nothing at the time.

Frank: Right. So it was just a guess on my part!

Mike: And now? Do we give the whole thing up? (Sarcastically) Does virtue indeed triumph over villainy?

Frank: I know you're being sarcastic, Mike, and I guess you think you have reason to be.

Mike: Quit playing the psychologist, Frank baby. Don't try to understand anything with that detached logic of yours. Because you just don't have enough of it yet for it to do anybody any good.

Frank: I understood you.

Mike: Shit, what's there to understand? Hell, I've told you a dozen times. You want to know something? You ask.

Frank: Anyway, now that we've got it out in the open it'll be a healthier thing for everybody. We can start to do something about the problem.

Mike: What problem?

Frank: Homosexuality.

Mike: Who says it's a problem?

Frank: It must be.

Mike: Shit!

(Frank and Mike exchanged words back and forth like tennis players volleying. Joe seemed somewhat removed from the action, but Rick and Jim avidly watched the verbal slugfest.)

Mike: Just for the sake of discussion, Joe. Suppose something should have happened between you and me last week?

Joe: It couldn't have. (Chuckles) You're not my type.

Mike: Don't cop out. Just suppose it might have happened.

Joe: (His eyes grew wide.) It couldn't have happened. Denton was here.

Mike: I agree it couldn't have happened; but let's just assume that maybe it did.

Joe: (solemnly) I don't know. I'd like to say that I would have jumped up and beat the crap out of you. (He shook his head.) I guess that's what I would have done.

Mike: But you're not sure?

Joe: Let's say that I am.

Mike: Okay. You've given thought to it now and decided that is what you would have done. But why?

Joe: Why? (angrily) Hell, that's a stupid ass question. No other guy is going to put the make on me.

Mike: Okay. That's the way you feel. How did you come to feel that way?

Joe: What is this? I feel that way because I know that's the way a man is supposed to feel. (he laughed sharply.) And if I need to tell a guy that, then that guy is bad off.

Jim: That's your feeling, man. Live with it.

Joe: You're goddamned right I will.

Mike: But men are supposed to love one another.

Frank: Sure, they are, but the point is that men can love one another without getting hung up in sex.

Mike: Agreed, but going beyond that basic point is the fact that men have great difficulty relating to each other simply because sex is in the way. You get so afraid that just because you like some other guy so damn much that some damn fool is going to come along and call you homo. Hell, it happened to me a long time ago and it bothered me. (He turned to Frank and pointed an accusing finger.) And, hell, isn't that what you were talking about with Rick? He feels close to Joe so, post ipso facto, he's gay.

Frank: How about you? You made some cracks!

Mike: Sure I did, but like we've said before, you and I are on different wave lengths. I make observations, you make judgements. For all practical purposes, Frank baby, you and I are in different worlds.

Frank: You can say that again.

Mike: It won't do any good. You and your kind are always making some moral judgement that's born out of your own insecurities. Then you make hell for someone who doesn't feel the need to be so constricted.

Frank: Meaning?

Mike: Meaning that if two men want to physically love one another, and if they are not hurting anyone else by their actions, what in the hell business is it of yours or anyone else's?

Frank: But I've heard that kind of crap before, Mike. It makes some sense, I admit. But the real thing is that you have to argue that way. You're caught up in a chain of circumstances that requires justification of your behaviour. Let me hear somebody who is not an admitted homosexual say what you've just said and I'll be more prone to believe their sincerity.

Mike: Crap! Frank, you and your kind couln't believe anybody would make that kind of statement unless he were already committed. You cannot argue rationally with irrationality. (He moved to become more confortable in his chair.) Besides, I don't think I have to justify my behaviour or my feelings to anyone.

Frank: But you do, Mike. The majority of homosexuals always have to justify their behaviour to the population at large. They're a minority, and they have to defend their disobedience of group mores.

Mike: You're making me sick.

(Frank threw up his hands in despair.)

Mike (continuing): You don't know what to think of me, do you, Frank? Well, hell, I don't know what to think of you. Okay. Leave it like that. As far as I'm concerned, you can go out and seduce a nanygoat and it's still none of my business. I'd like the same expression from you.

Frank: Seduce is a good word. That's what you guys do. You go out and grab a guy when he's drunk. Or you get him in some other kind of a situation where he's more likely to give in.

Mike: Shit.

Frank: Deny it if you want to, but it happens!

145

A STRANGE BREED OF CAT

Mike: So, it happens, and you're suggesting that Joe was set-up by Denton?

(The blow was telling and decisive. Frank virtually reeled from the verbal impact.)

Frank: (shouting) That's not it at all. I know Denton wouldn't do such a thing.

Mike: The way you were telling it made it sound like Denton was just hanging back waiting for the outrage to occur.

Frank: (in a rage) I didn't say that at all.

Mike: The way I see it means that you thought Denton had put good old Joe up as an object d'art for Todd and Rick and Jim and me to drool over. Now, isn't that what you meant to say?

Frank: You're putting words in my mouth.

Mike: (sarcastically) With my kind, you better be careful it's just not words. Or did you just finish saying something else that you didn't mean to say?

(Todd, Carlos, and Jim roared with laughter at Frank's discomfort, but Rick and Joe remained out of it.)

Frank: (forcing himself to laugh) Well, I'm not going to argue with you about it, Mike. My main concern was wondering if the group had let a game get out of hand. I've asked it and Denton said he was going to answer it next time.

Mike: Oh! So you'll be here next time?

Frank: Sure, I'll be here. Why not? Just because Denton may have this group rigged for homosexual-heterosexual confrontation does not mean that I want out of it. Hell, I want to help in any way that I can.

Jim: Don't do me no favours, Frank. I can't afford your kind of help.

Mike: What Frank means, Jim, is that when it comes to curing all of us dirty bunch of sexual perverts that he wants to be in on it. The stupid bastard really thinks it's something to be cured.

146

SESSION IV

Todd: Mike, maybe Frank is trying to be sincere!

Mike: Forget it. Sincere people give me gas. Most people who think that they are sincere don't even know the meaning of the word. It's like all those clowns who go around considering themselves to have concern. Hell, sincerity and concern are things you feel. They're not tangibles you go around trying to convince other people you possess in any degree.

Frank: Now what the hell does that mean? I've always thought of myself as a concerned citizen.

Mike: (laughs) Hell, I just knew that you did. But what it means, baby, is that if you really want to help someone, the way to go about it is to try to understand. You don't go up to them and say that the only way to handle the problem is the way that you yourself have learned to handle it. You don't go up with a closed mind and an attitude that stinks of the smell that my way is the only way to do it. What you do, baby, is you say something like what you're doing is your bag; I dig it, but have you tried another route? Get it?

Denton: Okay, that's it for today, guys. Hit the road. I've got things to do.

(The session had been so heated that it appeared the fellows couldn't wait to get out for a breath of air.)

SESSION V

The anxiety level was at a peak. Denton felt it as soon as he entered the room. He had willfully timed himself to be ten minutes late in order to ensure that he would be the last to arrive. Whether or not a psychological sub-grouping had taken place remained to be seen, but physical placement had been altered. Joe was flanked by Frank and Rick. Todd sat next to Rick. In the order of the circle from Todd was Jim, Mike and Carlos. The chair reserved for Denton and the chair labelled the hot seat separated Frank and Carlos. The undeclared statement of the two empty chairs separating the antagonists was as eloquent as the positioning of Todd, the enigma, between Rick and Jim. Denton couldn't help but wonder how the seating pattern emerged. He moved the hot seat from the circle, and sat in the remaining chair.

Denton: Guys, we won't need the hot seat any longer. Look, last week I promised I would respond to Frank's questionings this time around. I want to get started right away; because what has to be said is not only involved, it's also going to be time-consuming as well.

If you've observed me at all these past four weeks, you'll have had to notice that my place has been very much in the background.

A group cannot grow very much if the trainer continuously interjects himself into the discussion. If you guys are going to get anything at all out of these sessions, it has got to be because you do the work and the thinking; and not because I do either the work or the thinking for you. When I have come in, it has been for a reason. Now this reason may be that I want a position clarified, a statement made clearer or sometimes because I think you guys have bogged down and aren't getting anywhere. But today I'm playing a different role; much like several of you have played different roles in here. Okay? Today I'm playing the role of the teacher, and what I'm going to do in effect is to lecture at you for awhile. It's a difficult thing that I'm going to attempt to do, because once I've finished lecturing I want to be able to sit back and become a group member again. This you may or may not let me do. But since Frank posed the questions he did, I have no other choice but to jump into the role. Now, as I'm going through my monologue, I want you to feel free to butt in and ask questions. Okay? So this is point number one. Phase two has something to do with what I've already said. I'm not kidding myself into believing that you've allowed me to become a member of your group. A trainer never really becomes totally immersed as a group member, but you guys have worked very hard at keeping me in my place. Case in point: when all of you were yapping about who has had homosexual experiences within the last year, one of you (and it's up to you to remember!) did me the kindness of indirectly asking "How about Denton?" I wanted to answer the question even though it was phrased in a purposefully discreet manner, but, before I could, another member of the group stated emphatically that I should not (as he phrased it) "be put on the spot!" Now that's a hell of a thing to do to somebody: to exclude him from participation. Oh, yes, I recognize it as an intended mark of kindness. Only it didn't come out that way. It came out as "we don't care about you, Denton." And you know, that kind of hurts. And more important, it's the thoughtless kind of thing that people go around doing quite literally all of the time. Words have a way of back-firing, don't you see? What several of you genuinely meant as a kindness was perceived by me as keeping me in my place outside of the group. And this is only one of the many examples I could give; others could be cited, but this particular one applied to me. But if you'll think about your participation in conversations in this group, you'll have to agree that each one of you has been guilty of many unkindnesses. Much of the harsh language was intended exactly as harsh language; your actual intent was to strike out at someone in as vicious a manner as possible. Yet other times I think I heard you saying things you didn't really intend to say; whether you spoke before you gave thought to your words or if it was a matter of phrasing things poorly is of no great consequence. I heard the words and I heard the "Gee, I'm sorry's;" my personal feeling is that more often than not you were simply not getting across what you wanted to say. In the final analysis though, why is it necessary to lash out at people? You know, even if you don't agree with them, there is little to be gained through actual confrontation. And I know that this last gem runs contrary to much of the activist thinking of today. But change, if it's to come about, and regardless of what sphere you're working with, has to be engineered. Change for the sake of change is pure bullshit. So that's point number two.

Point number three gets closer to the heart of this matter of why we are here. Frank persisted in enquiring if each of you had seen me on a professional basis. (To Frank) You could have saved a hell of a lot of time, Frank, by simply asking me that question.

Frank: Would you have answered it?

Denton: Sure I would have, Frank. Each fellow is in here because I personally asked him to come. And each fellow, including you, was as prepared for these sets of encounters as I could possibly make him. No one was forced to come, and everybody knew he was going to have to give of himself to the group if we were ever going to accomplish anything. To that I would add that we've all agreed that what goes on in here stays in here, so under those circumstances I surely would have answered your question.

Frank: You've suggested we're all here to grow, and I go along with that too. I know there is plenty of room for me to grow; but are we all here for growth purposes?

Denton: I would certainly hope so. Unless you consider me one big phony. I've assured each one of the guys that if he did his damndest to make this an active group, it could be the greatest experience of his life. And, by God, I believe that!

Frank: Right. But are we all seeking growth in the same sense that I am?

Denton: I'd respond to that on two levels, Frank. First, I hear you asking me to enumerate the various concerns of each member of the group. I'm not going to do that because growth is struggle, and each one of the fellows is going to have to struggle with his feelings one hell of a lot and feel absolutely safe with every other member of the group before he shares himself. Second, I hear you asking me to define growth. That I can do, although to different people it means different things. To you it could mean becoming more confident around people, but to someone else it might have an entirely different connotation. In essence, growth suggests an improvement in a physical skill or a mental facility. I think it also means learning about one's self as well.

Joe: Denton, do you think it was fair for Frank to challenge you?

Denton: Challenge is maybe too strong a word. But I think he did right to phrase his concerns.

Frank: I'm so glad to hear that. I thought you were getting ready to pounce on me.

Denton: Be assured on that point, Frank. We're all in this together. We have to be, or nothing is going to come out of it. We've got to trust, to share, to criticize, and to argue for our point. We've also got to be prepared to change our minds, if need be, and we've got to have absolute faith that no matter what any one says or does we are not going to nourish any grudges, either in the group or out of it.

Frank: That's a pretty tall order, Denton. Do you think any of us are up to having the patience and fortitude of Jesus Christ?

Denton: Frank, let me ask you something. Have I said anything so very different now from what I said when I asked you if you wanted to join the group?

Frank: As far as I can remember, you're saying the same things. Only when you come up against the reality of a situation the meaning tends to become diffused.

Joe: What do you mean "diffused?"

Frank: I guess what I'm saying is that in theory it sounded beautiful, but in actual practice I'm finding it difficult to remember how beautiful the theory sounded.

Mike: Score one for Frank! He's learned to separate fantasy from reality.

Denton: Nothing's that simple, is it, Mike?

Mike: (laughs) Of course not. I'm just digging.

Jim: Proper thing. The bastard needs more of it.

Todd: Oh, come on, Jim. Let Denton continue.

Denton: As a matter of fact, I've only got one more point that I want to get across to all of you. Frank asked if this was a group where the "gays" would encounter the "straights," or words to that effect. Now that's a difficult one to answer, and I don't know if I can; but of course I'll try. The thing is that men who consider themselves heterosexual meet men who consider themselves homosexual every day of the week. More often than not they don't even know the sexual persuasion of the other.

Frank: You're saying you consider it a persuasion? A preference, in other words?

Denton: Sure. That's exactly what I'm saying.

Joe: Learned behaviour?

Denton: Exactly. I'm inclined to think so anyway. There have been some biogenetic studies, but I question if anything significant has resulted from them.

Frank: Then if it's a preference, why?

Denton: That, my boy, is a good question. I guess it is anyway. At any rate, I consider this group to be a microcosm of the world around us.

Rick: It can't be. There are no girls.

Denton: I'll agree to that, Rick. And I suspect what I should have said is that I consider this group to be a microcosm of masculine society. To go a step further, I think I could state that if indeed girls were present, the entire tone of the group would have a different complexion. For instance, it would be greatly debatable that we could have ever reached this point in our discussion if girls or women were present.

Joe: Why not?

Frank: Well, I think I can answer that one. All of us have something of an ego investment in our own masculinity. We would struggle harder to show how masculine we are if girls were present.

Joe: I don't mean this as a bad joke, but even Mike and Jim?

Carlos: Why did you leave me out?

Joe: Because you're more quiet, I guess.

Frank: I think they would!

Denton: Why don't you ask them? Or, one of them? Why ask Frank?

Joe: Sure, why not? I'll ask Jim.

Jim: What?

Joe: Haven't you been listening? I want to know if you'd be acting differently if girls were in the group.

Jim: It depends.

Joe: That's a hell of an answer.

Jim: Yours was a hell of a question! How in the hell do I know how I would act?

Frank: But Jim, you've given us to understand that you don't fight it anymore.

Jim: In a way, that's true. But in another way, it's not.

Frank: Then what you're saying is that you play games about it.

Jim: I think that's fair enough to say. I play games.

Joe: Then why did you say you didn't?

Jim: I'm sorry, but I just can't answer you. You know what I mean. I'd like to, but I can't.

Denton: Maybe I can help, Jim. Are you saying that your attitude towards your own involvement in sex is not always consistent?

Jim: That's true all right!

Denton: And would you also agree that you feel safe enough in here with us that you believed you could honestly be you?

Jim: It may be as you say. Probably there's some truth in everything you said about why I've acted the way I have. But I think also that Frank, Rick and Joe were coming on so strong that I just reacted out of spite. They've all made me fighting mad at one time or another, so I guess maybe I was fighting back. At least, that's how I see it.

Denton: Fair enough. It's okay to get mad as hell. The point is that you said what you thought.

Jim: Oh, but I haven't said all of it!

Denton: Of course not. But you've made a beginning, and that's important.

Frank: Denton, the way in which we handle our sexuality is a big part of the objectives of this group. Right?

153

Denton: Now, there you have it. Yes, sexuality is a prime focus of this group. Not like you said earlier homosexuality! Or heterosexuality. But plain sexuality, yes. Learning to accept ourselves as sexual beings is a part of growth.

Joe: Like Frank, I'm getting a clearer picture. I've got to admit I was confused for awhile, but I see what you're getting at. First time I came to see you it was about a sex problem. You helped me get straight on that one, and then I kept on seeing you.

Rick: What kind of a hang-up, Joe?

Joe: Later, eh? Now that I've gotten the idea, you don't have to worry about me keeping things to myself. I can understand how this group is going to be of value to all of us. Instead of sitting and talking to Denton by himself, we're going to talk together . . . . all of us. But before, I go on, I'd like Denton to tell me something about homosexuality.

Mike: You're ready to listen, eh?

Joe: Okay, Mike. I deserved that. But, you know, I've often wondered about it.

Todd: Everyone has. Isn't that right, Denton?

Denton: Yes, that's true.

Mike: So go on, Joe.

Joe: Well that's it. I just want Denton to give me some background information on the subject.

Denton: (laughs) Well, of course, you're inviting another lecture from me. But if you're willing to listen to me awhile longer, I'll be glad to make some observations and share some of my ideas with you.

Todd: I'm very interested. It may sound like Joe talking all over again, but I'm certain now that I can see the kinds of things this group can do for me. And all of a sudden I feel very comfortable with the group. Very safe, if I may use the word. I want to start talking right this very minute, and (to Joe) you've hit the very issue I want to talk about.

Rick: (kindly) You think you have a problem, Todd?

Denton: Okay, that's a fair question, Rick. But let me jump in right here and ask all of you to avoid the use of the word "problem" as much as possible. From now on, let's ask each other direct questions about how we feel and think and act.

Rick: Okay. Let me rephrase. Do you think you're a homosexual, Todd?

Todd: You know, this is foolish as hell. A guy ought to know, I suspect; but that's the trouble. With me I don't know. Sometimes I think I am, but other times I know I'm not.

Frank: You're plagued with self-doubt?

Mike: (laughs) That's my boy, Frank. I knew you'd be back to analyzing. You didn't let me down.

Todd: (ignores Mike) Yes, I am. And I want Denton to make his observations, because I hope they'll be of help to me.

Denton: Todd; maybe before I begin, you'd like to talk some. We're all ready to listen to you.

Todd: Really, Denton, I believe it would be of more help to me if it went the other way. I don't know how the other guys feel, but I'd rather you began talking.

Denton: Well, Todd, that's the way we'll do it. I think I'd like to begin by saying that in a world that boasts of its technical expertise and its scientific dedication to the discovery of truth, homosexuality is a virtually unknown dimension. Even the definition of the term is a matter of disagreement. I'll get back to that point later. Many men achieve a rather tenuous psychosexual differentiation, and it goes without saying that many men avoid any kind of patterning. In the time of the teens and the early twenties, psychosexual differentiation comes under stress. At times this stress appears as late as middle age, but this is not the norm. Follow me? Homosexuality, per se, resists definition. What one finds is that scores of different individuals assign myriad operational definitions to homosexuality, and then are somewhat amazed to learn that so much disagreement as to what it actually is does exist. If something can't be defined, how can it even be rationally evaluated?

Some thinking holds that homosexuality may be applied to any situation in which an individual has some kind of overt sexual behaviour with a member of his own sex. It matters not one whit that the incident was the sole experience, nor under what particular situation the incident came about. This is often referred to as the hard-nosed approach. A thirteen year old boy masturbating with his buddy is as involved in homosexual behaviour as is the drag queen, according to this school of thought! Understandably I reject this as any kind of an operational definition.

Frank: God, that was what I was doing.

Denton: Something like that! Let me explain how one of my professors in Clinical Psychology detailed the spectrum of sexuality. This guy was extremely good as a lecturer, and he was always able to get his point across. Anyway, I'm digressing. What he did was simply to draw a long line across the blackboard, which he called a continuum. A continuum indicates a continuous series. And that was his point. Simply that sexuality is a continuous series. At the polar extremes of the continuum were the positions of absolute heterosexuality and absolute homosexuality. In the middle of the continuum, the professor had drawn a vertical line, He termed this vertical line the mean of sexual expression. Most men, he argued, lived in houses somewhere on the heterosexual side of this vertical line. The main point he wished the class to conclude, however, was that for the great majority of men it was extremely plausible that they would make moves to the opposite side of the mean on various occasions of their lives. Age and stress were both factors, he explained, but there were other applicable reasons as well. It is indeed true that some men never operate on the side of continuum marked homosexual just as it is an established fact that some men never operated on the side of the continuum termed heterosexual. On each side of the line labeled the mean of sexual expression, the professor drew arrows that moved away from the centre position. Above each arrow he had written the word more, indicating that the further a man moved away from the central position which was the mean of sexual expression the more certain he was of his psychosexual differentiation. Thus, some men are more heterosexual in their expression than others and in the very same manner that some men are more homosexual in their expression than are others. Let me try it another way. As I recall it now, the main theme of the lecture had been to show that bisexuality was actually a very common phenomenon, and that the direction of sex expression is shaped and determined by significant environmental influences. And if a man be homosexual in the framework of the rationale that any single encounter employing overt behaviour is to be labeled homosexual, then, in like manner, the actual homosexually oriented guy would have to be labeled heterosexual were he on any occasion to have sexual relations with a female! The professor pointed out how utterly preposterous the situation had become. He said he preferred a different taxonomy. He suggested the terms overt heterosexual, overt homosexual and the bisexual. He presented additional stages as well, which meant to further describe areas of sexual activity but within the scope of the three broad titles. But with especial regard to homosexuality, I recall he termed latent homosexuality as a condition in which the individual desires overt involvement with a member of his own sex but at the same time refrains from any commitment. Another term he used was that of pseudo-homosexuality. Although he said he had nothing but his own observations on which to make judgement, but that it was his opinion that the pseudo-homosexual faced less damage of a psychological nature than did the latent homosexual. His definition of the pseudo-homosexual described the man who engages in overt activity only under alcoholic stimulation, possibly under the influence of drugs or depressants or while in a particular type of stress. He also spoke about situational homosexuality, where a man might temporarily manifest a type of sexual expression directed towards a member of his own sex because of the unavailability of women. His last category was what he called psychic-homosexuality. This is when a man quite literally talks himself into overt or covert homosexual expression.

Todd: How is that possible?

Denton: There are so many ways this could come about, Todd, that we could discuss all the ins-and-outs for the rest of our lives. I could suggest a couple of ways, maybe. Actual cases I have seen. One was a fellow who all through school was teased by his friends about his sissiness and the fact that he talked like a girl well up into his teens. Actually the guy was slower than his mates in physical development, but it was only later and after he had gone through a lot of trauma that he came to see what had happened to him. Another man was purely and simply painfully shy around girls when he was younger; because all of his friends were having dates and all, he began to believe that something was wrong with him. When each of these men developed insight into their purely sexual selves, really remarkable changes came about in their behaviour. In any event, psychosexual differentiation is a very subtle process. Also, any number of factors are involved in achieving a personally satisfying means of sexual expression. There are conditions existent in every male which, to say the least, cause ambivalence. Of course, Freud and others have stated that homoeroticism is a normal libidinal phase prior to the attainment of heterosexuality.

Frank: That would mean that homosexuality is arrested behaviour.

Denton: Yes, in Freud's thinking that might be the explanation. But most psychologists tend to agree that a pattern of sexual expression becomes preferred as a result of experiential determination. Many factors have pressed and weighed on the individual prior to the assigning of his commitment. Thus it becomes incumbent to a large degree upon any therapist to make no value judgment on the rightness or wrongness of either the homosexual or the heterosexual modes of expression, except a willingness to note that both forms of expression should be temporarily if not permanently accepted as somehow reflecting a pattern of behavioural responses which are of some satisfaction to the individual in his search for the reduction of sexual tension. It follows then that bisexuality is a to-be-expected phenomena.

Todd: You're saying that a man can be bisexual? Does that mean he can be attracted sexually to both females and males?

Denton: That's right, Todd. You see, human sex behaviour is determined by two factors: biology and culture. Another way of phrasing this is to state that the way in which you or I express ourselves on a sexual level is a combination of instinctive drives and by social influences.

Frank: The instinctive drive is procreation, right?

Denton: It's probably a lot simpler than that, Frank. The release of sexual tension and the gratification inherent in the resolution of the need are the major instinctual factors I should suspect. The concept of procreation is a double-edged sword in that it is a natural resultant of intercourse between a man and a woman, but again I suspect that procreation, per se, is a learned phenomenon. We have been instructed to produce our own kind by the church, for one thing. In our society there is something of a social pressure involved (especially for the man) in having his surname passed on to subsequent generations. Other cultures stress the need for a couple to have children so that in their later years they may be taken care of.

Frank: God, it's more complicated than I thought.

Denton: Not really. It's just that man throughout the ages has hung the taboo sign around those attitudinal sets and behavioural patterns that he doesn't understand. Sex has probably been wrapped in more superstition and taboo than any other area of human involvement.

Frank: And that's paradoxical as hell since sex is the most personal thing any of us possesses. What we've succeeded in doing is the construction of a large wall around ourselves which really prevents self-knowledge. (to Denton) Or is that an accurate assessment?

Denton: I'd say that it was.

Joe: Well, it sure as hell never occurred to me that a man could be bisexual. I thought there was only one way to have sex.

Denton: The point I'd like to get across, fellows, is that for most people there is only one way to have sex.

Todd: But you've suggested that is a problem, Denton.

Denton: No, Todd, I didn't suggest that as a problem.

Rick: Well, I'm getting more confused all the time.

Denton: Well, I'm sorry for that, Rick; but maybe if we look at the subject long enough some of that confusion will go away. Look, all I'm saying is that a man should become aware of his sexual identity. If he is attracted to women, great! If he is attracted to men, great! If he is attracted to both men and women, great!

Todd: If he's attracted to both men and women, would it be in varying degrees?

Denton: I should think so. My personal feeling is that he would probably be more attracted to one sex than to the other. It would be difficult to think that a human being could be so lacking in awareness that he ends up by being like the donkey set midway between two equally attractive bales of hay!

Frank: (laughs) He might end up starving to death that way.

Denton: (also laughing) True, but let's give man credit for having more sense than a donkey. It's on this basis that I feel that even though man can indeed have ambivalent feelings about sexual expression he is certainly to be expected to be inclined more in one direction than the other.

Todd: (To Denton) Going back to taboos. Do you really think that a man can fake heterosexual behaviour?

Denton: You know, Todd, I could answer that from my perspective. But what I'd really like to have take place now is for you guys to pick up on the conversation.

Joe: The fact that we might not have the right answers? Isn't that a danger?

Denton: Sure it is, but there's no harm in exploring the recesses of your own minds. If you get bogged down on the informational level, I'll be here to help out. On the other hand, it will be a hell of a lot better if each of you gets involved.

Frank: That makes good sense to me.

Todd: (eagerly) Me, too. (To Denton) Now how about answering my question? (General laughter)

Denton: Okay, Todd, okay. Yes, I do think many men go through their lives forcing themselves to be heterosexuals; but I think the reverse is true as well.

Todd: You mean men are homosexuals when they really don't want to be?

Denton: I don't know that I would put it exactly that way though. There's not the same social pressure on a man to be a homosexual as there is to be a heterosexual.

Mike: (entering the conversation) In fact, it's just the opposite.

Denton: Right.

Joe: So what you're saying is that some men force themselves to be exclusively heterosexual out of social pressure.

Mike: That's exactly what Denton is saying, Joe.

Joe: By why, for Christ's sake? I mean, everybody ought to be able to do his own thing.

Mike: (quietly) Joe, do you remember the things that you and Rick and Frank have said about some of the other members of the group?

Joe: (earnestly) Wow! Yeah, well, you've hit home all right. Whatever caused me to act like such a bloody ass?

Mike: Joe, I know right now you're being serious and even apologetic. Maybe you've even had an insight! I don't know. Whatever, I hope the understanding continues. But don't you see how much crap a guy has to put up with if he shows any homosexual tendencies at all? Take Jim, for instance. He's taken a lot off you guys; he gets even more of it outside. Hell, people consider it a bloody disease; even worse than leprosy! Fathers have nightmares that their sons will grow up to be gay, and they sometimes force them to get involved in all kinds of athletic programmes and do all kinds of "manly" things.

Rick: Hell, maybe I'm like Joe in that I've developed some insight; but I've had feelings all my life that I've got to measure up to a standard.

Mike: Right, Rick. And do you think you always do?

Rick: I think I back away from thinking about it.

Mike: You're damn right you do.

Rick: But is that necessarily bad?

Mike: I don't know; I really don't.

Joe: But, Mike, you've come to terms with yourself, haven't you? I mean, you're gay and you don't fight it!

Mike: Joe, baby, this will come as one big shock to you; but I don't consider myself gay.

Joe: (incredulous) But you live with Carlos! How do you explain that?

Mike: Well, first, I don't explain it! If you get what I mean. To get to what you're driving at though, I consider myself AC-DC.

Rick: AC-DC?

Mike: Bisexual, Rick.

Rick: Oh!

Carlos: (to Mike) You've never told me that!

Mike: Look, Carlos, you didn't ask.

Frank: Carlos, you look like a truck hit you.

Carlos: Well, I'm kind of in a bit of a shock.

Mike: I can't see why, Carlos.

Jim: (to Mike) I sure as hell can. It's a question of being faithful.

Mike: Damn, Jim. Faithful is as faithful does! Isn't that how it goes?

Jim: But that's why Carlos was so damned pissed off at me. He thought I was trying to get you to be unfaithful to him.

Joe: Christ! This is complicated as hell. I don't know if I can ever sort it out.

Rick: I think I understand.

Frank: (ignoring Rick) Todd, a while ago you said you were about to burst to say something. Now you've gotten very quiet.

Todd: I'm listening.

Frank: How about talking?

Todd: The pressure's not there any more, Frank.

Mike: Maybe it would help if I started it, Todd. Do you mind if I tell the group about how we met?

Todd: I can't promise I'll react.

Denton: Fair enough. But I think Mike wants to tell it, Todd. You have any objections?

162

Todd: No. No objections.

Denton: Okay Mike.

Mike: Well, we met in a restroom.

Rick: Where?

Mike: That's not important, Rick, but it was on campus. Anyway we met in this restroom. It's a funny thing in the restroom trade, but you never know what you're going to end up doing or even if you'll meet anybody. Well, to make a long story short, I was in a stall and Todd was in the next one. We were sitting there, and then I made the usual pass. When he didn't respond like I expected him to, I decided he was scared we'd get caught. So I wrote him a note asking him if he wanted to go with me to my place.

Frank: Would Carlos have been there?

Carlos: I can answer that! I wouldn't have been, and Mike knew this. Otherwise he would not have suggested it.

Mike: I'm sorry if all of this is going to shake you, Carlos, but this is something which might be of help to all of us.

Carlos: If it bothers me, so what? As you say, let it all hang out!

Joe: Hold on, Carlos. You don't know the whole story yet. Why make a judgement before you get all the facts?

Carlos: That's easy enough for you to say. Me? I've heard enough.

Frank: But Joe's right, Carlos. It has to come out in the open now.

Carlos: Sure. Why not? Let's all hear what Mike has to say.

Mike: (to Carlos) I know this is going to be difficult on several counts, but I've made up my mind I'm going to tell the story. If you get pissed off about it, all I can say is that I'm sorry you feel that way.

Carlos: Like I said, get the hell on with it.

163

Mike: Okay. I appreciate the fact that you're mad as hell at me, and will probably get madder. But one thing I want you to remember. I have never once lied to you.

Carlos: I just didn't get the whole truth.

Joe: Look, how about you guys settling this later. We're getting bogged down.

Mike: You're right, Joe. Well, in any event I wrote Todd a note asking him to come by my place for a drink. Well, I kid you not. The guy went nuts. He started shouting like a madman.

Jim: What did you do?

Mike: (laughs) Hell, all I could do. I jumped up and tried to get out of there. Only thing is, Todd moved faster than me and collared me as I was going out the door.

Frank: Still shouting?

Mike: You better believe it!

Joe: What was he saying?

Mike: Just about everything about queers that you and Rick have said. Only he was shouting, man. He had me in his grip leading me along, yelling at the top of his bloody lungs.

Rick: But you look big enough to have taken him, Mike.

Mike: Baby, I tell you he was like a madman. He had such a hold on me like you wouldn't believe. Besides, I guess I was just stunned by it all.

Frank: Or maybe you just wanted to get caught?

Mike: Oh, stop that psychoanalytic jargon, will you?

Frank: (laughs) Okay, you're right. So what happened then?

Mike: Well, we ended up in Denton's office. Todd practically threw me through the door. The next thing I knew we were in Denton's office trying to tell him the story.

Frank: Trying?

Mike: Well, Todd didn't say too much. I had to do most of the talking. Then Todd said he wanted to forget the whole thing.

Todd: I didn't know what else to do under the circumstances. Denton didn't seem to think any kind of action should be taken against Mike. What the hell else was there to do?

Rick: (being helpful) Why didn't you tell your side of the story?

Todd: I thought I did.

Mike: Like hell you did, Todd. It was like the tip of an iceberg. You were holding back. Now why in the hell can't you tell us exactly what happened from your point of view?

Todd: (resigned) Well, I can try. I wish I would have blurted it out earlier when I had my mind made up I wanted to talk. Needless to say, it's a hell of a lot more difficult for me to talk about it than it was for Mike.

Frank: You're among friends, Todd.

Todd: I've got to admit that makes it easier. (directly to Mike) I have felt really guilty about the whole goddamn thing. Believe me, Mike, I've thought one hell of a lot about it.

Mike: I'm sure you have! Come up with anything?

Todd: Well, I covered up a lot the other day.

Mike: That comes as no news flash. But I am glad you've thought about it.

Todd: I didn't really think it would be news to either you or Denton. (To Denton) You've got it all sorted out too, don't you. You know, putting two and two together?

Denton: (soberly) Sometimes the trouble with putting two and two together, Todd, is that you can easily come up with five. Especially when there are unknown quantities. See what I'm saying? To my mind, there were several unknown quantities that day that you and Mike came into my office. The thing with unknown quantities is that the longer you speculate on them the more possibilities there are to explore. The best way is for a man to go on only what he's told. You may have some distorted perceptions to work through, but the odds are a bit better than in a pure guessing game. Follow me?

Todd: Yes, I see. And the answer is that you didn't speculate. Only I guess that maybe you did. Well, in any event I'll fill in all the details now. (Smiling) No more guessing on unknown quantities, fellows. The truth is that I knew it was Mike in that booth next to me.

Mike: (Surprised) You knew?

Todd: Sure. I had seen you hanging around. I wanted to be there, and I wanted you to be there.

Mike: Then, what the hell?

Todd: All right, I'll be frank as hell. I wanted you to blow me. (appears relieved) There, I finally got it out. (To Mike) I hope it's okay with you, but I've decided to spit it all out. It won't get you uptight?

Mike: No way, baby. No way.
(The group remained silent during the exchange. Only Frank looked as if he wanted to interrupt.)

Todd: Well, it just happened so differently from how I had worked it out in my mind. I got scared, and that's the bloody truth.

Mike: (incredulous) You got scared? And that's the reason you pulled all that stupid crap out in the hall?

Todd: It sounds stupid, Mike. But that's the honest to God truth. I got scared. And I'm scared right now.

Denton: Relax, Todd. You've got no real big reason to be scared of any of us, do you?

Todd: Well, I'm scared now in a different way from what I was the other day. If you know what I mean. Right now I'm saying things that I've never said before, and I guess that's the reason I'm scared. But I know it's got to come out, and I'm convinced that it will help me if it does. The other day I was doing something that I had never done before. And that scared me. I guess it's about the same thing.

Denton: (kindly) About the same, Todd.

Todd: You know, it's crazy as hell. I planned everything, and I knew before I went in there what I wanted. Then the time comes that Mike does what I've been wanting him to do, and I screwed it up. It doesn't really make sense. I made a damn fool of myself, in addition to seeing that Mike got made an ass of as well.

Mike: Like I said, don't worry about me.

Todd: Easier said than done. (snickers) Hey! Do you know that I've had god knows how many phone calls from guys asking me to go out with them? One guy told me I looked cute when I was mad, and that he'd just love for me to drag him down the hall that way.

Frank: How did those guys get your name and telephone number?

Todd: Hell, I don't know.

Frank: Do you think that Mike had them do it in order to get back at you?

Todd: I thought about that. But I don't think he did. (To Mike) Did you, Mike?

Mike: Hell no! That's bullshit!

Todd: Someone must have recognized me. (Shakes his head) Anyway, it burns me up that I made such a bloody fool of myself.

Rick: Well, how about getting on with the story, Todd?

Todd: Right. I guess I got carried away. Anyway, sitting there with my pants down around my ankles, I kept wqiting for Mike to make a move. He didn't, so I edged around on the seat so that the light flashing down from the ceiling through a reflection of my erection on the floor. Mike couldn't help seeing it if he was looking. (blushes) I don't mean that it's that big. It's just how it happened and how the light works in that restroom.

Jim: So then what happened?

Todd: Nothing at first. Like I said, I figured Mike could see me. I've sat in the booth where Mike was many times and seen guys flashing around like I was doing.

Jim: But you said this was your first time.

Todd: It was my first time to try to go the whole route. Actually what I've done before is just jack off; but it seems I have a stronger ejaculation when I do it in there.

Jim: Wow! Oh wow!

Todd: (laughing) Well, I guess it's funny after all. Anyway I've thought about letting a guy give me a blow job in there. It was going to be a brand new experience. I've wondered and wondered what it would feel like.

Jim: Wow! A real babe in the woods, eh?

Todd: You can call it that. Anyway, I guess I got the idea from reading about it and then thinking about it. I've even seen it done a few times. But I've always been too scared to get involved. But that day I had my mind made up that I'd go through with it, and that's why I was flashing it to Mike. (nervously clears his throat) That's the way I've seen it done.

Frank: So if you had your mind made up, what happened?

Todd: (laughs) Well, the first thing I know is that Mike stuck his god damned head under the partition. That kind of shook me up.

Mike: Hell. You mean to say that my putting my head under the partition shook you up? What the hell was I supposed to do?

Todd: The way I had seen it done is that the guy gets down on his knees, sticks it under the partition, and the other guy starts sucking on it. You didn't do it that way.

Joe: My God! There's a goddamn science to it!

Todd: Well, the way I had seen it done is that the one guy signals the other guy with his hand that he's to get down on his knees and slide it under.

Joe: Kee-rist!

Todd: Well, when Mike put his head under it got me scared. That's the only way I can explain it. He then reached over and grabbed me rough as hell.

Mike: (sarcastically) And you were expecting a love tap?

Todd: Hell, how was I to know what I was expecting? You had already loused it up for me. Besides, I was so damned excited that I ejaculated.

Jim: You probably shot it all over yourself.

Todd: As a matter of fact I did. That made me made as hell too, because it ruined my plans of getting him to suck me. See what I mean?

Joe: I hear you, but I swear to God it's hard to believe what I'm hearing.

Jim: (laughing) What you're hearing, Joe, is the twentieth century virgin queen.

Joe: That I can believe. In fact, I'm ready to believe just about anything now.

Frank: Hey, guys. Let Todd get on with the story.

Todd: Well, that's it. I knew I couldn't wait around to build up a hard again. It would have taken a few minutes at least. I know I could have gotten one on, but I was so damned mad that he didn't do it the right way in the first place.

Mike: Let me get this straight. You mean that if I would have let you kneel down and squat under everything would have gone okay?

Todd: Sure. That's what I was expecting.

Mike: (shaking his head) Brother, I just can't believe it.

Todd: Well, that's the truth. I was so damned pissed off about the way you went about it. Then I come all over myself. And then you wrote me that goddamn phony lousy note.

Mike: What was wrong with the note, for god's sakes?

Todd: I didn't want to go to your goddamned place. I wanted you to take me in that place. Period.

Frank: So then what happened?

Todd: My temper got the best of me is all. I started yelling at him, and then he tried to run out of the place ahead of me. That made me even angrier. I grabbed him at the door. I guess I was just going to drag him outside and beat the shit out of him.

Mike: That would be the day.

Todd: Okay, Mike, have it your way. But I do like to fight and I'm good at it. And I can take you any day of the week. Sometime we'll have a go at it just for the hell of it. Okay? Anyway, that's what I thought I was going to do. I was going to beat him up real good. I even thought that after I did beat him up that I'd then make him suck me. You know, all kinds of things were running through my head, but I knew I wanted to beat him up. Then we passed this office, and the sign on the door said Counselling. I'd never been in there, but by that time there were so many people in the hall and there was such a racket going on that I thought maybe I better get in out of the hall. And that's it.

Frank: You mean you weren't thinking of psychotherapy for Mike?

Todd: (laughs) Didn't even enter my mind. I guess all of a sudden it dawned on me that I was making a bloody ass of myself.

Joe: So what it boils down to is that you got real mad?

Todd: Right. And that's kind of in character for me. I'm always losing my cool. But I don't stay mad long. I live and let live, except for the few minutes that I really get pissed off.

Frank: Todd, does the fact that you went looking for Mike bother you?

Todd: Well, it isn't fair to say that I went looking for Mike. Any guy would have done okay. It's just that Mike was there.

Frank: Okay. But does it bother you that you went looking?

Todd: Hell, yes. It bothered me then and it bothers me now. Oh, I'm not saying that I didn't plan the whole thing. I wanted some guy to suck me. I guess if I felt anything about Mike being there it was relief that it was him. You know, he's a little smaller than me. I guess I figured I had a secret to keep and he would keep it for me, or I'd pound him into the ground.

Mike: Like I said, baby. Any day.

Todd: Okay, Mike. I could be wrong. But I think I could take you. Okay?

Frank: (interrupts) You wanted it kept a secret?

Todd: Sure I wanted it kept a secret. Just like right now I wouldn't be telling you guys all of this if I didn't trust you.

Frank: And how do you feel about sitting there shooting off your mouth the whole time thinking you can trust us?

Todd: (smiles) Oh, you're not going to get me mad, Frank. No, I feel like I can trust you guys all the way. And I really feel great right now. You may not believe it, but I've been sitting here since the first day waiting for a chance to spill my guts. And believe me, it feels real great.

Frank: So you feel it's okay to talk to us, eh? But isn't there anybody else you can talk to?

Todd: Are you kidding? With whom? As my mother would say, "it's not a fit subject for conversation."

Frank: And you, Todd? You don't think it's a fit subject for conversation?

Todd: Maybe here it's okay. In fact I know it is, because it's done me a lot of good to talk. But I can guarantee you it's not a conversation you can carry on very many other places.

Jim: Why not?

Todd: (explodes) Why not? Well, hell. Isn't it something a guy should be ashamed of? Running around a rest room with a hard dick trying to find some guy to blow you isn't exactly termed polite conversation.

Frank: You find it threatens you?

Todd: Sure it threatens me.

Rick: Todd, have you ever thought you'd like to do it to some other guy?

Todd: Suck somebody else? Man, are you crazy? Hell no, I never thought about it. And if I did, I sure wouldn't let myself think about it for long.

Frank: It's interesting that the very thought of it can upset you so, Todd. You can let somebody else go down on you, but you can't stand the idea of you going down on some other guy. Very interesting.

Jim: It's the way it is, Frank. I felt that way once myself.

Frank: The way you say that makes me believe you have lots of regrets.

Jim: (smiles wanly) No regrets, Frank. Sorry.

Mike: You might be overstating the case, Jim. People have regrets all the time over all kinds of things. Why should you be any different?

Jim: You have any regrets, Mike?

Mike: Loads of them, baby. I'll tell you about them some time.

Jim: (snorts) Maybe I've sold myself a bill of goods? Is that what you're saying? Because if it is, I don't buy it. I know my likes, and I enjoy my life.

Denton: Well, sorry to butt in, guys; but it's time to go. It seems to be a damn good stopping point. It seems we regularly go over the time we agreed on, but that's no big deal. I'd like to say that I think the group owes an awful lot to Todd at this moment. He's brought us a long way this afternoon.

Todd: Mike did too, Denton.

SESSION V

Denton: Well, to be fair about it, everyone did his share. Of course, when one of us doesn't talk much he deprives the rest of us of the chance to get to know him better. That's one thing we should all pay attention to. Sometimes we have to help get the other guy started.

Frank: Right. Like Mike helped Todd get started.

Denton: Exactly. And I feel that a couple of members of the group haven't opened up at all.

Frank: Maybe that will change now that Todd has broken ground.

Denton: It's possible. But each of us here is still going to have to help the process.

Joe: Well, I'll do my part. I feel I owe this group a lot.

Mike: That feeling is easily shared, Joe baby. (looks at Carlos) Maybe at the moment things aren't right for all of us, but, if we all stick together, things just have to work out.

Denton: Well said, Mike. Now let's clear out for the day and we'll all get together next week. Okay?

(The group left the room almost as if they were departing from a hallowed presence. There was a pervasive feeling of holiness attached to the afternoon's proceedings. Denton felt it, and he saw it in the eyes of all of the other group members; except for one. Carlos looked stunned!)

SESSION VI

The group members arrived, with the exception of Frank, in pairs. Denton went to the group room early, more to keep from being detained in his office than for any other reason. Whether by design or whether by accident was enigmatic, but Joe came in with Rick, Mike arrived with Carlos, and Frank wandered in by himself. Todd and Jim were the last to arrive, and they presented the appearance of having been deeply involved in a conversation that was being disrupted by their attendance at the session. For a period that lasted maybe five minutes (but seemed horrifically longer), no conversation ensued. Much shuffling of feet, some forced laughter; all symptomatic of general uneasiness.

Frank: Somebody's got to say something, so I guess it might as well be me. I've worried about something the whole week. (His words were seemingly a welcome break in the silence, but no one picked up on the comment. Quiet of an oppressing nature again descended on the group.)

Frank: Well, damn it. I tried! Doesn't anybody want to say anything today?

Denton: How did you try, Frank?

Frank: Well, I asked a question.

Todd: I didn't hear you ask a question.

Frank: In a way, I guess I didn't. But I did say I was worried about something.

Mike: Then the next gambit was for someone to ask you what you were worried about! Right, Frank?

Frank: I thought we were supposed to learn to care about each other. If I'm worried, somebody ought to care. Remember how Denton said he felt left out when we agreed that to involve him might put him on the spot? Well, that's how I feel right now. Left out!

Mike: Then you did want the question asked?

Frank: Hell, yes. If I say I'm worried about something, I think the least one of you guys could do would be to ask me why I'm worried.

174

Mike: Then let me ask you why you said you were worried instead of coming right out with the question.

Denton: Gee, we're sure playing games today, aren't we?

Rick: I can see what Frank is saying. It's hell to be ignored when you see everybody else getting attention from the group.

Joe: Christ, Rick! What are you saying? If you've been left out of a lot of the discussion it's because you chose it that way.

Rick: Not true, Joe. I've done my share of talking and general mouthing, but, like Frank, when it came to the crunch, the group let me down.

Joe: Hell, I don't know where anybody let you down. Give me a for instance.

Rick: Like hell I will. All I'm saying is that I understand how Frank can feel left out; because I too have been left out.

Joe: (to Denton) Do you know what he's talking about? (Denton nodded his head.)

Joe: For Christ's sake! Does anyone else? (No response to his question.)

Joe: Well, it's up to you to tell us, Denton. Rick won't.

Mike: (interrupts) Joe, you're almost proving Frank's point you know.

Joe: Now how in the hell am I doing that?

Mike: Simple. Frank was telling us he was worried. No one responded to him. He said it was almost as if we didn't care. Still no response, other than my asking him why he didn't come out with what was worrying him rather than just to say he was worried.

Joe: So?

Mike: So you didn't do one damn thing to help Frank open up.

Joe: I was giving him time.

Mike: Not true, Joe. And I'll tell you why it's not true. A few minutes later when Rick said he knew what it meant to be left out you moved in like a tiger. You were all over the place trying to find out what Rick meant.

Joe: Right. He's a damn good friend of mine. You know that!

Mike: Exactly. You showed your care and concern for Rick by trying to help him spit out how he felt; but with Frank, you didn't say or do one goddamn thing.

Joe: (penitent) Wow! I've done it again. Sorry, Frank.

Jim: Well, now that we've reached this point, who do we listen to first?

Joe: I think we should listen to Frank first.

Mike: Why?

Joe: A matter of priority. He came out with it first.

Mike: What about the priority of friendship? Like you said, Rick's your buddy. Why shouldn't he come first?

Joe: You know what, buddy? You've got me right up against the wall. I can't answer your question.

Carlos: (laughing) Good old Joe. You're damned if you do and damned if you don't! How does it feel?

Joe: (snickers) Frustrating as hell. And that's the damn truth.

Rick: (to Denton) Do you really know what I'm talking about?

Denton: I can't be absolutely certain of course; but does it have something to do with last week when Jim was talking and you said "I think I understand," and nobody picked up on it?

Rick: That's right.

Denton: (apologetically) Maybe I should have picked up on it?

Rick: No, I'm glad you didn't. Don't misunderstand; I feel better knowing you heard me, but I appreciate the fact you didn't say anything. It just wouldn't have been the same.

Joe: What the hell, Rick? I still don't understand.

Rick: It's okay, Joe. Let's leave it for now. Okay?

Mike: All right! Then that leaves the floor open for Frank, eh? What are you worried about, Frank?

Frank: Well, it's you and Carlos I've had concern over actually.

Mike: You want to know if my comments last week had any bearing on our relationship?

Frank: That's it, Mike.

Mike: Who are you asking? Me? Or Carlos?

Frank: Both of you, I guess, but one at a time naturally. I really was going to ask Carlos first, because he's the one I was most concerned about. But now I'd like to ask you first. That is, if you don't mind.

Mike: No, I don't mind; but the simple truth is that it hasn't affected me in one way or another. You see, rightly or wrongly, I think I know myself pretty damn good. I don't want to sound patronizing to you guys, but I think every one of you with the possible exception of Denton have a far greater distance to go in really knowing yourselves than I do.

Frank: You're putting me on!

Mike: That, baby, I am not doing. Call me a colosssal clod if you will, but I like myself, I know myself quite well and further, I like me as I perceive me. That doesn't mean I'm not open to change; it just means that I don't think I'm as naive as you guys.

Rick: But don't you care how Carlos feels?

Mike: Sure I care. You guys seem to think I've done him an injustice; and, if the truth be known, Carlos shares your enthusiasm on that point. Yet the main thing to be resolved is that I don't feel that I did Carlos any wrong.

I've never lied to him, never exploited him, and I have never been guilty of not letting him know exactly how I feel about any given subject he asks me about. (to Frank) And I bet that's more than you can say about your relationship with your wife.

Frank: Okay, Mike, but let's not get hung up on me until I've had a chance to ask Carlos the same question.

Carlos: Well, I'm not like Mike, and I guess that's why some of his openness last week kind of shocked me.

Jim: Is that past tense?

Carlos: No, Jim, it isn't past tense. It's present tense, and for all I know it might be future. I've been thinking about it all week, and before I got here today I had decided I was going to unburden some of my feelings on you guys. In a way I guess we've all been brainwashed into believing that if we share our feelings with one another some good is going to come from it. I guess I'm banking on that; because it's hard as hell for me to talk much, let alone spend much time thinking about myself.

Frank: Are you telling us you don't like to think about yourself?

Carlos: I've never thought about it in those terms before, but maybe it's true. And I think all of you know that I'm quiet as a rule.

Todd: But not all the time.

Carlos: No, not all the time. Even though it's going to be difficult for me, I'd like to tell you about me. (pauses, almost as if he's waiting for someone to protest) You know, it's a damn funny thing. I mean the way this group came about, and the fact that Mike is in it with me. I guess Denton in his wisdom foresaw that something like this was going to happen . . . . you know, me having to tell my story in front of Mike.

Todd: But you knew Mike was going to be in the group?

Carlos: Oh, sure. Denton told me he would be.

Todd: How did you react to that?

Carlos: Well, I guess Denton reassured me that no matter what happened I'd come out the better for having been involved in this kind of interaction. (smiles) And then too, to be honest I felt the fact that I was quiet would keep me safe from ever talking like this to all of you.

Frank: So you don't feel Denton has let you down.

Carlos: Oh, no! The fact is that although we've talked a hell of a lot about me, I've always felt that Denton was not helping me as much as he could. Again, I'm not suggesting he let me down in any way. In fact I really think he asked me to join the group because he sensed what I was thinking. He knows me better than I know myself, and I've got it figured out that he knew that this is what I needed.

Frank: But you have your doubts?

Carlos: No, I can't say that. Right now I'm unsure of myself, but there's not a doubt in my mind that Denton knows exactly what is best for me. I've got very strong feelings for Denton, and I'd probably jump off the bridge into the river if he asked me too.

Frank: Do you feel the same way about Denton that you do about Mike?

Carlos: The only answer I can give is a yes and a no. You see, Mike just happened; but Denton didn't.

Frank: Can you explain that?

Carlos: I'll try! It has to go back to the first time I saw Denton. As I said that was quite some time ago. I had been worried about a lot of things, my sex life being just one of the things I was worried about. Somebody told me to go the Counselling Centre because maybe they could help me to become motivated. I didn't know who I was supposed to see, but it ended up that I saw Denton.

Frank: You'd never seen him on the campus or anything?

Carlos: No, first time in my life was when I walked into his office. The thing that first impressed me was all the books he owned. The office was nice enough, and it would have been better if the bookshelves had been built in rather than just being a placement of four metal bookshelves. But I liked the

179

appearance of the books nonetheless. Anyone who owns that many books just has to be intelligent.

Joe: Damn, I thought the same thing; but I also wondered if he had read them.

Carlos: No, I didn't question whether he read them. You see, down in the valley you can always tell an educated man, or so my father said. My father had once pointed out the unmistakable signs to me, and then throughout the years had reinforced them. "You see, Carlos," he had said, "a smart man doesn't get dirty or dusty. He doesn't have to work with the hands. So, he wears a black suit." And another time my father said to me: "A man is as smart as the books which he owns. Show me a man who owns a lot of books and I'll show you a smart man." Thus went my father's criteria.

Frank: (laughing) Was Denton wearing a black suit?

Carlos: (earnestly) No, he wasn't. And I said, "Well, you're not wearing a black suit;" and Denton said, "Should I be wearing a black suit?" And I told him about my father. (Carlos looked short sitting in the chair. Of course he was short for a man anyway. He was probably no more than 5' 8. Carlos had a dark complexion, but he wasn't really as dark as the typical Mexican. His skin was more sallow than it was brown. Jet black eyes and very black hair emphasized the dark aspects of his complexion, making him at first glance appear darker of skin than he actually was. Carlos boasted very broad shoulders, again probably emphasized because of his short height. Yet his hips were almost as broad as his shoulders, and this mistake of anatomy distracted from a picture of a boy with a good build.)

Frank: (urging) Go on, Carlos.

Carlos: I don't think I can.

Denton: Do you want me to help, Carlos?

Carlos: Maybe if you were to talk to me directly like we did in your office that first visit?

Frank: (enthusiastic) Yeah, role-play.

Denton: Well, it's not exactly role-play, Frank. All of this actually went on.

Frank: Yeah, that's the wrong term. I guess I should have said something like re-creating the first visit.

Carlos: Will you help me, Denton?

Denton: Sure, but it might not go exactly like it did the first time.

Carlos: It will, believe me. I've got the words etched in my mind.

Denton: How do we begin?

Carlos: I can do it. I remember looking at your diplomas. They were very impressive. Then I wondered if the diplomas were still in place on Dr. Almendariz' office walls.

Frank: Who was Dr. Almendariz? (Denton brought his finger to his lips to indicate to Frank to keep quiet. Carlos didn't see the gesture for his eyes seemed riveted to the ceiling.)

Carlos: (continuing as if Frank's interruption had not occurred.) Then I looked at Denton's desk. It was neat and uncluttered. Not like Dr. Almendariz' desk at all. I guess I must have been grinning or something, because Denton made a statement just at that time. (to Denton) Remember what you said?

Denton: (softly) You smile a lot, Carlos.

Carlos: Yes, that's right. (returned his gaze to the ceiling) Then I told him, "Sure why not?" You see, we Chicanos grow up in a life that's pretty tough. My Father used to say that while a man struggled to make his life better he should grin all the time to show how easy it was to work hard.

Denton: (softly) You loved your Father deeply?

Carlos: (now almost in a trance) I still do. My Father's alive. So is my Mother. So are all my brothers and sisters.

Denton: Why didn't you go to school closer to your home, Carlos?

Carlos: Just wanted to get away.

Denton: From your family?

181

Carlos: Not so much. (sighs) But from a lot of other things.

Denton: Such as.

Carlos: Memories mostly, and mostly of Dr. Almendariz.

Denton: Dr. Almendariz?

Carlos: Yes. He's a doctor back home. Mexican, you know.

Denton: Okay.

Carlos: Well, he wasn't a doctor like you. What I mean to say is, he is a medical doctor.

Denton: Your family's doctor?

Carlos: Well, he was the doctor the family went to when anybody got sick. But he wasn't a doctor to us all the time. Poor people don't have family doctors.

Denton: I see.

Carlos: Well, anyway, he kind of played with me.

Denton: Oh?

Carlos: You know what I mean?

Denton: Maybe you better tell me.

Carlos: Well, I had a bad cold.

Denton: Okay.

Carlos: And it went into my chest.

Denton: And?

Carlos: I finally had to go to see him. We waited until it looked like I would never get over it. You know, he costs money to go to.

Denton: Okay.

Carlos: Well, I went to see him and he gave me an examination.

Denton: I see.

Carlos: All over. Do you follow me?

Denton: I think so. Go on.

Carlos: Well, he got me real excited. Because he wasn't examining my chest all the time.

Denton: It was more than a chest examination?

Carlos: That's an understatement. Anyway, he told me it was all my fault for getting like that when he was examining me. He told me he really understood, because a lot of muchachos did the same thing when he examined them. I sure can understand why too. But he told me I had to do something about it before he could continue the examination.

Denton: What did he mean?

Carlos: I asked him what he meant. He said I should jack it off. Only I didn't want to.

Denton: You didn't want to?

Carlos: No. Oh, not that I didn't use to do it all the time. It was just that I didn't want to do it in front of him. But I guess he made me.

Denton: How did he make you, Carlos?

Carlos: Well, he made fun of me. He said that it didn't bother him for me to jack off in front of him. He said that boys had to do it all the time, and that sometimes it was the only way he could continue the examination. And then he made fun of me by saying if I was such a stupid fellow that I couldn't even masturbate before a medical doctor so that he could continue his examination, that he would just go and leave the room while I did it. But he told me I ought to be ashamed of myself for disturbing a medical doctor's routine, and that he had a lot of better things to do than wait around for me to cooperate with him while he examined me. And he said he was going to send my papa a double bill, and tell him that I wasted a lot of time. He said he'd leave me to my own papa.

Denton: And?

Carlos: Well, I knew papa would get mad as hell if he got a double bill. It was hard enough for him to pay one. So I went on and did it with no further arguing.

Denton: You masturbated in front of Dr. Almendariz?

Carlos: Well, I went away from him to do it. I went and stood where I could. It was right by his diplomas and I read them while I did it. I read the wherefore's and the whereto's and the thus's. The doctor came over and stood by me at first. Then he pulled up a little stool and smoked a cigarette while I pulled on myself. When it was all over, he stuck some cotton in my ears. He wrote me a prescription for the drug store, and then told me to quit playing with myself so much. That's the reason he gave me for my getting excited during the examination. He never let on that his rubbing it was the cause. (Sadly) Have you ever heard anything like that before?

Denton: Did you ever see Dr. Almendariz again?

Carlos: No. But I dreamed about him.

Denton: Okay. And what do you think about it.

Carlos: Then? Or now?

Denton: Then.

Carlos: Then I was really a scared kid. I guess I didn't know what to do or think. He was a doctor, and he was supposed to know what to do for me. I don't really even know that I thought it awfully strange that he watched me jack it off. But I was scared, because I knew playing with it was a big sin. He handed me a towel when it was all over, and I recall he laid the towel very carefully on the wash basin. Almost like he was being very careful with it. He came back to me and put his hand on me. He said he didn't understand why it took such a long time for it to get soft again. He rubbed it for a little while, and then he put the cotton in my ears. That's all.

Denton: And now? What do you think now?

Carlos: Now what do I think? Now I guess I can't understand why he didn't blow me. I'm sure I must have scared him off in some way. I bet a million dollars he's done a lot of teenagers that way. Only it was something you wouldn't ask another boy about.

Denton: So you think he wanted to? It wasn't an accident after all.

Carlos: An accident that I got hard? (He shook his head.) No, it was no accident.

Denton: And you never saw him again?

Carlos: Never. Most of the time I was pretty healthy.

Denton: But you're convinced it was a homosexual contact?

Carlos: I'm sure of it now. And it was my first homosexual contact.

Denton: I see.

Carlos: But now I have a roommate that I live with. You know.

Denton: I guess you're saying that you and your roommate have sex together.

Carlos: That's right. Only he doesn't believe that he's only the second one.

Denton: Oh?

Carlos: No, he doesn't.

Denton: But it seems important to you that he does believe it.

Carlos: Yes, it is important. I told him about Dr. Almendariz, and how that's how I discovered I was a homosexual.

Denton: The one experience with this man convinced you?

Carlos: You don't understand. I was scared, but I enjoyed it too. And like I said, I dream about him.

Denton: Going through the examination again?

Carlos: Yes, and wishing I hadn't scared him off.

Denton: I think I understand.

Carlos: It's screwy, isn't it? And it's foolish for me to be dreaming about Dr. Almendariz when I'm living with Mike.

Denton: Mike?

Carlos: Mike Stewart is my roommate.

(The dialogue between the principals was intense, although for each it must have had a deja vu quality. The other group members reacted as if they were watchers at a table tennis tournament as the conversation flowed, viewing first one move and then the other. The drama silenced shuffling of feet or noise of any kind. Mike seemed caught up more in the intensity of the situation than any of the other members; but no one seemed disengaged from the scene.)

Denton: You are living with Mike, but dream of Dr. Almendariz who you feel made you a homosexual?

Carlos: Yes. He made me a homosexual. But I am living with Mike now, so that means I'm continuing.

Denton: Well, it means you're living with Mike.

Carlos: Yes, that's true; but Mike's attitudes are different.

Denton: What does that mean?

Carlos: The way he looks at things, and the way he acts like he doesn't give a damn about anything. I know that Mike has probably had a lot more time to think about things than I have, and there is no question but what he will think about himself and attempt to analyze his behaviour.

Denton: And you're saying that you don't?

Carlos: And probably won't. And I know that I have to get over that. I thought you could help me.

Denton: You're making good progress, Carlos.

Carlos: I've never talked to anyone like this before. Not in my whole life.

Denton: Not even with Mike?

Carlos: Mike doesn't want me to pass my troubles on to him. He is happy-go-lucky, and if I tried to talk to him like this he'd find some way to cut me off. Oh, not that he'd be mean or anything like that. Mike's never mean. But he'd crack a joke or something, and the message would get across to me.

Denton: You and Mike get along well, I suppose?

Carlos: Beautifully most of the time, but there are the times when I get worried. And when I get worried, I do my best to keep him from knowing. He's always happy, and it bugs him when he thinks I'm not. It's a big game I play. I'll probably end up having ulcers on top of ulcers.

Denton: Maybe not. All you have to do is to learn how to handle your feelings.

Carlos: Sounds great, only I don't do it. Let me give you an example. Only once in my life before I met Mike did I have any kind of sexual experience. That was with Dr. Almendariz, like I told you. But yet Mike doesn't believe me when I tell him that.

Denton: So why is it so important to you that Mike believes you on that score?

Carlos: (sadly) It is more important to me that Mike believes me than anything else in the world. You see, Mike is a lot different from me. He's had a lot of experiences, a lot of lovers. I haven't, Mike is the only one. Not counting Dr. Almendariz of course. But Mike can't believe what I say is true. He sometimes tells me that I lie to him. He says if he can't believe me on one count, he can't believe me on another. Maybe he's only kidding around, but it bothers me a lot. You see, Mike has this thing about people telling the truth. And he kids me about this all the time. For some reason or another, he refuses to believe that I haven't jumped from one set of experiences to another like he has.

Denton: It's difficult for him to think that you haven't had as many experiences as he has. Is that it? (Carlos nodded his head.) But Mike is older than you. Isn't he?

Carlos: Three years. Actually two and a half.

Denton: That might make a difference.

Carlos: True. But Mike is so much different from me. He's got a great personality, and everybody likes him. And he is always saying something funny.

Denton: (redirecting the conversation.) So you might say that Mike gets annoyed with you, even though he pretends to be kidding.

Carlos: Yeah. He claims I want to go around acting like a virgin, and that I don't really fit the role. I don't really know what he means by that. I've asked him but he won't answer me.

Denton: So all of this is important to you?

Carlos: It's important to me in that Mike is the most important person in the world as far as I'm concerned.

Denton: You love Mike?

Carlos: More than I could ever love anybody else. More than I've ever loved anyone.

Denton: Is it possible, Carlos, that you understand that Mike's reluctance to believe you on this count might be a way of his telling you that he doesn't love you?

Carlos: (sadly) It must be true, Dr. White. He denies it. He says he loves me. He says he loves all of humanity even. But I don't believe he loves me any more than he loves anybody else. Do you see what I'm trying to say?

Denton: I think you're saying that you really don't think Mike loves you enough.

Carlos: Exactly. And even worse, he's going to leave me.

Denton: Leave you?

Carlos: Yes.

Denton: How do you know that? Did he tell you?

Carlos: No, he wouldn't tell me

Denton: Then how do you know?

Carlos: It's something I feel. (He cried softly, his voice muffled in sobs.) And I don't want him to leave me.

Denton: But if he hasn't told you, isn't it possible your fears are unfounded?

Carlos: You feel things, Doctor. You know that. And I feel Mike is going to leave me. That's another reason I'm here. I thought maybe you could help me.

Denton: Gee, I don't know how. You know, Carlos, that this is something you'll have to work out with Mike.

Carlos: Deep down I know that, but I've got to have someone to talk to.

Denton: Listen to me, Carlos. You have people to talk to. Not only me. (Tenderly) Everybody in this room is greatly interested in you, buddy. Not just me. Not just Mike. But everybody.

(For the first time since he had begun, Carlos looked around at the other group members. There were tears in his eyes, but he did not try to brush them away.)

Everyone of us wants to help you in any way he can. Do you understand?

Carlos: Yes, but in the final analysis Mike is the only one who can decide whether he's going to stay or not.

Mike: Carlos baby, there are no gilt-edged guarantees on anything.

Joe: Good God, Mike. You could solve this whole god-damned thing by just saying the right words.

Mike: That's another place where you and I can't get it together, Joe. I don't go around saying right words.

Frank: Then maybe you should try.

Mike: Give me one reason why?

Rick: Are you planning to move out on Carlos?

Mike: Good Lord. All of a sudden I'm the heavy catching hell from all sides. You'll have to pardon me if I sound cynical, but you three guys having concern over Carlos just about makes me want to vomit. It wasn't so long ago that anyone of you would have slit his throat because you considered yourselves so goddamned superior. Now you're jumping all over trying to get at me because there's a general notion I'm going to be leaving him. Christ! Are you guys for real?

Rick: (Angrily) Just answer the goddamn question!

Mike: You go straight to hell, you mother!

Frank: Look, that's not going to get us anyplace. Let's try to keep it on a cool level.

Todd: Yeah, we should have learned by now that all the shouting and swearing is no damn good. (to Carlos) How did you meet Mike?

Carlos: (smiling) It's funny in a way. It was an accident, of course. It was out in one of the parking lots. He was trying to get his car started and I offered to help him. Actually I don't know anything about cars, but I thought I could help him push it if nothing else.

Todd: You were going to give him a push with your car?

Carlos: No, I don't own a car. But I walk through the parking lot to get to the bus. It's the shortest way.

Todd: I see.

Carlos: Well, we didn't actually get it started. A guy driving a car came up behind us and asked if we wanted a push. Mike told him he thought a push

would start it, that the battery was low. So Mike told me to get in real quick.
I did, although I don't know why. He was going to get a push which is what
I had stopped for in the first place. But I did. I got in, and the other guy
started to push. The car started pretty soon after that. Then I told Mike
that he could let me out anywhere along the street because I had to catch
a bus. But he said the least he could do was to take me home, that after all
I had made an offer to help and he was plenty grateful.

Todd: And did he take you to your home? Or apartment?

Carlos: Actually I didn't have an apartment. It was just a room. It was all
I could afford, but it was nice enough. I guess. But we didn't get there at
all. I told Mike I had only a room, you know. Just in conversation. Well, he
said that as a matter of fact he owed me a drink. So before he took me home,
he suggested we go over to his place for a beer. I don't like beer and I told
him so. He said he could fix rye and ginger or scotch and soda as well, so
what would it be? I said scotch would be fine, so we went to his place instead.
You know, I told him it wasn't necessary; that he didn't really owe my anything 'cause I hadn't done anything. But he laughed and said something
about my heart being in the right place anyway. And I was real glad to go,
because I got so lonely before I met Mike that I thought I'd go batty.

Denton: It's lonely being in a strange city.

Carlos: It sure is. Anyway, we went to Mike's apartment and it turned out
to be a real nice place. He fixed us drinks, and we started to talk. Then he
fixed more drinks and before long the whole afternoon had passed. Later on
it became time for dinner, and he insisted he would fix something for the
both of us. It was no more trouble fixing for two than just for one, he said,
and, of course, that's true. So we ate some soup and salad that he fixed.
After dinner we sat around and talked some more. We even had a few more
drinks. I was feeling really good, because as a rule I never drink at all.

Frank: But you drank a lot because the conversation was good. You found
you had some things in common?

Carlos: Something like that.

Frank: You're probably a pretty lonesome guy, way up here. Do you have
many friends?

191

Carlos: Any friends would be more like it! (laughs softly) Well, at the time I met Mike I'd have to say I didn't actually have any friends. There were people I knew in my classes, and things like that. Once in a while I'd see somebody I knew drinking coffee in the cafeteria and sometimes I'd get to talk to someone that way. But friends outside of class was one thing I did not have.

Todd: But then Frank's right. You were lonely. (nods sympathetically) I know what that's like myself. But I'm from here so that makes it a lot better.

Carlos: Sure. You have family, if nothing else.

Frank: But anyway, Carlos, you and Mike found out you had some things in common, eh?

Carlos: I guess. We talked about school and teachers. Even hometowns, although Mike let me do most of the talking there. Mike doesn't say much about his family or anything like that. And then we got around to talking about how much the cost of living was; you know, how you can barely make ends meet trying to go to school. I guess maybe I brought that subject up, because I was having it so damned rough. The only thing Mike said about that was that he had kind of been looking around for a roommate, because the cost of everything could be cut if things were shared. Mike said he hadn't found anybody yet though, and he guessed maybe he hadn't been looking all that hard. Well, I jumped at the idea. I was pinched for money, like I said, and I hinted around that I'd like to move in. I still am of course, but it is a hell of a lot better now. Anyway we talked about that for awhile, and then got into talking about likes and dislikes. You know, that kind of thing. By the time we polished off some more drinks, I guess it was keenly agreed on that I'd move in sometime during the weekend.

Frank: It was a mutually agreed on thing.

Carlos: Sure. It made good sense.

Joe: And you moved in the following weekend?

Carlos: No, it didn't happen quite like that. We had been drinking a lot, and I was getting tired and sleepy. I told Mike that I'd best be getting on to my place. He said it was so late and all, why didn't I just stay. So I agreed to.

192

Joe: Hell, yes. That made sense. You were going to move in anyway, so why not right away?

Carlos: Right, we had agreed to move in together. Well, Mike's apartment has only the one bedroom. I had just assumed I'd sleep out on the sofa in the living room. It made into a bed. But Mike said that was stupid as hell. Every morning we'd face the hassle of getting that damned chesterfield made up. We'd just share the double bed for the time being, and if that didn't work out we'd get some bunk beds or something. I remember laughing and telling him that I didn't snore, and that I slept so soundly that even if he did I wouldn't notice.

Mike: (annoyed) Oh, knock it off, Carlos.

Carlos: (to Mike) Look, Mike. I've begun the story. It's hard as hell for me to get it out in the first place, and in the second place I think it might be good for me to talk about it. Now, I'm really sorry that this is getting you mad at me; but the purpose of the group is to handle things like this, isn't it? I've got to learn how to handle myself better; you've said that yourself. Maybe the guys can tell me the things I do wrong.

Rick: Look, Mike. You can always leave if you want to.

Mike: It's not that I want to leave. I just want Carlos to shape up.

Frank: Sure you do. He's talking about a relationship between you two, and you're afraid that you'll come out on the bad end of the stick.

Mike: Oh hell, why argue? Go on, Carlos.

Carlos: I'm doing this because I have to, Mike. I'll try to tell the exact truth all the way down the line. I wouldn't say anything to hurt you. You should know that.

Mike: Hell, I'm not afraid of being hurt. You're the sorrowful one, not me.

Frank: Okay. That sounds fair enough. Carlos is going to tell the truth, and he has no intention of saying anything that will make you turn out looking like a louse.

Joe: And if he does say something that's not true, you can correct it. Sounds fair to me.

A STRANGE BREED OF CAT

Mike: Okay. Go on, Carlos baby.

Carlos: I guess it is a bit embarrassing.

Mike: Not to me.

Frank: Like hell. It shows on your face.

Mike: Next you'll want to try phrenology!

Frank: Admit it, Mike. You're mad as hell.

Mike: I admit no goddamned thing. (sarcastically) Didn't you hear him say I'm happy-go-luck? (soberly) But you've got to admit it's a bit on the personal side.

Rick: (explodes) Christ Almighty! It's been a hell of a lot more personal than this and you haven't exploded.

Frank: Let me explain, Rick. Mike's been playing a role all this goddamned time. You see, he's the happy bisexual of the group. Militant perhaps, but happy. Mike feels he has the best of two worlds going for him.

Mike: Right. I'm no narrow-minded bastard like you!

Jim: (mimics) Mike swings AC-DC.

Joe: Right. He talks about the rest of us feeling so goddamn superior. But all the time he's been coming on like I'm some kind of narrowminded freak.

Frank: Not only you, Joe. He has the same contempt for Jim and Carlos that he has for you and me. That part of it hasn't shown through yet, and that's the part that Carlos is going to show us about him.

Mike: Oh, shit! You and your goddamned analysis. I don't feel like I'm superior to anybody in this room. Okay. I take girls to bid; I take boys to bed. I like them both in different ways. Does this make me superior to you?

Frank: Only because you think it does. You think that because the rest of us don't think your way that we are all narrow-minded as hell.

Mike: The only thing I say about all this, Mr. Analyst, is that I'm a hell of a lot more honest with my emotions than the rest of you. You shit all over yourself if you think about a man. It might work the reverse for Jim. I don't know. I think all of you have a lot to learn about yourselves. God knows Denton tried to tell you.

Joe: Okay, if we all have so bloody much to learn about oursevles why don't you knock it off long enough so we can hear what Carlos has to say. Anybody got any objection to that?

Mike: You know damn well nobody would have any objection other than me. And it's all about me. The rest of you are crapping all over yourselves waiting to hear Carlos spill his guts.

Carlos: Mike, please.

Mike: (imitates) Mike, please. All right. Get on with the bloody story. But don't say I didn't warn you.

Frank: Is this a threat we hear?

Mike: It's a statement of fact you hear. What I do with my life is my own business. If I want to hold a grudge, I can.

Frank: Meaning that if Carlos tells this story you're going to hold a grudge.

Mike: I might. Who knows? (To Carlos) Go on, for Christ's sake.

Carlos: Well, it's not long or complicated as a matter of fact. It's just that when we got to bed things began to happen.

Joe: What in hell does that mean?

Carlos: Well, I must have gone to sleep right away. I had drunk more than I usually do, and liquor always makes me sleepy. But I woke up after a while to find Mike laying right up against me. I could feel that he had this hard on.

Joe: How could you feel it?

Carlos: Well, he was pressing it up against me. He had one of his legs locked around me, and he was pulling against me real tight. I realized I had one on too, and it shook me up. I guessed that Mike was asleep. I was kind of embarrassed that I was awake and he was asleep. I thought a couple of minutes about it; you know, what I should do. Finally I rolled over on my stomach to get away from him. I wanted to move away without waking him, but almost fell off the bed in the process. The only thing was that Mike moved with me, and both of us were nearly falling off the bed. I decided the only thing to do was to get up from the bed and go sleep on the couch. But before I could get away, he rolled back further on his side of the bed and pulled me with him. He had his arm around my waist, and he's really strong. So I got pulled back into the middle of the bed. His eyes were still closed, and I was feeling guilty as hell. The next think I knew he had his hand around my cock and was jerking at it. It felt good as hell, but I was afraid he'd wake up and find out what he had been doing and then both of us would feel stupid as hell. I took his hand and moved it away. It came right back just like before. Then he moved into position where my hand was up against his cock. He started a movement against my hand while he was still jerking me.

Jim: (drily) And you thought he was asleep with all this action going on?

Carlos: Yes, I did. But I knew he wasn't asleep when he told me to grab hold of him and make him feel good.

Frank: What did you think then?

Carlos: Hell, I didn't know what to think. I thought he was awake, but then again he could have been asleep and talking. I just didn't know. Anyway, the next thing I knew he was down on me. It didn't take but a minute or so before I exploded. I didn't do anything to him. After it was over he lay back in bed with his head resting between his hands. I guess he went to sleep. I lay there for a long time thinking. I guess I really didn't know what the hell was going on. Anyway, after a little while he started snoring lightly and then I must have gone on to sleep.

Frank: But you were confused enough to stay awake long after he had gone to sleep?

Carlos: Well, quite a while I'd say. You know, I had a lot to think about as I recall. You know I was getting ready to move in with Mike, and then this first night some damn fool thing like this had happened.

Jim: It was all one accident to you? I find that hard to believe.

Carlos: Well, that's what I thought about it anyway. Maybe it was stupid of me, but I believed that somehow or other I had caused it. I do remember wondering if Mike would be mad the following morning that it had happened. Call it anything you want, but I thought that if Mike woke up the following morning and remembered what went on he'd call off our moving in together.

Jim: Christ! You are stupid!

Rick: I don't think so. I could see where that could happen.

Jim: Rick, you've got to tell us more about that.

Rick: (turns red) Hell, if a man's asleep it could happen. You've got to admit that.

Jim: (sarcastically) Sure. Only I never get that sleepy.

Frank: Oh, knock it off, Jim. Let Carlos go on.

Carlos: Well, I guess that was the last thing I was thinking about before I went to sleep. You know, how I had gotten a chance to cut down on my living costs and then this thing happened that would screw it all up.

Jim: (Nastily) And undoubtedly you thought about Dr. Almendariz?

Carlos: (laughs) As a matter of fact I did. Not that that proves anything. At least I don't think it does.

Jim: Only that you're always being taken advantage of.

Frank: So what happened the next day, Carlos?

Carlos: Well, I was a bit shaky at breakfast in the morning. I kept waiting for Mike to say or do something. Only he didn't.

Frank: And you didn't either?

Carlos: No. I was relieved more than anything.

Frank: Relieved that he didn't say anything?

Carlos: Right. At the time it proved to me that he had been asleep, and that he didn't remember any of it. But I continued to be shaky anyway. I didn't get over the feeling until Mike asked me when we were driving down to the campus if I wanted to wait until the weekend or if it didn't make just as much sense to move that afternoon.

Joe: So what did you do?

Carlos: Well, Mike met me after last class and we went over and got my things. I didn't have much to move. My rent was paid until the end of the week, but it made sense to move in right away to cut down on eating costs. Then, too, Mike had a car and I could cut down on bus fares.

Frank: You were going to help out with car expenses?

Carlos: We had talked about that. But Mike said he drove anyway, so why the hell should I have to pay? It wouldn't cost any more to have a passenger in the car.

Rick: So it was pretty near the beginning of the fall semester that you moved in with Mike?

Carlos: Right. About three weeks after classes began.

Joe: Are you still there?

Carlos: Right.

Frank: And the sex thing? When did you learn that Mike hadn't been asleep?

Carlos: (laughs) The first night. Neither of us made any pretense about it after we once got into bed.

Frank: Did you tell Mike how concerned you had been?

Carlos: No. Actually it didn't come as any real big surprise after all, for I was somehow expecting it.

Frank: Eh? But you said Mike had ignored it all day long.

Carlos: True enough. Mike hadn't said anything about it, but I had been wondering if he had really been asleep after all. You know how sometimes you think about things. I wasn't convinced that he had been awake, and I wasn't convinced that he had been asleep. The concern was still with me that maybe I had done something once again like I had done with Dr. Almendariz. I know it might not make sense to you. I was worried that he had done something that he would have cause to be ashamed about. But he didn't seem to remember anything. Then it worried me that such a popular guy like Mike seemed to be wouldn't want a roommate like me for very long anyway. I've always been something of a drag; even I have to admit that. I don't know. I was thinking about so damn many things that nothing made sense after awhile. It was just one damned thing after another. But anyway, when it happened that second night it didn't really come as a big surprise. I was halfway expecting it.

Rick: Are you telling us you just gave in then?

Carlos: (To Rick) No, it would be wrong if I said I just gave in. I didn't; my eyes were open and I knew what I was doing. Besides I liked what I was doing. I'm not going to say I expect any of you guys to understand, but I guess I was thinking how lonely I had been without a friend and how broke I was. Things would definitely be better on those counts. I liked Mike right away. I'm not about to deny that. And my feelings for him have gotten stronger every minute that I have known him. I'm not going to deny that either. Purely and simply I decided to stick it out.

Frank: But at first you didn't enjoy the sex thing?

Carlos: No, that's not true either. I did. The only thing I remember about those first times is that I went through an awful guilt period. I felt everybody in my classes knew what was going on. Mike told me that was stupid as hell. As far as sex itself was concerned, Mike made no demands of me. I'm not being coy, but he didn't ask me to go down on him or anything like that. When it happened it was because I wanted it to happen.

Rick: Damn, you kind of slipped into it.

Carlos: (laughs) That's a hell of a way to put it, but I guess that's a fair enough way to phrase it. I don't know. At first it seemed that it was a much better thing for Mike to be going down on me than for me to be jacking off all the time. I thought about girls a lot, and I've got to say that at first I had some wild fantasies. I could close my eyes and see all kinds of girls from classes that were actually the one in bed with me. Pure and simple,

I'd feel his body and think of a girl. That's what I used to do! Now I close my eyes and see Mike. (simply) I hurt Mike by telling this story, I guess. And I'm sorry as I can be. I never should have told it.

Frank: You should if it makes you feel any better.

Carlos: I don't know whether it's made me feel any better or not. But I know that I wouldn't do anything to hurt him. I love him too much. (very simply) I'd do anything for him.

Frank: Mike, how do you feel about all this? Carlos is asking in an indirect way, and I think we'd all like to know. Are you mad at him? Does any of this come as a surprise to you?

Mike: To be truthful, I don't really think I'm mad. Annoyed perhaps, but not mad. As far as any of it coming as a surprise, I guess not. I knew about the money thing and I knew how he felt about me. I guess it feels good that he said it in the group like this.

Frank: It makes you look pretty good, doesn't it?

Mike: Well, I don't know what you mean by that crack. It's only natural for you to want people to like or love you. I guess the fact that he said it in the group means that he's no longer ashamed. I never have been. Read into it what you want, but I've got very strong feelings for Carlos too.

Frank: You mean you love him?

Mike: I guess in a way that I do. But love has some implications that go beyond sex, if you see what I mean.

Frank: Oh, I agree with that. But how about after today? Do you feel as strongly now as you did before? Do you feel like he let you down talking before the group the way he has?

Mike: Not really. I don't feel like he let me down. I kind of have mixed feelings about it. I've never made any kind of pretense with any of you guys, but having it all spelled out in black and white does mean something different than working it out all in your own mind. And if this happens to help Carlos handle his feelings a bit better, then it will be a great thing that it happened. I do know that I think it's great that he was able to talk first to Denton and then to the group. I have mixed feelings about my own involvement, but I can handle those.

Frank: You think it was great that he was able to talk when you yourself are unable to do so?

Mike: Oh come on, Frank baby! You're reading things into what I said that aren't really there. Spill my guts to this group? Why not? It wouldn't bug me in the least. You've heard me say plenty, haven't you?

Joe: For my part, I'm beginning to wonder if you've said anything. We've heard nothing about you personally, except second-hand information.

Mike: Things build, Joe baby. Who knows what you might hear before these sessions are over? But getting back to Carlos! Getting him to talk is like pulling teeth. This is the first time I've ever heard him talk so much.

Joe: Carlos says it's because you cut him off.

Rick: Yeah. You're so busy pretending to be such a good guy that you don't have time to listen to anybody else.

Mike: Well, hell! Like I said, I'm coming across as the heavy in this production number. All you mothers are sitting around analyzing me now. Damn if what Frank's got isn't contagious.

Frank: First you bitch because the group doesn't attempt to understand homosexual behavior, Mike. Now it seems to me you're bitching because we are making an attempt to understand. I don't know what you want from this group. Do you?

Mike: It's not a question of what I want from this group, baby. I've said it before and I'll say it again; I don't think I have half as much to gain from this group as anyone of the rest of you guys. Now before you go reading things into what I've said I'll tell you flatly; I want to be in this group, and I want to share if I can. I have nothing to hold back. I've shared already, and I will continue to share; but the flip-flops in positions that you guys are doing makes me want to vomit. As far as I can see, most of you are continuing on your merry way letting your emotions rule you no matter what you hear in this place. Now because both Todd and Carlos have opened up, you seem to all be falling all over yourselves trying to have sympathy for them. Even empathy, for all I know. And that's what I call letting your emotions rule you. I have seen nothing to suggest to me that any basic attitudes have changed, but those are the very things that need changing. And this final bit of shit about me being in such a bad position because I didn't come through like the shining angel in either of their scenarios just about does me in. I don't like having all you bastards jumping all over me at one time.

Todd: That's a bit unfair, Mike. I don't see the group pouncing on you like you say they are.

Mike: It depends a lot on where you sit, Todd baby. And I tell you that several of these mothers are just itching to tear into me!

Frank: You're paranoid! You know that?

Mike: Some so-called paranoids have damn good reasons for feeling paranoia. Just like some so-called inferiority complexes are based on actual fact. Just think of it! Some goddamn fools don't have inferiority complexes: they really are inferior. (laughs at Frank's expense)

Joe: I think you're wrong about the pouncing bit, Mike.

Mike: All right! So I'm working up a sweat for nothing.

Rick: Joe's trying to help, Mike.

Mike: Right! And since you're his alter ego, how about telling him he got his message across the first time? All by himself.

Jim: Well, I think Mike has a point. I think several of you do have it in for him.

Frank: Good God! You of all people! You don't think he's been acting like a rat?

Jim: What is this "you of all people" shit?

Frank: I'm sorry for that.

Jim: Okay, I'll accept that because I really think you mean it. But I don't see where Mike has been acting like a rat.

Frank: Christ, look how he's been treating Carlos!

Jim: Oh, for Christ's sake. What's he been doing to Carlos other than living with him? From where I stand Carlos has no complaints. Like he said, he's cut his living expenses and he has somebody to keep him company. He's not lonely anymore, eh? Hell, he's even got a live-in chauffeur.

Joe: Oh, you're a funny one you are. You don't feel a damn thing for Carlos.

Jim: Hell yes, I feel for Carlos. I probably know better than most of you guys what it feels like to have a hopeless love. And I don't mean to be funny and I sure as hell am not trying to put you on. It might sound dramatic as hell, but that's the only way I can phrase it. And besides that, it's true! But I can't see where all of you get off feeling so uptight over Carlos' plight. Every one of us knows that it's possible to become too dependent on somebody else. We're becoming dependent on each other in here, and I guess that's okay. It's a luxury to allow yourself to be really free with another human being. Do you know what I mean? Now, having said that, I'll have to add that I haven't heard one bloody thing that would convince me that Mike was leading Carlos on. It seems to me that Mike was very straightforward with him. All right, maybe Mike doesn't like to talk about their relationship. Big deal! Maybe he'll learn to talk about it in here. But who cares? As long as the relationship is alive and kicking, what the hell is there so much to talk about?

Frank: That's a step backward, Jim. People like to talk about the way they think and feel. You say it's a luxury, and I agree. But it is something we're supposed to be learning to do in here. And it seems to me we've reached a point with Mike where he's going to clam up on us.

Jim: No, I don't think so. Besides, there's a difference in the way people can open up with each other. Some people can talk and tell it the way it is without whining. Have you ever really listened to Carlos? I'd say he was a real whiner. In my opinion everything he says comes out with a great big built-in plea to pity poor Carlos.

Joe: Okay, so he whines. But he's had a hard life.

Jim: Crap! We've all had hard lives. And what about that thing about smiling that Carlos told us his father believed in? Hell, his father had it a hell of a lot harder than he does, I warrant. You know, I don't believe that social work crap that preaches that because a man has had a hard life that the world owes him a living. But Carlos believes it. Only his father didn't, if what Carlos said about him is true. And as far as I'm concerned, it's the whining that Carlos does and not the things he says that bug the hell out of Mike. If, indeed, he is bugged.

Rick: (sarcastically) But you've got a vested interest here, don't you, Jim? You're itching to move in with Mike, aren't you?

Jim: (laughs) I might if given the chance. Who knows?

Rick: It somehow surprises me that you're so honest about it.

Jim: What has honesty got to do with it? A rational basis for living would be the more appropriate phrase.

Rick: Whatever you want to call it. But my point is that it doesn't really matter what you say about Carlos as long as it comes out in the end that you're living with Mike.

Jim: That's what I like about guys like you and Frank and Joe, Rick. Life is so simple for you! You're too thickheaded to understand a problem until it's literally pounded into your head; but once you get the first glimmers of understanding you are all able to come up with a pat answer that seems to fit.

Rick: (To the group) As far as I can see, whatever Jim has to say about Carlos is bound to be biased because he wants Carlos out so that he can move in with Mike.

Joe: My God! Is all this really happening?

Jim: (ignores Joe) Maybe I would move in; maybe I wouldn't. That's got absolutely nothing to do with it. Everybody, including me, acts within his own vested interests. I'm no different from anyone else, in that respect anyway. And what I'm telling you boneheads is that Carlos has no legitimate beef with Mike. And none of you have any reason for ganging up on Mike. Mike's done nothing to hurt Carlos. And you can't come up with one shred of evidence to indicate that Mike has exploited him. And for what it's worth, you insensitive clods are not really feeling sorry for Carlos. You're just using him as a tool to get at Mike! It's Mike everyone of us is jealous of!

Joe: Shit! Speak for yourself. Maybe he can turn a trick both ways. You turn it only one way because you can't do any better. I turn it only one way because that's the way I want it.

Jim: Right! And the moon is full of green cheese.

Joe: The guy's crazy as hell.

Frank: Well, look at it this way, Jim. You think it was okay for Mike to be chasing around restrooms the way he was?

Jim: Was Carlos doing any of this chasing around restrooms?

Frank: Don't ask me. Ask him.

Carlos: You don't have to ask me. I can tell you. I wasn't.

Jim: You're one in a million, sweetheart.

Frank: So you see, Jim, there is a bloody difference.

Jim: Damn, I don't see what that proves.

Frank: Do you need me to draw you a picture? Hell, Mike's living with Carlos; but at the same time he's running around on him.

Jim: So you're saying that Mike is guilty of infidelity.

Frank: Right.

Joe: Oh Christ! I can't believe I'm hearing what I'm hearing.

Jim: (To Joe) Yeah, I bet you can't believe what you're hearing. The old infidelity bit. Shocking! And especially to an oversexed stud who literally jumps from bed to bed and broad to broad one bloody night after the other. (drily) What do you call it? Sharing of blessings?

Joe: I'm glad you noticed it was broad to broad.

Jim; How could I miss it? You've got your buddy to back you up every inch of the way, don't you? (snickers) Although I guess I shouldn't have used the word inch. It's probably too suggestive for you.

205

Joe: Go to hell.

Denton: (interrupts) Fellows, I think this is a good stopping point for this week.

Rick: (sarcastically) Saved by the bell!

Jim: Who, me? You silly bastard. If anyone's saved, it's you.

Denton: (firmly) The reason I'm calling a halt at this point, guys, is that I've been listening to you for the last ten minutes or so and nothing new is coming out.

Jim: It was about to.

Denton: Okay, maybe it was, Jim. But it'll hold, don't you think?

Jim: (sarcastically) Sure it will.

Denton: In any event, it's time. And it seemed to me like we were on a kind of plateau. But it makes no difference. I would have called time anyway. Okay?

Frank: Before we go, Denton, couldn't we take the time for you to evaluate this session for us?

Denton: I don't think it's something I can evaluate at this time, Frank. I think what we all need to do is to go home now and give some good thought to what did go on at this session. The one comment I'd make is that I think we made a whale of a lot of progress today. I can see things beginning to happen that are good indicators of personal growth for future sessions; but I can't really evaluate right now. I'd be giving you some of my thoughts, and this would undoubtedly bias your own clear thinking. Read me?

Joe: (laughs) Well, as long as you're pleased and we're pleased, I guess something good is happening. (To Jim) Buddy, you play rough at times, don't you?

Jim: I can give it and I can take it.

Joe: Right! I'll give you credit for that.

Carlos: (rises from chair) Denton, thanks for hearing me out. (To the group) Thanks for listening, guys.

Mike: (laughs) I guess I'll have to agree on that one.

Todd: Damn, it's just like old homecoming week, isn't it? A few minutes ago everybody was fighting all over the place. Now we're agreeing the session was a good one.

Rick: Well, didn't you think it was?

Todd: Oh hell, yes. But it's like Denton said, I've got to go home and think about it.

Denton: (laughs) Okay, fellows. It's been a long session, and it's been a good one. Let's break now. Okay?

(The members arrived and seated themselves. There was no joviality; everyone seemed ready to go to work.)

Joe: Well, how do we begin today?

Todd: I sometimes wonder how we ever begin.

Frank: It seems to me that we just kind of start talking and then someone grabs the ball. And you know who is always initiating the action.

Joe: Denton seems to be the one grabbing the ball a lot. Look how he talked to Carlos last week.

Rick: Almost as if the rest of us weren't here is how he did it.

Frank: (to Rick) Did you get the feeling you were eavesdropping?

Rick: No, I don't think so. But man, I was really caught up in it. When I thought about it later it seemed real spooky.

Jim: Didn't seem spooky to me.

Mike: No, I can't say it sounded spooky to me either; but I did get the feeling that I was listening in to a private conversation.

Joe: Do you think we shouldn't have been listening?

Frank: How could we have helped from listening?

Mike: Then it logically follows that you don't like the way Denton drew Carlos out. Isn't that what you're saying?

Rick: Gee, I hadn't thought about it that way; but now that you mention it, I guess I'll have to say that Denton should not have done it. Hell, he almost had Carlos hypnotized.

Joe: How should he have handled it?

Todd: Well, I think we ought to ask Carlos about how he felt being drawn out. You know, about the same thing happened to me and I thought it was a great experience. One of the best that ever happened to me as a matter of fact.

Frank: But if you use that as the only criterion, Todd, then what you are actually saying is that the end invariably justifies the means.

Joe: Hell, I don't see it that way at all. Denton used some kind of special technique on Carlos that enabled him to loosen up and share his concerns with us.

Frank: So it worked and Carlos got to talking. Big deal! And there was no special technique in it at all. The only thing he did was to sit and talk to Carlos, pretending that the rest of us weren't there. But what would have happened if it hadn't worked? Suppose Carlos hadn't opened up?

Rick: But he did, Frank.

Frank: So the end justifies the means! That's all I'm saying.

Joe: Then let me ask you again, Frank. How should Denton have handled it?

Frank: (petulantly) The group should have done it.

Rick: You don't make sense. The group did get involved.

Frank: But only after Denton had that little seance of his going.

Mike: Okay, Frank. What's really bugging you?

Frank: I told you. I didn't like the way Denton had that confidential chat with Carlos while the rest of us were looking on. It made me feel like an eavesdropper. The technique was lousy, the group failed in its purpose, and I'm fed up. I can't see where any of this is getting us any place, and I'm getting behind in my studies because I spend so damn much time in here playing games.

Mike: I hear your words, Frank baby, but they have a false ring to them.

Joe: Yeah, I get the same reading. What's wrong with you, Frank?

Frank: Nothing's wrong with me. I'm fed up on this group stuff though; and I'm even more fed up with Denton playing God over there. He tells us all this crud about how the group will draw us out, and how we'll learn to handle strengths and weaknesses; and that we'll all be able to relate on an interpersonal basis much better than before once we get through with all of this. But if you ask me, its a pile of nothing. The only thing I've learned about me is that some of you think I'm a know-it-all. Well, screw you! I knew that about me before I came in here. It seems we've spent most of our time either cursing at each other or talking about somebody's sex life. My sex life is nobody's goddamn business. You guys can go on and expose yourselves, but I'm a happily married man; and this talk about homosexuality is boring me silly. I don't want to learn about it; I don't want to hear about it. Todd is a stupid ass to play around with something he knows he shouldn't be messing with. That's what I think about Todd! As for Carlos, he's a fool; but he knows what he's doing. He's just taking the easy way out, and all this talk of love is crap.

Joe: I don't get it, Frank. Up to now you've never said anything to suggest you want out of the group.

Frank: Joe, I came in here this afternoon to bust this group wide open. I'm sick of it, and I want all of us to put an end to it today.

Rick: Maybe no one else wants to put an end to it, Frank.

Jim: Right. I don't.

Frank: (to Jim) Sure you don't. You can make a grandstand play for Mike in here.

Joe: Christ! Are we back to that again?

Frank: My question is, do we ever leave it? We're always talking about how Mike is unfaithful to Carlos and how Jim is trying to push Carlos out of the picture with or without Mike's help. Todd shoots his big mouth off about his encounter with Mike, and we even wondered about when Rick is going to make his play for Joe.

Joe: (angrily) It seems to me that a lot of that speculation has been made by you, Frank; especially that bit about Rick.

Rick: Yeah, and I've noticed you've been the one who kept feeding most of the questions once someone got started.

Frank: I've made my mistakes too, I admit that, but Denton was the one who pulled all this together. He's been the bloody sage over there who allowed all of us to be pulled into the vortex. He's the one who carried on that dialogue with Carlos last week that made me finally get fed up.

Mike: What made you get fed up on that particular count, Frank?

Frank: His bloody sex life, screwed up as it is, is his own bloody damn business. Denton had no right to pry all those details out of him.

Joe: Why not? Didn't we all agree we'd share all of ourselves with each other and that we'd have trust in each other? I can't see why you're taking out after Denton for something we all agreed to participate in.

Frank: But we're playing the game completely by Denton's rules. Like I said, he's set himself up as God and all the rest of us are pawns. He establishes rules and we have to follow them.

Mike: You're talking as if you think he conned us into this.

Frank: Whether he conned us or not is something none of us will ever be sure about. However, it goes without saying that he says one thing and then does another.

Joe: What do you mean by that, Frank? I can't see where he's done that.

Frank: Of course not. We've all been brainwashed.

Mike: (sarcastically) But you, dear Frank, with your superior mentality were able to resist being brainwashed.

Frank: Think what you want, Mike. I went along with it for awhile, but I'm not going to stand by and let it happen any longer.

Todd: For God's sake, Frank! Let what happen?

Frank: Let Denton play God over us. Telling us one thing and then doing another; having us get bombarded by stimuli which is always almost purely sexual. Oh, let me tell you. I've really thought about it.

Mike: Then how about telling us about it instead of making all those sweeping generalizations.

Frank: We've got to end this group today!

Mike: Frank, how about answering my question?

Frank: What question?

Mike: Simply tell us why you think Denton is telling us one thing and then turning around and doing another?

Frank: Well, it's obvious the group has failed in its purpose.

Joe: But for Christ's sake, how?

Frank: We were supposed to talk about our problems.

Todd: Don't you think we have? I certainly feel better after having talked about mine.

Frank: Your problem was of your own making. Anybody that bloody stupid deserves having a problem to worry about. Any fool can go around making problems for himself.

Mike: Okay, leave Todd out of it. What about Carlos?

Frank: (explodes) You have the guts to ask "What about Carlos?" You two are thicker than thieves, and yet you ask "What about Carlos?" You know you're crazy as hell.

Mike: Instead of being so damned sanctimonious, why don't you ask Carlos what he thought about the session?

Frank: I don't give a good goddamn what Carlos thought about the session.

Joe: I think that's a hell of a thing to say.

Frank: I've got problems too, for Christ's sake. Why do I have to listen to everyone else's?

Mike: Look, Frank. Nobody's put a muzzle on you. Good God, look how you're shooting off your mouth today. You haven't heard anyone tell you to shut up and quit monopolizing the time, have you?

Frank: If you'll notice, smartass, Denton's keeping out of it today. He hasn't said one damn thing.

Mike: So what does that prove? Denton doesn't usually have too much to say.

Frank: That just shows how observant you are. Oh, he makes a big deal out of sitting back and studying us: he treats us like guinea pigs. But then he gets started and nobody else gets a chance to say a word. He is so damned holier-than-thou that he makes me sick. And that conversation with Carlos last week was one of the sorriest things I've seen in my life. It was disgusting.

Rick: Now wait a minute. How was it disgusting? I don't feel that way about it at all. I learned a hell of a lot from what they were saying, and I didn't consider one bit of it disgusting.

Frank: What they were saying was not disgusting, Rick. I didn't mean that at all. But what was sickening to me was the way Denton pulled it off. He couldn't wait for the group process to work. Oh no! He had to wade in like Jesus Christ to get Carlos to open up.

Carlos: Frank, you're way off base. Denton didn't do anything but encourage me to get started. If I hadn't been able to turn to him, things might not have worked out.

Frank: Right. Exactly my point. He intervened in the process.

Carlos: Wrong, Frank. I was the one who asked for help.

Frank: (shrugs) Makes no difference. As far as I am concerned the group is finished anyway. I've gotten very little out of it, but I have spent one hell of a lot of time. Now I think maybe some of you guys feel good about it right now; but when you really back off and think about what's been going on you'll come to the same conclusion that I have reached — Denton's been exploiting us.

Todd: I don't think like that at all. As far as I'm concerned Denton has been a big help.

Frank: Sure he has to you. You're another one who's gotten a chance to talk.

Joe: I can't understand why you feel you haven't had a chance to talk to the group, Frank.

Frank: You don't, eh? Well, I'll tell you. Denton always finds some one else. Never me. Everybody's got problems, but not good old Frank. It's because he decides he wants to hear somebody else, and then he forces the rest of us to go along with it.

Mike: You really think the group has failed, don't you, Frank?

Frank: As far as I'm concerned it has. I can't think of one damn thing that's happened to me as a result of it.

Mike: (kindly) I can tell you one thing it's done for you, Frank.

Frank: Thank God for little favours! Please enlighten me.

Mike: Okay. You're still a know-it-all and you're still trying to be a bloody analyst, but look how free you've become of Denton's pervasive influence. When we first started in this group you hung on to Denton's every word as if your life depended on it. You were so scared of the man and what he could do to your professional future that you were kowtowing all over the place. But look at you today — you're taking out after him as if he was the worst villain you'd ever met. Doesn't that tell you anything?

Frank: It tells me I'm fed up with all his damned righteousness!

Mike: Okay, maybe I'm the analyst now; but it tells me something completely different. It tells me that you're coming to grips with yourself and that you're transferring a lot of your weaknesses to accusations against Denton. Pure hostility!

Joe: Maybe Frank is following you, Mike, but I'm not. I understand the part about his being less afraid of Denton, but this thing about transferring weaknesses to Denton is above me.

Mike: Frank has always had a thing about authority. He probably grew up in an autocractic home where it was the accustomed thing to accept authority without question. If you had an older relative, you accepted his viewpoints without question; your teacher always knew better, so you didn't give him any trouble either. If a man had a better job or was further along than you, then it became absolutely necessary that you give him the respect due him! Translated this means that you accepted everything he says or does; you may not like all the crap that you have to put up with, but you kept all of it to yourself. You never argued your points with a superior. Yet you see this is what Frank is doing this morning. He's not arguing with Denton; he's telling the group — within Denton's hearing — all those things he's long felt about him but never had the guts to say before.

(During Mike's explanation Frank self-consciously began staring at the floor. It appeared that he was withdrawing from the conversation.)

Rick: But he still doesn't have the guts to tell Denton directly.

Mike: The important thing is that he's getting there. You might say that right now he's testing just to see how much he can get by with.

Todd: That makes sense.

Jim: On the other hand, if he's got something to say, why doesn't he come right out and say it?

Mike: Just like you're not going out on any street corner and announce to the world that you're gay.

Jim: Oh, but that's a different damn thing.

Mike: Fear by any name is self-defeating, Jim baby. For Frank, it's as much of a problem to admit he's afraid of Denton (and anybody else his gut felling tells him has power over him) as it is for you to level about some things you think are personal.

Joe: I see Jim's point, Mike. A guy is not going to clobber you because he thinks you're afraid, but he might if he thinks you are gay.

Rick: You're naive, Joe. People who know your weak points invariably end up by taking advantage of you.

Carlos: It might even be human nature for all I know; but it is true. One thing that is beginning to filter through my skull is this business of being your own man. You can't control everything that goes on around you; but if you're in reasonable control of your own feelings, you can handle whatever comes your way.

Todd: Right. I'm beginning to see that too. That thing that Mike and I got into wouldn't have happened if I had had control of myself. I caused that whole bloody scene, but at the time you couldn't have got me to admit it.

Joe: (to Mike) Then what you say Frank is doing is letting his feelings that Denton is in a superior position come out through an attack on him?

Mike: Sure. That's the real reason people have trouble relating to other people. I know I've been accused by this group of feeling superior to everybody else. I reject that as a statement of fact, and I will continue to reject it. But what I will say about me is that I know myself quite well, and that usually I'm in fairly good control of my emotions. I think I learned long ago that when I was having a hassle with somebody or when I didn't understand somebody else's attitude towards me that if I really cared about what was going on, I'll examine me instead of trying to speculate about what was wrong with the other guy. And you know it works almost 100 percent of the time. (laughs loudly) Of course there's always the exception like Todd was talking about. There was no way I could have taken the time to have figured that hassle out. But seriously, what you've got to do is figure out how much the person means to you. If he or she means something and its worth your time, you start examing how you may be coming across and what you can do to improve the situation. If you decide the person means nothing to you, the answer is obvious. You just back away and write it off. There's no point in hassling unless a very solid principle is involved. If you go around uptight, it's your own bloody fault ninety percent of the time. And so that's what I'm saying about Frank. He obviously has felt beholden to authority all his life, and this is the first opportunity the poor bastard has had to challenge it.

Jim: Even at that he did it in an indirect manner, Mike.

Mike: Sure, it comes back to testing.

Todd: But look, Mike. You can't go around continually challenging authority anymore than Frank can go around telling his major professor to shape up.

Mike: Why not?

Joe: On the one hand you'd be locked up as a nut, and on the other hand you'd be kicked out of graduate school. That's why!

Mike: Joe baby, you're making it too black and white. You're trying to make it all too simple. And life simply isn't that simple, regardless of what some clowns would make you believe. Look! First off, what is authority?

Joe: Well, authority to me means that someone or somebody has a kind of control over me.

Todd: Right. And this someone usually has been given the power because in one way or another he has earned the privilege.

Jim: I wouldn't go along with the word earn.

Mike: Neither would I in all cases, Jim, but let's not get hung up on words. Let's just agree that a person in one way or another "earns" the right to be an authority-figure. Okay?

Jim: Okay.

Mike: So it's up to me then to recognize this authority over me. In other words I accept or reject.

Joe: That sounds even simpler than what I said.

Mike: But that's just the beginning, Joe. If I accept, there's no sweat. For example, I accept the fact that the police enforce laws set up by society for everyone's good. Maybe I don't agree with all of the laws, but even those I strongly disagree with I find myself trying to rationally understand why they are on the books. Now suppose I reject a particular law. What do I do then?

Joe: You disobey it.

Mike: Maybe, but more important I work to change it. I don't go around hassling anybody. I don't enter into civil disobedience nor do I make a bloody ass of myself by carrying arounds signs or tearing up property. Any meaningful change has to be thoughtfully engineered.

217

Joe: All right. I'll buy that. But what do you do when you have somebody in authority over you that you think is taking advantage of you? If I'm following what we're talking about this afternoon, it seems like Frank resents Denton being in authority over him.

Jim: Frank never said that.

Todd: True, but a lot of what he said implied that he resented the hell out of Denton.

Rick: Yeah. I think that's a fair statement.

Mike: Okay, we'll agree that Frank resents Denton.

Carlos: It sounds to me that not only does he resent Denton being in authority over him because he is his major professor but that he strongly dislikes Denton's role in this group.

Mike: I think one thing leads to another. First, Frank is resentful of authority, even though he'd be the last to admit it. Then second, Frank dislikes Denton's authority in this group. The point is that Frank couldn't take out after Denton on the usual academic stamping grounds, but here in the group Frank felt safe in taking him on.

Joe: Oh, I get it. Frank felt some of us would swing to his side.

Rick: Yeah, but I think more important is the fact that Frank felt safe in this group to say what he thought about Denton.

Mike: Only he was flogging a dead horse.

Joe: Now what does that mean?

Mike: According to the way I read Frank, his outburst came on two levels. One level is that he has something to say to us. I think that's the important one. The second level is that he was using Denton as a scapegoat in order to get our attention.

Joe: You're saying Frank didn't mean any of those things he said?

Mike: He meant some of them all right.

Todd: But you're saying he wants to tell us something.

Mike: Right.

Joe: Well, why didn't he just come out with it instead of all this beating around the bush?

Mike: Why don't you ask him?

Joe: Okay, I will. Frank, you want us to listen to you?

Frank: (looking up, tears in his eyes) Thank you, Joe.

Joe: Frank, what's happening?

Rick: How can we help?

Frank: (rubs the moisture from his eyes) All of you already have.

Todd: Gee, we haven't done anything.

Carlos: Not so much as I could notice anyway.

Frank: What you've done, my friends, is to hit the nail right on the head. (to Mike) In all sincerity, Mike, you were the one who did it. Just about everything you said was true; even the thing about me wanting the group to listen to me.

Todd: You thought we weren't? Gee, it seems to me you've talked just about as much as anyone. I've listened to you.

Carlos: So have I. Although a lot of the time I haven't agreed with you.

Mike: I understand, Frank. You've been throwing out a lot of words, but not many of them have meant anything.

Frank: That's about it! And it seemed like everybody was getting a chance to talk except me. And today there was something I really wanted to talk about.

Rick: Why didn't you?

A STRANGE BREED OF CAT

Frank: That's a good question, only I don't know if I can answer it.

Mike: Try!

Frank: Well, I think I did try. When we first came in I wanted to start right away, but I believe Todd jumped in first and asked how we would get started. That took the ball away from me initially. You know, it kind of set me back. Then I guess it was Joe who was saying how great it was how Denton was able to get things rolling. Both Todd and Carlos had things to say and Denton was able to get them started. I guess it was then that I lost my cool. It sort of happened that I got to thinking that Denton is my major professor, knows me quite well, and yet didn't seem to give a damn about any problem I might have. He wasn't trying to get me to ventilate.

Joe: Well, what about the authority thing? Was Mike close to the truth on that too?

Frank: You'll have to give me some time to think about it, but on the surface I'd say he was quite close to the actual heart of the matter. I do have a tendency to overreact to authority. I'm not my own man, I'll agree. Sometimes I don't think things out well enough. I guess today's little episode was a prime example of how I don't get it together all the time.

Mike: Feel like talking now, Frank?

Frank: Mike, believe me. There's nothing to say right now. But thanks!

Rick: I wonder if Denton wants to say anything.

Denton: (laughs) Only that I feel like Mike has replaced me.

(General laughter)

Mike: I've been sitting at the right hand for so long that some of it was bound to rub off!

Jim: Say, that's right. How come you let Mike do the very thing you were bitching at Denton about, Frank? Seems to me good old Mike was doing a lot of speculation at your expense.

Frank: No, it wasn't the same thing at all. Mike wasn't talking to me like Denton was talking to Carlos.

Jim: He sure as hell was talking about you.

Frank: There's still a difference.

Mike: What you really wanted, Frank, was for Denton to talk to you like he did with Carlos. Isn't that right?

Frank: That's about the size of it, Mike. I've got something that's been driving me up a tree. I didn't expect everybody to notice, but I expected Denton to pay attention. He seemed to be interested in everybody but me. We've spent a lot of time hashing and rehashing a number of things, and Todd and Carlos both got to talk at great lengths about themselves. Everybody has talked about himself to a degree. All except Frank, and nobody in this group seemed to give a damn.

Joe: That's not true; and you know it, Frank.

Frank: That's how it looked to me, Joe. And then being put off again today was the final straw.

Denton: All I can say, Frank, is that I'm truly sorry. If there's anything I can do right now to help, I'll be glad to; but somehow I get the feeling you'd rather be left alone.

Frank: Actually, I'm suddenly very tired. It's about time for us to wrap this session up anyway. I did have some things I wanted to talk about, but right now I feel too drained to go off on another emotional binge.

Mike: Was it an emotional binge, Frank?

Frank: I don't recall ever being so spent. I'm really serious. Maybe the words Mike and the rest of you guys were saying were on a different plane than I would have been on, but the impact is the same.

Joe: I don't follow you, Frank. I'd really like to, but I just don't follow you.

Frank: Let's leave it at that then. Please? Something real strange has happened to me. Just in the last couple of minutes. Sometimes you can be talking about one thing and thinking about another. You know what I mean? Well, it's just happened to me. That's why all of a sudden I'm so tired.

Todd: We'd like to help, Frank.

Frank: Believe me, this will pass. I'll get over being tired, and next week or one of these weeks I'll be able to fill you in on the details. It's like I said a minute ago. I was listening to your words, and a lot of what Mike said especially was true. It was hitting home, but all of a sudden — BANG! It became even more true and I developed some insights into the likes of which you've never seen. Wow! Talk about Saul on the road to Damascus. I'm sorry. That's all I can say now. I'll have to do some thinking first. I'm like that, you know. And then maybe I'll do some acting. I thank all of you more than I can possibly say.

Denton: Frank, are you all right?

Frank: (a catch in his voice) Yes, I'm all right, Denton. Thanks for caring. You're a great guy. You're all great guys.

(Denton moves from his chair and goes to Frank. He places his hand on Frank's shoulder. Frank looks up at Denton, and tears flood his eyes. Frank stands, lays his head on Denton's shoulder and begins sobbing. Mike exchanges looks with Joe, and simultaneously they go to place their arms around Frank. Todd joins in, followed by Rick, Jim and Carlos. Pain which cannot be expressed in words tears at each of the members, and it appears that only their close-knit unity of the moment can afford the strength needed to meet the crisis.)

(Denton was the last to arrive for the eighth session. Business with the Academic Dean had detained him. He greeted the group with a breezy "Hi.")

Mike: We were just going to go on without you. We didn't know if you'd make it or not.

Denton: I'll always make it, Mike. I just had a little something over at Administration.

Frank: We never could go on if you didn't show, Denton. I mean, you wouldn't want us to go on if you weren't here, would you?

Denton: Well, I can't see the possibility of my not ever being here when I'm supposed to. But I guess if the situation ever arises, I'd just have to leave word with Janet.

Frank: You wouldn't want us to continue without you?

Joe: Hell, we ought to try it just one time for kicks.

Rick: (sarcastically) You've really flipped your wig, fellow.

Joe: (laughs) Who in hell turned you one? What's biting you anyway?

Mike: Maybe he's decided you use him too much.

Joe: Shit. Some more of that crap, huh?

Frank: Hey, let Denton answer my question, eh?

Denton: I don't think the group ought to meet without me.

Joe: Why? Hell, like you said yourself, you don't do anything. You just hide and watch.

Frank: Maybe. But he's here to set limits.

Joe: Limits. What limits?

Jim: You just don't see them, baby. Me? I feel them.

Rick: But then you'd feel anything, wouldn't you?

Mike: What in hell's wrong with that guy? (He turned to Joe.) You two break up?

Frank: (insistent) Leave him alone for a minute. I think that it's important we hear what Denton has to say.

Joe: What's to say? He said, don't meet without me. So, okay, we won't meet without him. Okay, Frank?

Frank: Okay. Just as long as everybody's got it straight.

Joe: Big deal. Now, if we can get on with it, I want to tell you guys something I've learned from the group. Okay?

Jim: Hell, he's not a slow-learner after all. What you been up to, pretty baby?

Joe: Well, one thing I've learned is not to beat the shit out of any guy who says something like that to me. (good naturedly) But the hell with you. If you don't want to hear what I've learned from you mothers, then I won't bore you with the details.

Rick: You guys are carrying on as if nothing happened here last week. Where's this big concern for Frank that we all had? As far as that's concerned, Carlos has been lost in the shuffle as well. We have never learned from either him or Mike what happened as a result of Carlos' bringing up the subject in here. It seems to me that we are always going up the brink of something, and then we either back off the following week or we just ignore that any damn thing ever happened. There's something wrong about it.

Denton: I don't know if I'd go that far, Rick. It's a problem that we only meet once a week. We'd be a lot better off if we could all get away for seven or ten days together. We could avoid the discontinuance and the feeling of disjointed sessions that way. We might even be able to build up more of a sweat. But I know what Rick is saying, and I fully sympathize with him. We get involved with Todd and then we let it drop; next comes Carlos, and then we get no additional feedback. Last week Frank made a kind of a call for help, but this week we begin almost by acting as if none of this happened.

Mike: So I guess the question before us is how do we handle all the old business?

Todd: My God, you've turned into a parliamentarian before our very eyes.

Joe: It's a legitimate question 'though.

Carlos: Does anything really have to be done about it? That's my question, and I think it's equally legitimate.

Rick: Well, you could probably answer that better than anyone else, Carlos. What I mean is, didn't you feel somewhat slighted when you came back that week after you told the group about your involvement with Mike and learned that not one of us asked about what had happened since?

Carlos: Maybe it's the Mexican in me, Rick, but sometimes its just as kind to say nothing as it is to say something.

Rick: You're telling me you were relieved that nobody asked you?

Carlos: Oh, if someone would have asked I would have come out with how I was feeling.

Rick: (terse) I'm asking now!

Carlos: Everything is fine, Rick. Believe me.

Rick: And Mike? Was he mad?

Joe: Why don't you ask Mike that?

Rick: (to Joe) I was asking Carlos because it was his opinion I was interested in. If it was Mike's opinion I wanted, I would have asked him. Okay?

Joe: (annoyed) Christ, I'm sorry.

Rick: (drily) Yeah, I'm beginning to think so.

Carlos: (interrupts) Mike played it cool; just like he plays everything cool. I've begun to understand that now, and it makes things a lot easier for me.

Rick: You're saying he was mad but he didn't show it?

Carlos: Oh, he was mad and he showed it. Only he pretended he wasn't mad and tried not to show it. I guess that doesn't make any sense but that's the way it was. Mike played it cool; just like he plays everything cool. You know?

Rick: He's like Joe super-cool sitting over here. A goddamn sphinx.

Joe: Man, something's bugging you.

Rick: (mimics Mike) Right on, baby.

Joe: Well, are you going to give with it or not?

Rick: Man, no! I'm just settling back in my chair waiting for one of your goddamned sea stories. Only before you got started with the details I thought we ought to hear from Frank and Carlos since they've managed to take you off stage centre for the last couple of weeks. But I did my duty now! I've asked Carlos. Someone else can ask Frank if they want to, but I'm ready for the inevitable make-out story.

Mike: (quietly) The target for the day seems to be Joe.

Rick: (to Mike) Not from me he isn't. From this point on I vow to say not a word.

Joe: (sarcastically) Can we count on that?

(In answer, Rick covers his mouth with his hand.)

Jim: Well, so much for Rick. I think I'll join him in a pact of silence.

Joe: Will someone tell me what the hell is going on?

Todd: It's too complicated for me. (to Frank) But I'll ask the second part of Rick's question, Frank. How are you this week? Get things worked out?

Frank: More or less, Todd. More or less.

Joe: We never knew what the problem was, Frank.

Frank: True enough. As a matter of fact you may never know. How does that grab you?

Mike: Joe baby, you're getting shafted from all sides.

Jim: I wonder why!

Joe: What's happened to your pact of silence?

Frank: (interrupts) You know, I was thinking about what Rick said about not following through with Carlos and me. I think I know the answer, and maybe Denton will agree. Anybody want to hear it?

Todd: Sure, why not?

Frank: Well, I think we're all kind of swimming around in some kind of pool that none of us knows very much about. We don't know how long it is or even how wide it is. It seems to be deep, but none of us have gone down into the depths for any period of time. Most of the time we swim alone with our own thoughts occupying us, only occasionally brushing into somebody else. How does that sound so far?

Mike: Sounds like we need sonar in order not to bump into each other.

Todd: No, that's not right. If we had sonar we wouldn't bump into each other at all; and if we didn't have the occasional bump we wouldn't have the interaction. Right, Frank?

Frank: That's how I see it, Todd. (to Denton) What do you think about the analogy?

Denton: So far, so good; but I'd like to hear you explain it more.

Frank: Well, the bumping is the interaction; and we do a lot of that. But every once in a while one of us badly needs a breath of air, so we surface with a lot of kicking and splashing. About that time all the other swimmers come up to see what all the kicking and splashing is about.

Todd: The surfacing is when somebody feels he has got to say something. Right?

Frank: That's how I see it! And some of us have surfaced and some of us haven't.

Joe: Then you think every one of us will surface before we end these sessions?

Frank: It's not inevitable of course, but I think it to be highly likely. What do you think, Denton?

Denton: A lot depends on how long we allow these sessions to continue. Then, too, I believe it can be stated that not all of us have the same need to ventilate. You've noticed that some of us talk more than others, but there's nothing significant in that. You've got to believe that your actions in this group are right and use that as a gauge; not how much or how little you talk. It's very possible to become better clued into yourself by just swimming around, to use Frank's analogy, and never surfacing.

Frank: That kind of thing happened to me last week. I surfaced all right, but the insights I gained were those that were almost parallel to the flow of words.

Carlos: I'm not sure I understand what you're saying, Frank.

Frank: Not much to understand, Carlos. I surfaced from the pressure; some tension was released simply by surfacing, and then Mike started saying some things which all began to apply in a completely different context. It was then that the tension almost completely dissipated.

Joe: But if I hear you correctly you're telling us you have no need of surfacing right now.

Frank: That's exactly it, Joe. I have no need right now.

Denton: And you feel no compulsion to force it.

Frank: Quite the contrary. I'm very content in just swimming around.

Mike: Well, I guess that answers Todd's question.

Todd: It sure does, and I guess it satisfies Rick as well.

(Rick maintains his stony silence.)

Joe: So really all you're saying, Frank, is that someone surfaces when he feels the need. After the need is met, he's very content to go back to his swimming. He doesn't necessarily want it to go on and on.

Frank: Speaking for me, that's exactly how I see it. Right now I have no need for support. I know I can count on you guys if I need support, and that means a lot!

Todd: Sounds beautiful! But what happens if two or more fish want to surface at the same time?

Frank: Then one has to be ignored. That's what happened to me, don't you see? Carlos and I were surfacing at about the same time. Carlos got the attention and I got the shaft. At least that's how I perceived it at the time.

Carlos: And I was the number one fish.

Frank: Right, and it pissed me off with Denton because I felt Denton should have noticed me instead of Carlos. Then I thought about it; and then I came up with the fish analogy.

Todd: It makes good sense, Frank.

Rick: (breaking his self-imposed silence) So, guys, I'm sorry. I've thought about it too, but it didn't come out like Frank's version. It explains to me how we've been acting. We weren't really ignoring anybody, eh?

Carlos: I didn't feel that way. I was content to let it ride.

Frank: That's about the way I felt. I had my time at bat; and, for the time being anyway, was happy.

Rick: Was?

Frank: Was, right. Still am!

Rick: Well, what do we do now that we understand each other so well?

Todd: Translation?

Rick: It looks to me that we're in the process of forming a mutual admiration society.

Joe: We could be doing worse. At least we're not shouting at each other anymore. (chuckles) I can't believe I heard everything that some of you guys have said, but the fact that we're not shouting should mean something. Whether we're forming a mutual admiration society is something else again, but I think we're learning to respect differences of opinion.

Mike: I've said it before, Joe, and for your benefit I'll say it again. I don't think you're learning a goddamn thing except maybe you're not calling names anymore.

Jim: For Joe, that's progress.

Rick: I'll say!

Joe: (to Rick) You know, I'd sure like to know what's bugging you!

Rick: Where did you get the idea that something is bugging me?

Joe: You started out this afternoon raising hell, and you're keeping at it.

Rick: (sarcastically) I said I was sorry.

Joe: Right, but then you turn around and make a dig at me every chance you get. What in the hell have I done to you?

Rick: ". . . . . let me count the ways."

Todd: I don't think that helps anything, Rick.

Jim: Who says he's trying to help?

Rick: (to Jim) I've decided to break my vow, you stupid bastard. I want to be in a mutual admiration society in between you and Joe.

Jim: (to Joe) Does it strike you as odd that we're on the same side of the fence, Joe old boy?

Joe: Not a goddamn thing surprises me any more. Only thing is I can't figure out what Rick is so uptight about.

Rick: What's uptight about me?

Joe: It seems to me you've got something to say to me. Only thing instead of saying it you keep making digs at me.

Frank: It sounds to me like Joe hit the nail on the head.

Mike: Like I said earlier, Joe. You're the target.

Todd: Gee! Where did all the sweetness and light go?

Mike: And Lord! Here's our man Rick taking up with a confirmed homosexual.

Jim: (in mock horror) My God! I thought I had missed being confirmed.

Rick: (laughs) I daresay that's the only trick you've missed.

Jim: Up yours, buddy. (joins in the laughter with Rick)

Mike: (drily) What a pair of jokers! A thousand comedians are out of work and these two decide to go into the business. (laughs in spite of himself) A real pair of winners, I must say.

Rick: (very seriously) The only thing left for an encore is for you and Joe to take up together, Mike. Just think, fellows. The really great studs among us could opt for a twosome.

Joe: Christ, Rick! Knock it off.

Mike: Yeah. If you've got a point to make, go on and make it.

Rick: (to Jim) See! They're getting together already.

Jim: (snickers) Poor Carlos. He'll get shafted again.

Rick: It sure as hell looks that way.

Mike: Goddamn it! Knock it off. You've had your fun.

Jim: What's the matter, Mike? Don't you like being teamed with Joe? The way I see it you two deserve each other.

Frank: You were only half right, Mike. Joe's half the target, but you're the other half.

Joe: Okay, but why?

Frank: Rick tossed out that they were both great studs. I suspect that's the reason.

Rick: You've got a big mouth, Frank. You know that?

Joe: (ignores Rick's comment to Frank) I don't consider that an insult.

Todd: (to Mike) And how do you consider it?

Mike: (laughs) As the gospel truth.

Rick: (to Jim) See! They deserve each other.

Jim: Right on, baby.

Joe: You know, this scene is really beginning to piss me off.

Todd: Mike, this may sound like a stupid question.

Rick: It wouldn't be your first one.

Todd: Christ, why me?

Joe: Why anybody?

Mike: Ask your question, Todd.

Todd: This besexual thing. That's what I want to ask you about. (Looks at Rick) But I'm feeling guilty right now. It seems to me that Rick was trying to float to the top as Frank would say it, and maybe I interrupted.

Rick: Don't you worry about me, sonny boy.

Joe: Maybe it's best if we leave Rick alone for awhile.

Jim: Push both of us to the back burner.

Mike: Now what in the hell is that supposed to mean?

Jim: You're so with it, Mike. You figure it out.

Joe: Oh, hell. Let's get on with it. We're just going around in circles. (to Mike) Why don't you field Todd's question? I'd like to hear some more about it myself.

Jim: (very sarcastically) I bet you would!

Mike: (to Jim) Why don't you knock it off? You know it might be beneficial to all of us if you and your buddy over there went back on the silence kick.

Rick: I hope you're using the term buddy very damn loosely.

Jim: He is; for two reasons. First, he doesn't know the meaning of the word; and second, he knows that you and I are poles apart.

Frank: (laughs) Now there's a Freudian slip if I ever did hear one!

Jim: Go to hell; you and your Freudian slips.

Carlos: Joe's right. We're going in circles.

Mike: Okay, I'll try to break it by answering Todd's question. (to Todd) You want to try asking it again?

(General laughter)

Todd: (after the laughing dies away) Well, I was curious about your statement about being bisexual. I just wanted you to tell us something about it. Hell, I don't even know what I want to ask.

Mike: (chuckles) I can imagine. You just don't know how it's possible to be sexually attracted to men as well as women. That's it, isn't it?

Todd: That's most of it. I guess maybe I am naive, but I just don't see how it's possible. I mean, you know, to have it both ways.

Mike: (laughs) A decent way to put it, Todd. But, you know as far as I am concerned it's a rather simple answer. There probably are a lot of psychological factors involved, so to get a technical answer you'd have to ask Denton. But down on the level where I'm at, I guess you'd have to say it was pure hedonism. I don't think being bisexual is something I've arrived at because I either worked at it or because I'm so damn smart. As far as I'm

233

concerned everyone has the capacity to warmly relate to a fellow human being.

Todd: Relate yes; but having sex is something else.

Mike: Sex is one of the finest ways to relate, Todd. Sure, you can have intellectual communion — if you want to call it that — with anyone. I've met girls I've had absolutely no sexual interest in; but I've found them to be good conversationalists, or maybe they're just a lot of fun to be with. This is what I meant by intellectual communion.

Joe: There's always some degree of sex involved, Mike. Even if you don't bed a chick you think about it. At least that's the way I see it.

Mike: It may be that you see it that way because you've been brainwashed into believing that women are sex-objects, but not much of anything else.

Joe: No, I don't agree. You seem to be saying that I think women are good for only one thing, and that's not true at all. I'm not saying they can't be anything they want to be. They can be doctors or lawyers or welders or anything else they want to be. What I am saying is that when I look at a woman one of my thoughts somewhere along the line is what she'd be like in bed.

Mike: Right. And I ask you again, what makes you think like that?

Joe: Hell, I don't know what you mean by what makes me think like that. I think it's pretty damn natural to think like that! Now that doesn't mean I want to go to bed with every one of them. Sometimes I'm not the least bit interested.

Rick: Christ. I never thought I'd hear you say anything like that.

Joe: Well, maybe not; but I'm being honest. I've even dated some girls I wouldn't take to bed on a bet.

Mike: Then why did you date them?

Joe: Well, like you said, they were fun to be with.

Rick: But you've always said you wouldn't date a girl more than three times if she wouldn't put out.

Jim: (sarcastically) He's probably also said he wouldn't waste his time on the fat and ugly ones.

Joe: Okay, guys. In all honesty I've got to admit I have said those kinds of things. But I was just shooting off my mouth. I didn't mean anything by it.

Rick: Then why did you say them?

Joe: Hell, bull-sessions! Trying to impress somebody! How in the hell should I know? (to Rick) You've done the same things. I've heard you.

Rick: Yeah! Well, in my case I was trying to live up to what the other guys were doing.

Carlos: In other words you weren't making out like the other guys so you pretended you were?

Rick: I'll admit to you guys that it's true.

Mike: But you wouldn't want it to get out of this room, would you?

Rick: (defensively) Well, we're all leveling with each other, and that's what I've got to level about.

Mike: But you still think Joe makes out like a bandit?

Rick: (getting angry) He says he does, and I believe him.

Mike: (drily) Well, all I've got to say is that you better quit believing a lot of that crap he tells you. Right, Joe?

Joe: (grins) I improvise.

Mike: You better believe it, baby. You improvise one hell of a lot, because you're playing a role. You like to be top dog in the woman department, so you'll lie like hell in order to appear like you are. And then in order to keep up with you, all the other guys start making up stories about their own exploits. Some of the guys like Rick become pretty good at making up stories. Oh, they might need an occasional boost to their ersatz masculinity; but most of the time they can get this simply by making a dig at some other guy's masculinity.

Jim: Right on. Look at the strong way Rick comes on about queers.

Carlos: Joe does the same.

Mike: Right, but Joe doesn't need to come on as strong in that department as Rick has to. And the reason is simple: Joe's more brainwashed in the balls department than Rick is.

Joe: You're crazy as hell! Mike, do you know you're just as crazy as hell?

Mike: (ignores Joe's comments) But something else happens too. Let me use Todd as an example. Do you mind, Todd?

Rick: Hell, go on and use him. He's the one who brought all this up anyway.

Todd: No, I don't mind.

Mike: I could use Carlos or Jim just as well.

Jim: (drily) I'd be just as happy if you'd use Todd.

Mike: (laughs) Well, I had planned to, but don't act like such a bitch.

Jim: I like being bitchy.

Mike: (continues) Like I said, some guys are pretty good at making up stories about their sexual adventures with girls. To keep up with all the stories they hear their buddies tell, they go off alone and make up convincing stories of their own. In a manner of speaking they make up lies to match the lies they're constantly hearing.

Joe: But they're not all lies. In my case they sure as hell aren't all lies.

Mike: True enough. But there are enough lies going around that if a guy wants to become even in the swapping of stories he's going to have to be doing some tall tale telling of his own.

Joe: You said you were going to use Todd as an example of something.

Mike: Right. And so I shall!

Rick: When, dear God, oh when?

Mike: (to Rick) Now, smartass, now! (to Joe) You see. Some guys are not natural liars. They're not all that inventive or ingenious. When they hear all these adventures the other guys are having, they begin to believe something's wrong with them.

Rick: (disgustedly) Shit! Do you mean to tell us that Todd was running around the restrooms because he couldn't make up stories?

Mike: Don't act so damn stupid, Rick. Haven't you ever felt second-best to Joe in that department? Haven't you ever wondered what he's got that you haven't that allows him to make out like a bandit while you come in such a poor second? And are you ready to admit that one of the reasons you play second-fiddle in your friendship is because you think he's somebody you've got to imitate? Maybe that's the reason you're pissed off with him today because you're waking up.

Rick: Crap!

Frank: I can see what Mike is saying. It makes sense.

Joe: It doesn't make sense to me. No guy goes running around trying to be gay because he can't shape up with his buddies.

Mike: As usual, Joe, you're trying to make things too black and white. Too simple!

Jim: (icily) That's the only way he can understand anything.

Joe: Denton, all this crap doesn't make sense to you, does it?

Denton: I'm interested in what Mike has to say.

Rick: (in dulcet terms) It's a fairy story.

Mike: Look, smartass. It's enough of a fairy story, as you call it, to have had a profound effect on your life. Just look at the friendship you and Joe have. You're the second partner in the relationship whether you want to admit it or not; and a lot of the reason that you're second best is because of your believing that you're second best in the stud department.

Jim: Yeah, Rick. You do play second fiddle to Joe. That much shows all over the place.

Frank: Jim, I think you're being too personally antagonistic. Why can't we talk about these things in abstract terms?

Rick: How abstract is Mike being? Hell, I don't call his remarks about me abstractions.

Mike: You're right, Rick. You can deal in abstractions only in a degree. Sooner or later you've got to get into reality.

Rick: And getting into reality means getting personal?

Mike: In a group like this that's trying to work with how we feel both here and now, there's no other way.

Jim: Okay, Mike. You've got a point in what you say about Rick and the way he allows Joe to dominate their friendship. I can see that. But what about you and Carlos? You know damn well you dominate him.

Rick: Yeah, Mr. Smartass. How about that?

Mike: Look, if I dominate Carlos . . . .

Frank: There's no "if" about it, Mike. You do; and you know goddamn well you do.

Mike: Let me finish, will you? All right, I'll try it another way; this time not in the subjunctive. Okay? Now it appears that Carlos is dominated by me. Right?

(General agreement signified by echoes of "yeahs.")

Mike: (continues) Well, all right; but whose fault is it?

Frank: There doesn't necessarily have to be a person at fault. Some people want to be dominated by others.

Rick: Gee, that's neat. I play second fiddle and Carlos wants to be dominated. You guys are all nuts!

Mike: What Frank says is true of course; but it can go beyond that. And I'm telling you it does. In Todd's case he is beginning to believe something's "wrong" with him, so he tries to experiment.

Frank: And if his experimentation is successful in terms of pleasure, he'll be in a position to convince himself he's gay!

Mike: Right. And Carlos? Well, he's already convinced himself he's gay.

Joe: And you're saying he isn't.

Mike: I'm saying he's never messed around with girls, so how in the hell does he know? Like I said before, I believe all human beings have a bisexual basis; but they get screwed up and never achieve their actual sexual being.

Frank: The way you tell it sounds as if you're advocating bisexuality as the final stage of psychosexual development.

Mike: Look, Frank. I don't have the psychology background that you do. So when you say things like that you lose me. However, in my own mind, I've worked it out that sexuality causes a lot of stupid problems for people. I've talked around quite a bit, because as you know I'm not bashful. I've also gone through a lot of the feelings that Rick has. Believe it or not, I did! And then I had to work out some feelings like Todd seems to have. One day it dawned on me I really didn't have to be one way or the other; I could be both. And though it sounds simple, it wasn't. There was a hell of a lot of agony along the way.

Frank: You don't think you have any hang-ups then?

Mike: Sure I've got hang-ups. Doesn't everybody? But I can tell you one thing for sure: sex isn't one of them. I don't prematurely wreck any possible friendships with women because I'm trying to prove my masculinity by channeling all my efforts at getting them into bed. Getting this need to prove myself masculine out of my veins has enabled me to have warmer relations with women.

Frank: I can see that. But how about men?

239

Mike: It works the same way. Possibly better. I'm not so worried about anyone considering me queer that I'm prevented from relating well to other guys.

Rick: Translation: jumping into bed.

Mike: That's not true at all. I would suggest that the number of men I've had relations with is much less than the number of women I've been to bed with.

Joe: Christ! You don't know.

Mike: Why is it important to keep count?

Frank: You've got a good point there. Why is it important to keep count, Joe?

Joe: For kicks, I guess.

Rick: To add some truth to your collection of sea stories, I bet.

Joe: Knock it off, Rick.

Mike: It strikes me that the way I think puts me in a damn good position. I'm not hung up in proving anything. The sea stories, as Rick call them, that other guys tell don't bother me; I don't have to stretch my imagination to cover them. Nor do I have to consider myself inadequate because I'm not matching up to a model. The other side of the coin is that I'm not scared into believing I'm something I'm not.

Rick: (sarcastically) Good old Mike. He plays no favourites.

Mike: It doesn't work that way, Rick, but I'm not going to try to convince you otherwise. It is impossible to argue rationally with the irrational.

Rick: You're the one who's been irrational.

Mike: Well, I don't see it that way. I see it as being a case where I'm not hung up on proving how much of a man I am. I see it also as a case where I'm free of the misinformation and taboos that normally plague friendships between people of the same sex.

Rick: You solve the problem by willingly jumping into bed with anything and everything.

Mike: (angrily) Like I said, Rick, it's not that simple. I select the people I'm friends with . . . .

Rick: (interrupts) And the ones you go to bed with!

Mike: Fair enough; but I don't allow myself to play second fiddle to anyone.

Rick: (flushed) I'd like to push your goddamn face in.

Mike: And do you think you're man enough to do it, Rick? You see I can talk on that level too. And if you want to take me on and try to push my goddamn face in, well you just come on and try.

(Rick moved not a muscle.)

Mike: Personally, I think you're a coward.

Rick: I may be a coward, but at least I'm not queer; or whatever you want to call it.

Frank: Knock it off, Rick. You don't understand the problem, so therefore you hate it. That's what people always do. When you don't understand something, you hate it.

Rick: (in disgust) Where was all this goddamn tolerance that you're talking about last time we met? You sure have changed your tune.

Frank: I haven't changed my tune. It's that I trust Denton. He's in control of what's going on. I've recognized that, so it has absolutely nothing to do with changing my tune.

Rick: You're nuts, Frank.

Frank: No. It's just that you don't seem to want to learn what makes people tick.

Rick: I don't want to know how a queer ticks. I just want them to leave me alone.

Mike: Who's bothering you?

Rick: As far as I can see, it's just a matter of time.

Jim: Don't kid yourself, baby. I for one have better taste.

(Rick shot Jim a dirty look. He made no reply.)

Frank: Why do you want to remain outside the group, Rick?

Rick: What the hell do you mean remain outside the group? Damn it, I'm in it as much as you are. It's just that it's now pick on Rick day, and I'm goddamn sick of it.

Mike: You don't act like you're in it. You're snapping at everybody. You're like a bitch in heat.

Jim: (snickers) Maybe he is.

Rick: (Shouting) That's what I mean. See? That mother can say just about anything he wants to. And so can the rest of you. Insult the shit out of me. But let me say anthing about any of you and you all jump on me all at one time.

Joe: That's not true, Rick.

Rick: The hell you say! And you're just as bad as those three damn fairies over there. Only you don't say what you really think. (to the group) Joe never says what he thinks. He only says those things that he thinks are going to make him look good. He wants to use people, not be buddies to them. (to Joe) Go soak your goddamn head.

(Rick was in a rage. He was perspiring profusely, and his face was very flushed. His clenched fists waved above his head.)

Joe: (pleading) Rick, for god's sake. Calm yourself.

Rick: (gets hold of himself) Sure, I will. In the meantime, go tell your fucking sea story to your goddamn queer buddy over there.

Mike: (forcefully) You better quit calling me queer, friend.

Rick: (convulsed in tears) Well, aren't you?

Mike: (very calm) Let's just say I go both ways, Rick. Okay?

Todd: What's wrong with him calling you a queer, Mike? Don't get excited. You should know I'm just asking, and not because I'm trying to put you down. You said the term didn't bother you.

Mike: (smiles) The whole thing revolves around the attitude of the individual using the term. Hell, you know that I see nothing wrong with a guy showing another guy that he cares for him in any way he wants to; he can even have the same close relationship that the heterosexuals have, if he wants to. But it's his bag; that's what I'm saying. Some people can use the term, and it comes out okay. But when somebody uses it and makes it mean filth and dirt, then I'm ready to slug it out. Okay?

Todd: I see your point. I guess I agree.

Denton: May I say something?

Frank: Sure. Join the fun!

Denton: It looks to me like Rick and Mike are hung up on a lot words.

Joe: That's the damn truth! Maybe everybody is.

Todd: Quiet, Joe. Let's hear what he has to say.

Denton: Well, I'm just referring to the idea that if you two keep using words on each other in the same old way that you'll find you'll never get around to communicating.

Rick: (sobbing) I'd fight him.

Mike: Oh, shut up, Rick. I don't want to fight you. I want to learn how to make you like me.

Rick: (puzzled) How can you want to learn to like somebody when you know they hate you?

Denton: Sometimes people just say they hate each other, Rick. Sometimes

243

they don't mean it at all. But they know the words, and somehow the words match the emotions. Or, at least they seem to.

Joe: Are you saying then that Rick doesn't really hate Mike? Or that he doesn't really mean those cracks he made at me?

Denton: The way I see it is that Rick has got some kind of a gut level feeling, and he's reacting to it with the kind of thing he's learned somewhere along the line. Most of us learn words, associate them with emotions, and somewhere they become glued to one another. One comes to mean the other.

Joe: What do you have in mind, Denton? The same thing as with me and Mike?

Denton: No, Joe, if Rick is willing, I'd like to get him to wrestle with Mike. You know, a no-holds barred contest. We'll make an attempt to get off the word level.

Mike: I'm ready.

Denton: I said it was up to Rick. You can agree only if Rick is willing.

Mike: Sorry about that.

Denton: Rick?

Rick: Why not? It just doesn't make any sense to me though.

Joe: (earnestly) It doesn't have to, Rick. Just do it, eh? There's probably something down in your gut you have to work out. Do it. Okay?

Rick: Okay. Where do we go, Denton?

Denton: Anywhere out in the middle of the room will be okay. Just move away from all the furniture.

Todd: But Rick's a lot bigger than Mike. It's not an even match.

Denton: Arguments in life are rarely even. But if Rick can put Mike down in two out of three falls, then it's an advantage to Mike that he knows it.

Frank: What does that prove? That might makes right? I thought we were supposed to be moving away from that kind of thinking.

Denton: In a way it proves that might makes something, Frank. But I don't think right is the word. When two people are hostile to each other, if they can find a way to work off the hostility directly on the person to whom it's related, it's very possible that the steam will blow away from the hostility. See what I mean?

Frank: I guess.

Denton: Let me try it another way, then. If the hostility is actually directed to its target, with it out of the way maybe some reason can come into the picture. It sure is true that as long as two people are involved in some kind of a confrontation that they cannot be reasonable. Now, what I'm saying is to get the confrontation out of the way at the outset; then there's room for the honest light of reason.

(Denton lined the two boys up, face to face. Rick's face was flushed and he looked angry still despite the passage of several minutes. Mike was cool, and looked as if he might be equal to his task.)

Denton: There are only a couple of rules. One, the wrestling has got to be clean, and both of you guys know what I mean by that. I won't put up with any punches or anything like that. Two, when I decide the fall or call for a quit, it's got to be accepted right away. Okay? (He placed one hand on each of the youth's shoulders.) You're to wrestle until I decide when one of you is pinned. Okay? And we will go two out of three. Ready? (He removed his hands from their shoulders and backed away.) Begin.

(Rick made a lunge for Mike's shoulders in an attempt to spin him around for a headlock. But Mike deftly moved out of reach and came back in, getting Rick's head in that very position. He slid around in back of the bigger youth, pulling his head backwards which resulted in Rick losing his balance. Rick fell to the floor with Mike's lock on his head still in place. Mike brought his legs into play, applying a scissors around Rick's waist. As a result of the dually applied pressure, Rick lay helpless in Mike's grasp.)

Denton: First fall goes to Mike.

(Mike broke and was to his feet very quickly. Obviously a bit stunned that Mike could pin him, Rick was slower. Rage had left him, and in its place was a strong determination to compete.)

Denton: Okay. Second fall, fellows. Begin.

(Rick moved faster the second time. With an outstretched arm, he gave Mike a hard shove that spun him around. Seizing the advantage, Rick moved in and grabbed Mike under the armpits. He easily lifted the smaller youth off his feet and threw him to the carpet. Mike landed and Rick was on top of him.

(He got an arm lock around Mike's neck. Pulling backwards, he forced Mike to roll over underneath him. With a surge of force he pushed Mike's hands sidewards as far as they would reach and then he knelt on Mike's shoulders. Mike was pinned, and though he made a stab at unseating Rick, the weight kept him pinned.)

Denton: Break. Second fall goes to Rick.

Rick: (smiling) You better believe it, Mike baby. And so will the third one.

Mike: We'll see about that. Talk about it after you've done it. Okay?

Denton: Third and final match, fellows. Okay? Begin.

(Mike was careful of the lunge executed by Rick that had spun him around on the second round. This time he dodged the expected push, but the dodge only succeeded in throwing him off balance. Rick moved to take advantage of Mike's imbalance. Throwing his whole body into a tackle, he brought Mike crumbling down. Mike was able to move away, but Rick made another lunge and had him solidly around his middle. Rick applied sufficient pressure to make Mike's face turn crimson. He suddenly relaxed his pressure, and Mike made the exact move that Rick desired. Mike tried to crawl away. Making a quick spin of position, Rick grabbed him in another scissors between his legs. Rick's legs were solid muscle and were able to exert tremendous pressure. Mike threw his shoulders back, allowing them to touch the carpet. It was too much for him.)

Denton: Break.

Rick: (standing over Mike and looking curiously down at him) I really never thought you'd be that easy.

Mike: I wouldn't have been if it had been my kind of fight. I do better with fists. (He smiled sheepishly and extended his hand to Rick.) A fair fight.

Rick: (He grabbed Mike's hand. He pulled him to his feet, and then Shook the hand.) A fair fight, Mike.

(Mike went to his seat.)

Carlos: You okay?

Mike: Sure, I'm okay. But that big mother nearly choked me to death.

(He smiled warmly at Rick.)

Rick: (Returning the smile.) But I am a lot bigger. Hell, I should have gotten you every round.

Denton: So, Rick, how do you feel?

Rick: Great. The last two rounds made me feel great anyway. The first time around made me feel like an ass.

Denton: Oh?

Rick: Sure. I never thought he could throw me.

Denton: And?

Rick: Well, all of a sudden I kind of remembered something the coaches used to tell us. "Don't get mad," they said. "You get mad and you forget how to play the game." So I got over being mad and started concentrating on how I was going to throw him.

Denton: The game of life is the same way, fellows. When you blow your cool, you've lost the battle. For the time being anyway.

Rick: Yeah, I know. I've learned my lesson.

Denton: Good. But how do you feel now?

Rick: Well, like I said. I feel good.

Denton: Good because you won?

Rick: I guess so.

Denton: And how do you feel about Mike now?

Rick: Well, he's a lot stronger than I gave him credit for.

Denton: You're evading.

Rick: What do you mean?

Denton: Are you still mad at him?

Rick: No, I don't think so. Like you said, I worked out my mad on him.

Denton: And you're not mad anymore?

Rick: I don't think so.

Denton: Rick, tell me. When you were out there, were you wrestling with Mike the queer or Mike the opponent?

Rick: (turns red) I'll have to admit that the first time around it was Mike the queer I was fighting with.

Denton: And you lost?

Rick: Yes.

Denton: And the second round?

Rick: (laughing) Hell, after he threw me I was fighting with Mike the fighter.

Denton: Then you're kind of saying that a label caused you to lose your head, so to speak. But when you remembered what the coaches said about keeping cool, you were able to forget the label and concentrate on the opponent. Right?

Rick: You're right. And I see the point. (He smiled wanly.) I apologize, Mike. And, Denton, I won't forget the lesson.

Denton: Good.

(Mike nodded agreeably.)

Denton: I think it's an important point, guys. So let me spell it out another way. Okay? (He assured himself he had everyone's attention before continuing.) What happens to most of us is that we get involved in the use of terms and labels. Some of these terms and labels are good. Others are not so good, and some are just downright terrible. Okay. Well, Rick was using a word. Mike recognized how he was using it. In Rick's vocabulary you probably couldn't have found a word that had a more terrible meaning, at least in his perception. Mike, being only human, rejected the tone and content just as Rick knew that he would.

Todd: Gee, I do get it.

Denton: Sure. It's not difficult to spot, once you know what you are looking for.

Frank: (chuckles) Games! Games! Games!

Denton: Sure, they're all games. Nearly everything we do every day, Frank, is some kind of a game. The trick is to sit back and recognize the game and then play it in a way that makes it work to our better acceptance of the gut realities. There's always hope for change.

Joe: But you have to work at it.

Denton: Right. Now, the other day you asked me to address myself to this business of whether the group had gone out of bounds; or, let me carry it a step further, is it in danger of going out of bounds. You still want me to answer it?

Frank: You've already answered it for me; but maybe you want to try it another way.

Denton: Okay. But let me start off by saying that I'm going to have to go the long way around to answer it. There's no simple way to handle it. So if you all agree that you want a long winded lecture, I'll begin.

Frank: I think I'm speaking for everybody. If I'm not, anybody can disagree. But since we're all in the learning business, I think we need to know everything we can that might help us relate better to others. Gee. Just look. Carlos and Jim seem to get along, and Mike and Joe have no more beef with each other. At least I don't guess they'll start back at each other.

Mike: We probaby will. That's the way these things work. Rub somebody else raw and see what colour of blood you get.

Frank: And Mike and Rick got a lot out into the open. So sure. Lecture if you must, but fill us in on the action.

Denton: (chuckles) Okay. Let's start with Mike and his attitude towards bisexuality. First, let's try to be objective about a comment that Mike made. What difference does it make to any other individual if Mike, or anybody else, chooses to relate on a sexual level with a member of his own sex? Sure, society has taboos against it; but then society has taboos against a lot of things. There may have been and there may still be reasons that society passes rules against anything. Yet from time to time all these rules need re-examination in the light of current societal needs and structures. Many of society's rules probably require change, innovation or abolishment. Maybe this particular attitude needs to be changed. Perhaps it will in time. But who's to say about the change? The point is that Mike offers a certain persuasion. Millions offer the same persuasion. I should suspect the criteria should rest with how much harm is being done to another human being. Murder is certainly a something society needs rules against; it is the supreme violation of another individual's right. Yet is homosexual persuasion that much of a violation of another individual's right that it needs be punished in any way? Speaking for myself, I say definitely not. An individual has rarely been involed in homosexual expression without some level of commitment, regardless of how he was able to rationalize it. In my several years of working with homosexuals, I'm not convinced that very much in the way of seduction of an innocent comes about. Another way of phrasing it is that not much conversion goes on. Individuals of like persuasion meet, and that's all there is to it.

Todd: Well, does this mean that a man can be homosexual without his really knowing it?

Denton: There again, Todd, you're getting into words. After all, what is the operational definition that you're using for homosexual? Is it an active type of wish-for experiences or is it a concern without justification? I mean, actual justification.

Todd: I guess it's the latter case. I guess I mean a case in which a guy is trying to figure out whether he's a homosexual. He's had no experience, but he wonders just the same if there is something going on that he knows nothing about. In a way, I'm asking if a fellow always knows?

Mike: Can I answer that, Denton?

Denton: Not right now, Mike. Maybe you can put your two cents in later.

(Denton was fully aware that Todd's hypothetical case was none other than Todd himself. Denton would have liked for Mike to speak on the subject, if for no other reason than from pure experience. Yet he knew the attendant trauma of Todd's plea for help and didn't dare risk Mike venturing forth on troubled waters without reasonable foreknowledge of what Mike would say. He didn't have this gift of clairvoyance. He couldn't take the chance.)

Denton: Actually, a guy can wonder if he's homosexual simply because girls don't turn him on the way he thinks they should. It might even be the reverse side of the coin. He might not turn the girls on the way he thinks he should. A man can pick up homosexual patterns of behaviour in this manner purely be default. As most of you know, substitutive behaviour is not completely unknown in the dynamics of human behaviour. If you can't have one thing, you pick an acceptable substitute. What I'm suggesting then is that a man could turn to the more easily attainable; that is, in his perception at the moment of the more easily attainable. It doesn't necessarily follow that this will happen, but it is a possibility. What I'm suggesting is simply this: a man could conceivably be following homosexual patterns of behaviour simply through fear that he could not be successful in heterosexual patterns of behaviour. He could actually be expressing homosexual patterns without commitment. He could be active or passive. I suspect it makes little difference. After awhile the pattern of behavior does become somewhat habituated.

251

Rick: What you're saying then is that a guy could become attracted to another guy simply because he is not making out with girls?

Denton: It's possible, Rick. Anything is possible, actually. And I'm saying, yes, this could happen. Initially I would suspect it would be less an attraction than simply a need for release. Masturbation serves that purpose for many, but masturbation is not satisfactory for many men. Maybe simply phrasing it as a need for release can turn one man in the direction of another man. Research into the sexual practices of inmates in the penitentiary when they are away from feminine contacts kind of supports the thesis that a man will turn in the direction of a less favoured sexual contact if the preferred sexual contact is absent. Many men who report homosexual experiences in prison and in similar stress situations report a return to heterosexuality when their conditions become normalized.

Todd: Gee. I never thought about anything like that. But it makes sense, doesn't it?

Denton: Sure it does, Todd. Besides that, there are levels of homosexual involvement. You've heard the terms cognitive, affective and psychomotor used as levels of behavioural processes. The same applies to sexual commitment and expression. There are levels of thinking, feeling and doing.

Frank: Can you give us some more on that, Denton?

Denton: Okay. Let's have a for instance. Mike said earlier that he had relations with women as well as with men. Don't you see that on the surface, at any rate, that there is a contradiction of terms?

Frank: Sure. I noticed it when he said it. And I don't see how he can do it. (General laughter greeted his remark. Frank joined in the laughter before continuing.) Well, I didn't mean it exactly that way. What I mean is it seems to me a man is turned on sexually just one way or the other.

Denton: A common misconception, Frank. Some men are most certainly tuned in on one mode of sexual expression as opposed to the other. But social and cultural factors are a big factor in one-way expression. But that is not the only answer either. Learned perceptions probably play the biggest part in determining sexual expression modes.

Mike: (interrupting) Frank, if you could only know the number of married men who regularly cruise the streets. I've even been out with a few myself. I'm being very serious, Frank. You would really have trouble believing it. And I know that some of these guys are so tuned in on men that even I wonder how they can turn on their wives.

Frank: Probably they don't.

Mike: (insisting) That's possible for some of them, Frank. But I swear to God it couldn't be possible for all of them.

Denton: Mike is absolutely correct, Frank. As you say, some of these married guys are really married in name only. Their marriage was a mistake, probably. There are any number of platonic marriages in case studies where the man is actually a practicing homosexual and the woman is accepting of the situation.

Joe: But how could a woman become accepting of a situation like that?

Denton: Well, it could be that the marriage is simply comfortable for her. She may be apathetic to intercourse in the first place. Or she could have learned to become apathetic. Probably there are thousands of reasons to be cited. Economics might be another. But I think it basically boils down to the issue that she would rather put up with the situation than leave the comfortable structure of marriage, whatever the reason.

Frank: I don't see how a woman can be apathetic about sex relations with her husband and have a happy marriage all at the same time.

Denton: That part of it is simple enough to respond to, Frank. There are probably as many marriages in effect wherein the woman gets little pleasure from the sexual experiences she has with her husband as those in which there is true sexual compatibility. This is fairly basic documented stuff.

Frank: Oh, hell, there are all kinds of manuals a guy can read to make sure that kind of thing doesn't happen.

Denton: True to an extent, Frank. But remember, one, some guys don't read; two, others don't profit from what they read. Frigidity is a reaction to psychological factors most of the time. A man who is capable of arousing a female to her fullest extent is aware of techniques certainly; but most important, he uses them.

Joe: This is what I was trying to tell you early today when you wouldn't listen. This gal I was out with the other night reacted in a way that I had never seen a chick act like before.

Frank: Maybe it was just the girl.

Joe: Maybe. But maybe it was because I was doing things that I had never done before.

Frank: You could be right. Anyway, Denton, go on.

Denton: Well, maybe Mike would like to say a few things.

Mike: The only thing I can think of to say is that the first guy I ever had sex with was a neighbour of ours. He was married to a real nice looking woman. They even had two kids.

Denton: He was older than you?

Mike: Quite a bit as a matter of fact.

Frank: How old were you?

Mike: Seventeen.

Todd: How did it come about?

Mike: (shrugging his shoulders) It just happened.

Frank: Aha! Then he seduced you?

Mike: No, I think it was more or less of a situation that came about because I was available and he was available. Things happen when the time is ripe for them to happen. Not before, and not later.

Todd: Then this means you haven't seen him since?

Mike: I've seen him since. They're still neighbours of my folks.

Joe: Christ, can I ask you if your family knew?

e: (laughs) Not about him. Actually, I got involved a little later in a brother sister act. That was what cut the bonds.

nk: I'll be candid. This being bisexual is something of a new idea for me. you're confident that you are?

e: Hell, yes. I'm also confident humanity swings that way.

nk: You undoubtedly lean more one way than the other?

e: Towards men. They're less problems to a guy, and I'm pragmatic. But met quite a few girls who turn me on too. A lot of the time, for me anyway, whole damn sex act is pretty much of a mechanical thing. You can make of what you want to make of it.

: Where is your feeling for people?

e: It's there. The thing is, I've accepted myself as a fine human being. Once an can accept himself, regardless of what defections he might have, he can n to accept other people. With me, sex is a mechanical thing a lot of the time. er times it isn't. But people are people, and you don't have to have sex with a an being in order to value them. Sometimes it adds to the relationship, and r times it wouldn't. But you know, Joe, deep down inside your gut you r really know for sure that a person who plays a sex-intercourse or sex- tion game with you is reacting in a mechanical way or not. Whatever the game, y it. And if I can make something come better by working a little harder appearing less disinterested, then I do it. I don't think this equates with any- g other than recognizing and living up to a fellow human being's needs.

nk: That's very interesting. I don't know if I followed you all the way, but ink I got most of it.

e: Nobody completely understands somebody else. I guess that's another tery.

: But this kind of group sure helps.

: (smiling) I buy that. And not because I'm agreeing with Joe, either.

e: (laughs) Why did you feel compelled to say that?

Frank: Oh, hell. Let's don't get back on that trolley. Go on, Mike, but quit analyzing Rick unless you want to have to let him throw you some more.

Mike: (grimacing in a playful manner) No, I don't want to go through that aga But let me turn it back to Denton. Okay?

Denton: Sure, Mike. There are a couple of more things I want to say. One po I'd like to make is that Mike says he is bisexual but is turned on better by men most of the time. That is what you said, isn't it, Mike?

Mike: In a way. It adds up to the same thing.

Denton: Right. Well, the opposite side of the coin is that there are men who a mostly attracted to women but who can be turned on by a man once in awhile

Rick: Wow! But listen, Denton. Isn't it possible for a man to be purely heterosexual?

Denton: Sure, just like it's possible for a man to be totally homosexual. But e then you'll find variations in life styles much as you'll find with the totally con mitted heterosexual. Let me try it this way. The vast majority of males live a heterosexual life style. Now why they so do is another matter. I strongly susp many men are steered clear of experimentation because of societal codes that a translated over into areas of punishment in any number of ways. But I also suspect that of this majority who have heterosexual life styles, the large majori of this majority never give much thought to any other life style but the one to which they are committed by perception and conviction. But, as I pointed out an intervening variable such as a prison sentence might temporarily circumvent even this form of commitment.

Frank: But you said something about variations in homosexual life styles bein very much akin to variations in heterosexual life styles.

Denton: Right. You'll find the wolf and the real shy type, and all points in between.

Mike: (interrupting): And, I'd like to add that even then you'll find variation in mannerisms. For instances, some homosexuals advertise themselves through slinky walks and lisping voices. They don't really have to be wolfish to act thi way. It's a sign they wear of their availability. They more often than not wan somebody to come to them, rather than pursue some other guy. Most of them

, on purpose.

nton: You use the word "them", Mike. Why?

ke: You know why, Denton, but I'll tell the others. It's because there's as ch difference between a guy like me and creeps like them as there is between ht and day.

: Being in-drag is a way to go.

ke: Maybe. But I want no part of anything like that. A man is a man just a woman is a woman. Sexual involvement has nothing to do with crossing styles. That's my feeling.

: Live with it, baby.

los: (interrupting): I think I'd like to add something to all this. I really guess t somewhere along the line I could have easily fallen into the situation of, know, lisping and developing a particular kind of walk. You know, I'm et and don't make much of an impression upon people. I guess at times I've ught that at least this kind of thing would help me to meet guys I could be rested in. It's all a recent type of thinking, as a matter of fact. And maybe 's where I need help. You know, in the area of learning to respect myself as eone who people could like and not as a pile of nothing. I never have had ple like me much. I guess that's my way. And sitting here, I'm beginning to it clearer and clearer. But Mike is not that way at all. He is outgoing and ndly. You see what he's done here. He's had homosexual experience, and ral of you guys would have had nothing to do with him several weeks ago. ke's changed a lot of your thinking. Anyway, I think that he has. Everything has had a lot to do with it too. But what I'm saying is that Mike gets himself d. I don't. Since he is the way he is, I guess I'm a lot less than what I might I know this is strange sounding but even if I were interested in girls, and I ht add that I definitely am not at this time anyway, I'd have to find a woman o could dominate me to a large extent. I just am not a dominant man. I don't k I could ever dominate another man, and I'm almost as certain that I couldn't ninate a woman. If I were to get married, I'd have to be henpecked. That's there is to it. I'm the kind of guy a lot of people walk over. That's me. And ke could dominate me if he wanted to. Most people could. I'm just easily ninated. But my main point is that I'm less dominated by Mike than I would to be. But yet he won't go any further. (He threw up his hands in a futile ture.) Does any of this make sense?

257

Denton: Sure. Some people are just wanting to be dominated, just like there others who want to dominate. That's what I was saying Carlos, only you amp fied it beautifully. It doesn't matter the sexual living style insofar as levels of behaviour are concerned.

Carlos: I just think it would be easy for me to go into drag. It might make m more valuable human being.

Mike: That's not true at all, Carlos, baby. All that crap means is that you're trying to be something that you aren't. A guy is a guy, and he can't change th Period.

Todd: What's in drag?

Rick: Christ! It only means that a man starts dressing like a woman.

Todd: All the way?

Mike: Sometimes. But a lot of times it means just putting on makeup and thi like that.

Joe: Christ.

Frank: Transvestitism is the real term.

Todd: Okay, Denton, let me ask you this. Once in a while you hear a group c guys sitting around talking about how much they hate queers. Now I don't m Frank or Rick here because I think we all know this is a different situation wh you're supposed to come up with gut level feelings. But a lot of jokers spend their time talking about queers and how they hate them.

Mike: Sometimes it's more than talk. I've known guys to get rolled by these dumb bastards. It's even happened that some guy laid his hands on me.

Denton: Well, to answer your question, Todd. From a psychological point of view, fellows like this are having an identity crisis of their own. Putting it very bluntly, a man who has what seems to be a pathological hatred of homosexual is probably fighting against some very strong feelings of his own on this very level. If a man wants to fight a homosexual, it's probably indicative that he's acting out on a symbolic level other things he would rather be doing. Of cour it is possible that simple indignation as a result of conditioning could have a l

o with it; but I suspect that more often than not that when a man wants to
t it out with a homosexual, he is not as strongly committed to his heterosexual
ngs as you might otherwise be led to believe. And, talking in itself is a sym-
c level of doing. Also, let me point out that it's kind of a well accepted fact
people talk a lot about what they are interested in. Certainly and admittedly,
e's great interest abroad with most people about homosexuals and homo-
ality. But watch out for reaction formation. If an individual seems too
rested, it probably is an acting-out type of behaviour. He's coming to wrestle
some feelings of his own.

k: How about taking money, Denton?

ton: Taking money?

k: Sure, taking money to let a guy blow you? All right, let me tell you about
When I was in the Air Force I took money several times. There were these
fellows hanging around the base. At least they seemed to be rich to me. Had
of money compared to me anyway. They hung around the gates like flies,
the M.P.'s just couldn't keep them away. Anyway I learned about it. A
k way to make five bucks. But like Mike said awhile ago, most of it was just a
hanical kind of thing. So I guess that's why I reacted like I did. Maybe I've
a guilty conscience about it all this time. I don't know. But I do know, and
the God's truth, that there were just three or four times, and that was a couple
ears ago. And I haven't gone and done anything like it since.

ton: The thing about taking money is not too complex. You say it was an
way to pick up some money. Okay. Take it at that. Why is it so difficult
nderstand? Financial necessity, or perceived financial necessity, is a factor in
y kinds of behaviour. Even more relevant, you have heterosexual prostitution.
not homosexual prostitution?

e: Why not? When the old man told me to leave home, I used to go on pay
s all the time. (He looked at Joe.) Don't look so damn shocked, Joe baby.
y's got to live.

k: (to Joe) Sure, we're not all born rich.

You sure have something in for me, buddy. Want to tell me what it is?

k: (ignoring Joe, and turning to Mike) Maybe that's where you got the idea
sex is a mechanical thing.

Mike: Maybe. Nonetheless, I knew what I was doing. And it was an easy way to make a buck, like Frank said.

Denton: The thing about taking money in a lot of cases is that it absolves feelings of guilt.

Mike: Only I didn't have feelings of guilt!

Denton: Maybe you didn't. But the fact is that if a man can rationalize his behaviour by saying that it's a way to make money, the transition of his feelings into a behavioural pattern becomes much easier.

Frank: Then you're saying that many guys start this way.

Denton: Right. Getting money helps him to live with his feelings. After awhile money doesn't have the same importance to him because he's learning to live with a whole new set of feelings. In other words, the rationalization was successful.

Jim: But the for-pay ones are dangerous. I've had some experience with guys who want to be paid, and I've heard even more. I know that a guy better watch out for them. They turn mean easy.

Denton: And even that is not difficult to understand. Since this guy finds himself waging some kind of inner battle, if a situation arises in which he is able to displace a bit of the aggression that is inner directed to somebody else, it is only logical he is going to do just that. I would strongly suspect that if a man who allows himself to be picked up for a pay date finds any weakness or trepidation or concern on the part of the guy who picked him up, he would seize the opportunity to act out his construct of how a truly masculine male would behave. Since it is usually conjectured that the typical masculine response is one of brutalization the pay date would act out his feelings in a brutal fashion. The experience would temporarily make him feel like more of a man.

Frank: Man, that's fascinating as hell.

Denton: (consulting his watch) Now, we've only got five minutes, so let me wrap this up. Okay?

(The youths nodded in unison.)

Denton: Well! It's true to an extent that the basic design here was one in which

mosexual patterns of thinking would clash with heterosexual patterns of
nking. I candidly admit that it was set up this way. It was even meant to be
newhat balanced, but it's less of a balance than I had hoped for. I'm not going
amplify that statement any, so don't bother asking. (He smiled broadly.)
at's one of the options retained by the intervener. Say mysterious things and
ɔe for the best. Anyway, Frank jumped on to the design. I'm not surprised he
. Sooner or later the others of you might have grabbed the same idea. It's not
ıll bad that you did. Now, going on to the bounds or limits. In my opinion,
·re are very few limits to activities of a group like this. Sure, I wouldn't have
spell out to you that some things I could not have allowed to go on. Just like
ave intervened to stop the senseless bantering back of words a couple of times.
all the same thing. But to answer you truthfully and honestly, I never at one
ıe had any concern about the behaviour or actions of any member of this group.
ope that this really answers all the questions that you may have. (He sought
t the expressions around the circle.) Does any one have any comment that he
.hes to make?

ke: I do, Denton. You were lecturing, but it was a damn good lecture. And
now from personal experience that much of what you said is true as hell.

ınk: I'm grateful. It cleared up a lot of things for me.

dd: Me too.

:: (smiling) And Carlos spoke on his own! Wonder of wonders.

nton: Well, let's break. See you next time.

ɔnton left the room, but all of the others stayed on for another ten or fifteen
ıutes in an animated discussion of how far the group had come in the entire
a of communication.)

SESSION IX

(The group was together prior to Denton's arrival. There was a bit of animated discussion going on, but Denton could sense that the conversations were casual He sat in the one remaining chair.)

Denton: Well? Where do we begin today?

Rick: Before anybody gets started today I want to just blurt out an apology. I'm sorry if I got anyone mad because I was uptight.

Frank: I don't think an apology is needed, Rick. Everybody has his day in co

Todd: Gee, I don't think it's necessary either. Just as long as you got it out of your system, everything is fine.

Joe: (soberly) Did you get it out of your system? Or whatever it was that wa: bothering you?

Rick: (smiles wanly) Let's put it this way, Joe. I've thought about things one hell of a lot.

Frank: So that means whatever was bugging you is contining to bug you. Isn' that right?

Rick: Now hold back a minute, buddy. You're reading meaning into my word and you ought not to do that. I've said something was bothering me and I've s I've thought about it a lot. I did not say it was still bothering me.

Frank: Okay, I'll back off, Rick. But I still believe you haven't got it out of y gut yet.

Todd: You may be right, Frank.

Rick: Oh hell, guys. Look at it this way. Don't you think people can ever wo things out for themselves? Must there always be a group of people around to help you work out your problems? If that's true, it sure as hell does away witl solitary thinking.

Mike: I think Rick has a damn good point. Sure it's good that we have this gr thing going. It's an experience the like of which I'll probably never again have.

Jim: (drily) Good God, Rick. You must have thrown him on his head.

Mike: (laughs) Hey, Jim. Let me be serious, eh? You know like last week. Rick was uptight, and he had one hell of a lot of things to say. Much of it was directed at me, and I have to add that I took offense all over the place. Yet, even though I did take offense I was able to recognize that I was just a convenient target; not necessarily the real one.

Joe: Who do you think the real one was?

Mike: Hell, I don't know. Why don't you ask Rick?

Frank: It's entirely possible that even Rick doesn't know.

Rick: Even more to the point, Rick might know but Rick might want to keep it to himself.

Mike: Right. And I'm saying there's nothing wrong with that. The group is great, and I repeat that I'm sure it will prove to be one of the big experiences of my life. I feel closer to you guys that I have ever felt to anyone; but that doesn't mean I have to depend on you for everything.

Frank: You know, it is strange how closely knit we've become.

Todd: What's strange about it? I think it's great. This group has become the most important thing in the world to me.

Carlos: I agree. As far as I'm concerned it can go on forever.

Joe: I'd hate like hell to see it end.

Mike: That's my exact message, guys. Don't you see? It's got to end.

Jim: I guess because you say so.

Mike: Jim, it's not in my power to say who has gotten what out of this group. I can only speak for myself, and I say again that it's been one of the greatest things that has ever happened to me. I can only guess what I think others have gotten, and I'd say you probably feel less committed to the group and have gotten less from it than anybody else.

Jim: (sarcastically) Now who's playing God!

Mike: Okay, okay. I hope I'm wrong, but it still isn't going to change my message at all; because what I'm saying refers primarily to how Rick is feeling. He's saying that we all have to work things out from time to time on an individual basis, and I agree. Right now we have the group to fall back on, and it's been a beautiful experience. I feel more for you guys now than I would have ever thought possible.

Joe: I feel the same way.

Mike: But the point is that the group sooner or later is going to have to come to an end. We'll all continue to be friends if we're anywhere in the neighbourhood, so to speak. We've gotten kind of used to the idea of sharing our feelings and our ideas, but I don't think it's such a good idea for any one of us becoming so dependent upon the group that we will feel lost when it no longer exists as an entity.

Frank: So what you're saying is that we should begin a countdown for the dissolution of the group?

Mike: No, I'm not saying that at all. That's Denton's business. I'm only stating my conviction that if Rick has something on his mind that he's working on, we ought to leave him at peace to work it out. It's a grand idea to share; but if some one wants to hold back a bit to chew on by himself, then the rest of us should encourage him.

Jim: Like I said, he landed on his head.

Mike: What I learned from that session with Rick was how out of shape I am. (laughs) It takes being thrown on your ass a couple of times to convince you you're out of shape. (to Denton) Put that in your psychologists's notebook.

Frank: (very seriously) Its more important than that, Mike. It lets you direct your hostility to the exact place where you feel it should be directed. I did some reading on the subject since the last session. It's a physical striking out at a target which you feel needs to be somehow punished, and so that answers the need of extinguishing or at least diminishing a level of hostility which , if allowed to fester could become very deep-seated. In a group, like this, the intervener can manipulate to determine that nobody gets hurt. It's an effective way of handling negative feelings.

Todd: (jokingly) Good Lord, Frank. I read and I read, and yet I can never come out sounding like a textbook like you do.

Frank: It's a fault I have, Todd. You guys have been telling me about it now for "x" number of weeks. (smiles) But I'm trying to overcome it. Give me time, eh?

Joe: He'll make a deadly lecturer.

Mike: A built-in guarantee to put anybody to sleep.

Denton: I've been accused of that in my time too, but let me just add a little to what Frank has said. (Denton laughed) Now, last time I got scolded in a manner of speaking for my quote-unquote lecturing so I'll make it brief. The one fundamental thing that I want to add to Frank's words is that any kind of feeling can be handled once it's gotten out into the open. The first thing you've got to do is to recognize the feeling for what it is. Give it a fancy label, perhaps, but recognize it. As long as you deny having an emotion, you're unable to deal with it. Yet once you'll just admit it's there, you can begin doing something about it if you don't like it. A mother who hates her child, for example. This is a pretty damned unorthodox admission, but until she gets around to admitting that this is the feeling for the kid she's going to be living a lie and wrecking the kid's life in the process. And the same thing is true of any kind of a feeling. Drag it out and recognize it, admit it's there, and then do something positive about getting rid of it. But only after you've decided you really want to get rid of it. You might even want to live with it. Who knows?

Frank: Right. The rest of the article went on to say the very same thing. Hell, Denton, you could have written that message.

Denton: (smiling) Writing is not my bag. I don't have the patience. See? I recognize things too.

Todd: Where did you do this reading, Frank?

Frank: In the library. There are a few books on group dynamics. Not much though. Hell, surely not as much as should be there.

Rick: Not much has been written, Denton. I got the bug to do some reading on the subject, but the librarian said there isn't much available. She even asked me why I wanted to know.

Frank: What did you tell her?

Rick: I said it was research for a psychology class. She just shook her head. You know. (He imitated her head movements, indicating that he had flipped his wig.)

Mike: Denton, what would you think about writing a book about us?

(Peals of laughter)

Mike: (continues) No, I'm serious. Most of the material you can get your hands on about groups are fairly much professional books. There haven't been many attempts at reporting actual group sessions.

Denton: To be honest about it, Mike, I haven't given the matter a single thought.

Frank: Well, I don't think it's a bad idea. I could see where it would be of large practical use.

Joe: What do you mean it will be of large practical use? To whom?

Jim: Yeah. Who'd be interested in us?

Frank: (defensively) Well, it's just an idea. No use getting uptight about it. My thought was simply that we've done a lot in here; we all feel we've done a lot, and just maybe some of the things we've talked about might be of interest to people who haven't had the opportunity to participate in a group like this.

Todd: Could you do it, Denton?

Denton: Oh Lord, Todd. There are no tapes, no records. Nothing like that. It would be pure and simple recall on my part.

Frank: Yeah, that's true; but each of us could read the manuscript as it went along to see if it matches our recall.

Denton: That would be tricky.

Todd: But it could be done?

Carlos: I would really like to read about myself.

Denton: Look, guys. Maybe the idea has merit; maybe not. But let's not get hung up on it right now. Okay?

Frank: Okay. We'll do what Denton says. We'll leave it for the time being. (to Joe) Hey, Joe, you were going to tell us about this girl you took out. Now that Denton has clammed up about the book, how about giving us the gutsy details.

Joe: (grins) Rick doesn't like to hear my sea stories.

Todd: (affably) To hell with Rick. I need to hear some of that kind of thing. It might damage my ego, though.

Mike: (drily) I don't know if any of us are strong enough for this encounter.

Joe: In deference to those detractors of mine, I shall proceed slowly.

Mike: (laughs) But proceed with it you will, eh?

Joe: Sure, why not? It's a good story.

Todd: Story?

Joe: (laughs) The truth, Todd; the honest to God truth.

Mike: Well, hurry up and get it over with. You seem damned and determined.

Rick: (smiling) Go ahead. If anybody minded, it's too late now. You're going to go ahead anyway.

Joe: Well, Frank, you're an old married man so there's nothing in it for you. Mike and Carlos and Jim will just have to bear with me.

Mike: Relating on a sex level with another individual has nothing to do with masculinity or femininity, Joe baby. Or haven't I told you it's just a matter of individual preference.

Joe: You told me. It's just that I'm not completely sold on the idea. (He looked at Todd.) You, buddy, can learn plenty now. Do you hear.

Todd: Yes, professor.

Joe: Well, the business of working a girl up to a real hot level to where she would get as much of a kick out of it as a man does is something I never did give much thought to. As a matter of fact, it's true that I got the idea from that relating-game with Mike. In the past, I just knew what a man was supposed to do and I thought I knew what a woman was supposed to do. I guess I have to say that I thought a woman was just supposed to lay back and let you stick it in once you got her talked into it. Hell, I don't know what I thought; but I guess it came pretty close to that. Now I'm not saying I ever disappointed a girl. (He blew on his fingernails in an attempt to get over the success of his past accomplishments.) I've had return engagements, so it must not have been all that bad. But it's always been a matter of a little necking and a little petting, and finally you get your hands down in the girl's pants and start rubbing it for her. A girl is pretty interested if you get this far, I can tell you that. Anyway, from that point on it's always been a matter of getting her pants off all the way and then putting my cock into her. This sounds pretty damned cold when you spell it out, but that's the way I knew how to go about it. But I really don't believe I ever was instrumental in getting a girl to an orgasm before the other night when I did that bloody game with her.

Todd: (seriously) What do you mean, Joe? I didn't know much about a girl's orgasm. Does she have one just like the man does?

Joe: No, not in the same way of course. But she gets her kicks just the same. A man has his orgasm by exploding all over the place, but a woman gets tied up in a lot of just pleasurable sensations. Anyway, I picked up the idea and tried it, not really knowing what would come of it. It's a hell of a lot different than just having her lay there beneath you letting you kiss her.

Frank: Go on.

Joe: What more is there to say?

Frank: Well, handle it like a research project.

Joe: First, I don't know how to handle research.

Frank: Research is what you were doing. Research is experimentation with a definite perspective in mind.

Joe: Aha, I focus in on that. Okay. The main thing is, I took lots of time with her. We rocked, and then she said she was weak. I picked her up and carried her to bed. Then I took a lot more time with her. I just did a lot of things. Kissing mostly.

Mike: It's show and tell time, Joe. So you are one of those studs who kiss and tell.

Todd: Ignore him. Go on.

Joe: Hell, I can't draw you a goddamn picture.

Frank: No, but you can handle it in a precisely qualitative manner.

Jim: Whatever in the hell that means. Me, I'd rather have the picture. Just make sure to get in the phallic symbol.

Frank: (to Joe) What it means, is to tell it like it is, only with meaningful detail.

Joe: Well, after all the rocking and the hugging and the kissing and so forth, I worked my way down to her breasts and boy, I lived on them for a good long while. You should have seen those teats of hers. They were just sticking up straight like she was offering them to me.

Jim: (sarcastically) Which the bitch was! Things you offer usually do stick straight out.

Mike: (annoyed) Oh, hell, Jim, knock it off.

Joe: Anyway, she started bouncing around so much it was all that I could do to stay up on top of her. She jumped and tossed and squirmed and squealed like nothing I've ever seen before. Man, with all that she just had to be greatly satisfied. And as for me? Well, hell, let me admit it. I just never had anything to feel so good before.

Todd: Joe, I'm being serious of course. Like you know, I've never been to bed with a girl, and I'm just dying to ask you a question.

Joe: Shoot, buddy.

Todd: Well, where did you learn about a girl having an orgasm?

Joe: Hell, I learned that years ago I guess. But I didn't know how to bring her up to one, even if I thought I did. I can see that now. (He scratched his head.) But where? I don't know. Maybe in a bull session.

Denton: Todd, if I may, let me suggest that you check out some sex manuals from the library. I've got some on reserve, so just ask the librarian for one of the manuals that I have on three-day reserve. That way I'll be sure you're reading a good book, because a lot of junk is on the market. Okay?

Todd: Fine, Denton. I've wanted to before, but I've always been kind of ashamed to go up and ask for a sex book.

Frank: You know, Denton, I was wondering if the girl Joe was talking about could have been pretending all that ecstasy.

Denton: Probably not. A lot has been written about the way women pretend. That's true enough. A woman not experiencing orgasm in regular intervals often pretends she is in order to please the man. But I don't think that what Joe was describing was pretense. Too much muscular activity was involved, and he talks of squeals of delight. That kind of thing is almost involuntary.

Frank: Well, a woman doesn't have an orgasm every time.

Denton: Oh, gosh no. Figures have been cited to suggest that one orgasm out of every two sex experiences is a damn good average.

Joe: I'll be damned. So you really couldn't expect a girl to get her kicks every time out then?

Denton: It'd be unlikely, but it would depend on the woman. Some would.

Joe: I'm glad to know that. It would bother me if next time I wasn't able to bring the same thing out. Now that I know better, I won't be disappointed.

Frank: Hey, Jim, how about you talking for awhile?

Jim: What do you want me to say? Something anticlimactic?

Frank: (grins) Oh, I don't know.

Jim: Well, then, what?

Todd: I think it would be great if you'd tell us how you learned to accept that you were homosexual. Now, don't get me wrong. It seems to me that you and Carlos feel like you are definitely set in that direction, where Mike kind of runs back and forth. How about it, Jim?

Mike: That's a good idea, Jim. This is a group that our leader has told us was especially rigged for this type of thing. (He grinned at Denton, then at Frank.) Let's not spoil the show for the squares, Okay?

Jim: Sure, why not. Actually, I am a lot different from Mike. For a long time I chased girls, and I was popular as hell with them as a matter of fact. But I guess you'd have to say it was all in a platonic way. I went the whole boy-chases-girl bit. The only reason had to be that I was doing it for my family and for my friends. Everybody expected it. I had fun, but one day it occurred to me that I wasn't interested in girls in a sexual way at all. From then on it was a downhill battle. All I got out of it was a bad case of nerves. It's been going on for awhile. Then I met Mike. He was calm and happy and very likeable. I got it in my head I wanted to move away from home and move in with Mike. Home was just one bad scene. And that's the tiff that Carlos and I were having. Mike was the first human being that I ever felt was really interested in understanding me. To add flavour to the sauce, I found I could go to bed with him and get another one of my needs answered. Pure and simple. Carlos was in the way of my moving in with Mike, and it never occurred to me that I could have both Mike and Carlos as friends. Now I'm not going to sit here and lie and say that Carlos and I will ever be anything more than friends. Oh, hell, maybe we can get involved once in a while, but, face it, Mike is the drawing card for me. (Mike's face dropped to a position where the only place he could look was at the floor.)

Carlos: I'm glad you're being honest, Jim.

Jim: I am, Carlos, and I probably couldn't have said this to you unless we were saying it right here. But it's the god's truth. We'll be damn good friends if you'll let it happen.

Frank: (interrupting) You know, I'm not at all sure that Carlos hasn't got it figured out some way that in order to have a close buddy he had to go to bed with him. I may be wrong about that, Carlos. But if I'm not mistaken, you're making one hell of a big mistake with your life. It's like Denton said. Some guys turn to a particular life style because of external pressure.

Joe: So, then, what we have to learn is what external pressures are operating on him.

Frank: It's not that simple, Joe, I don't even know if I'm right. It was just a stab in the dark. But it sure is something for Carlos to think about.

Rick: Hell, yes. The guy may have been doing you a big favour by telling you he likes you only because you're Mike's buddy.

(Carlos was deep in reflection. Denton recognized that a significant point had been made to the youth. Now that the ball had been thrown to him, Denton wondered if Carlos would pick it up and run with it.)

Jim: At any rate, it didn't occur to me that we all three could get together. We kind of learn early that it's a dog-eat-dog world, and when you want something you have to fight for it. Well, I wanted Mike; and it seemed to me that I'd have to fight Carlos for him. Carlos sensed this and reacted. Otherwise he doesn't fight. (Takes a deep breath.) Whether I'm saying it right or not, what I mean is that it seems to me that sometimes people knock themselves out of what they can do or can be or can possess simply because they have their minds made up in advance that they have to proceed in a certain way. Now, again, take me for instance. When I was on the frantic boy-chases-girl bit, I kind of knew that I wasn't interested in girls on a sexual level. But I tried to be, really I did. And I kidded myself for one hell of a long time. Ever since I can remember I've liked to look at pictures of nude boys and nude men. I've never been turned on by a picture of a nude girl. They're not disgusting to me. They're just nothing. I'd walk down the street and look at the men walking my way and see what kind of a box they had. You know, how their cock showed up against their pants. I liked summers especially, because then I could go to the pool and look at even more clearly detailed boxes. The bulgier the box, the more excited I became. Just looking at a guy caused me to have an erection. But like I said, girls in even the briefest of bikinis did nothing for me. But all this stuff was wrong, because I had been told it was wrong. (He paused, and took a deep breath, steeling himself for the continuance of the story. He had the undivided attention of the group.) All the guys I grew up with began getting interested in girls. I didn't. At first it was okay, but after awhile the guys started saying I must be queer if I wasn't beginning to date and make out and things like that. Well, I didn't like that at all. Its' only since I've been with Mike in here that I've begun to see how important it is not to live a lie. Anyway, at the time it was important. I started making dates with girls. That was no big problem for me. As long as I didn't have to go to bed with any of them, anything else was okay. And I even made up some good stories. Probably hurt a few of my date's reputations with it all, but maybe not. Guys don't usually believe half of what they're told anyway.

(Rick looked long and hard at Joe. Joe didn't catch the stare.)

Jim: But the fact remained that I still like to check out the men's boxes, not the girl's bra line. So I started looking at guys sidewise, always trying to make sure nobody caught me. I was sharp enough that had I ever been caught giving a stud the once over, some story would have popped in my mind about the colour of his shirt or the cut of his slacks. It really didn't bother me all that much. So I dated quite a bit, and I trained myself to look at girls like my buddies looked at them. You know, giving them the once over. I especially did this when other guys were around to see me doing it. I got the reputation of being able to undress a girl simply by looking at her. What none of them guessed was that I could do the same thing with a man, only I was more interested. But all this looking and no doing was not getting the job done. I've never liked to jack off, but for awhile there I had a buddy I did it with two or three times a week. He didn't think about it the way I thought about it, but that didn't bother me none. He never would have stood still for letting me go down on him, but the other part of it was okay. But when he left and moved to Jacksonville I was really alone. So I began to sneak out of the house late at night, or I learned I could bring a date home early and then go cruising. There's a furniture store downtown that literally crawls with guys walking up and down the sidewalk. This is at night after the store closes. Some of these guys want to blow, others want to be blown. You simply have to pick one up and try to score. Sometimes you score right away, sometimes you don't. When you don't, you get frustrated as hell. On the other hand, when you do pick one up it's better if you move very slowly with him. He could be a pig. Just as bad, he could be one of the mean ones. You know, what they call tough trade. If these guys get half the chance they'll beat the hell out of you and take everything you've got. Even your car and they'll leave you stranded somewhere while they go off and borrow your car for the evening. They've even been known to strip a car once they get done with it. Man, they're after anything of value. This tough trade. So, you've got to be plenty careful. It becomes a game when you score to first talk in circles while you try to pick up some information about him. And he's doing the same on you. But he could be sizing you up for how much cash you've got rather than just seeing how much action you are willing to get involved in. Hell, some of these guys will even blackmail you if they get hold of your wallet. The crap of it is that you really have nothing to go on. How do you know the guy you've picked up is on the level or not?

Joe: How do you?

Jim: The truth of the matter is you don't. Not until the action is all over, and you start to leave one another. Some guys operate by getting in the car and taking over the first chance they get. Others will let you finish blowing them before they make their move. So the truth of the matter is that you don't. But every guy somewhere along the line convinces himself he can really tell for sure, only you can't. Sure, there are some signs; but even these can be imitated by a stud who really wants to imitate them.

Rick: Sounds like a risky business.

Jim: It sure as hell is. I've been involved in a couple of bad scenes. Once a guy I finally figured out to be a cop, because of the questions he started asking right away, got out of the car when I told him I didn't blow. But he must have had second thoughts about it, because he got into his car and started chasing me down the freeway.

Todd: How did you know it was a cop? Did he have a car? And what would a cop want with you?

Jim: He had a car. It was unmarked, but that doesn't mean anything. They use unmarked cars all the time, and they want cash just like everybody else. Some of them. The charge doesn't really matter. It's the idea you're being charged with something and it tends to blow your cover, if you know what I mean. And hell, he may not have been a cop. He may just have been a stud from the tough trade that I had temporarily gotten off balance. Anyway he chased the hell out of me, and I was scared shitless. He had a faster car than I did, and he was able to keep on my tail. Hell, I couldn't stop and I couldn't let him follow me home. Finally I made a turn off the freeway and started driving down dark residential streets with my lights off. I'm lucky I didn't run over somebody, I guess. Eventually, I lost the son-of-a-bitch, but I was scared for a week or so afterwards that I'd run into him. Another time

I lost a ring and a watch to a punk who was younger than I was. He pulled a knife on me. He didn't take the car though, but he threw the keys into some weeds on the side of the street and I had to go find them. Late at night, on a side street, it was a real bad scene. He had gone off, but hell, he could have changed his mind and come back. From then on I parked the car and walked along the sidewalk myself. But even that's not the safest thing to do. This one stud the size of Joe there got me in the car, and like usual we drove away to one of the residential areas just outside of downtown that has a lot of dark side streets. He parked the car way off the street and made me take off all my clothes. I didn't want to do that because the police do patrol and all. Also, somebody could look out a window and call the cops. It's just too risky to get yourself in a position where no matter what type of situation you get in you can't get out of pretty damn quick. Anyway, he made me strip and then I had to get down on him that way. I felt something cold pressing against my back and he told me it was a knife. He said that not to worry, that as long as I kept sucking on him everything would be all right. But he laughed and said that I'd better treat him real gently because the minute that he came he was going to ram that knife all the way clear to my stomach. He laughed like hell at that, and told me that's why he made me take the clothes off; so I wouldn't get blood on them. I tell you, that guy was a psycho.

Frank: So, what happened?

Jim: Well, like the man said, I took my time. I was so damn scared I didn't have to do anything but sit there and shake. Finally, he blew his load. He hit me as hard as he could, I guess, alongside the head and told me to get lost. That he had changed his mind because I was a good cocksucker. I asked him for my clothes, but he just drove off and left me there. Just in my socks. He was a real sadistic bastard, he was!

Todd: What did you do then?

Jim: Well, I called a buddy. You see, there was this service station just down the street that was open twenty-four hours a day. Hell, it was late at night and only the attendant was there. A real old geezer. I'm sure he thought I was a mental case. Anyway I got him to let me use his phone after he calmed down. He gave me an old shopcoat to put on, and I stayed in the back of the building until my buddy got there. But Christ! Did I have to run back and forth through the bushes getting there! Was I ever scared? And then it seemed to me that the guy who had done me in was cruising up and down the street looking for me. I kid you not. When my friend got there, I told him to peel ass.

Rick: What happened to the shopcoat? And what did you tell your buddy?

Jim: Well, I left the shopcoat with the old man and rode bareassed in the car. What I told my buddy was that I had been out with a broad and her boyfriend had caught us screwing. Hell, what else? I told him the guy had just pulled her into the car and that he had probably grabbed up my clothes to teach me a lesson.

Joe: (chuckles) That's a damn weak story. I'm surprised he believed you.

Jim: (shrugged) But he did. I guess that's my version of a sea story.

Joe: Did you ever see any of those guys again?

Jim: I don't think so. If I had, they would have given me more trouble.

Frank: You mean you wouldn't even be able to recognize any of them?

Jim: It's a funny thing, you know. You never remember what a fellow you've been out with only once or twice looks like. You might remember his car or his voice or something, but it's a damned fact that you don't remember his face. It's for sure that I don't. And I've talked to other guys who say the same thing.

Todd: Wow! What a story.

Jim: Yeah, and I'm glad I got a chance to tell it. It's a damn good feeling talking about it as a matter of fact. I really appreciate the fact that you listened. I feel as if a load were taken from my chest.

Todd: Well, how about telling us how you met Mike then?

Jim: We met in a restroom down at a store downtown.

Todd: And?

Jim: We just drove out to the Park. That's all.

Rick: But you obviously met again?

Jim: Sure. I broke one of the cardinal rules of the game. I gave him my name and address and phone number, and told him to call me anytime.

Jim: You never get names or anything like that?

Jim: (shaking his head) For more reasons than one. First, you don't really know if you can trust the guy. But even if you feel you can, he might have a big mouth. Your name can get in the wrong hands that way. A second reason is that if somebody gets picked up by the police and has your name on him, then you can count on the fuzz watching out for you. But chances are the guy will go on and incriminate you anyway without much urging.

Mike: It's true. Everybody is so damned scared about getting picked up that they'll do just about anything and everything to avoid possible trouble.

Todd: Okay. So you and Mike got together. But didn't you know you both went to the same College?

Jim: Not at first. That came out later, so then we started to meet on campus. But at first he'd just call and we'd arrange to meet somewhere. It got to the point that it was more just conversation than sex, but there was that too. We both liked to talk a lot, but it got to be that I enjoyed listening to Mike talk more than anything else in the world. Anyway he became the most important person in my life in just a very short time. Maybe the fact that that he was the first guy I ever trusted enough to know that I was homosexual had something to do with it. It probably isn't all that simple, but I'm certain it's part of it. Anyway, I'm sure you can understand the feeling you're bound to have for an individual who you can learn to trust in a world where the rule is to trust nobody.

Carlos: And you see what's so damn funny about it is that Jim and I think pretty much about the same about a lot of things. But when I learned of his interest in Mike and Mike's interest in him, I just kind of bristled. And then he had to dislike me because he could see that I was in the way of his and Mike's relationship. He hated me and, whether I was reacting to him being attracted to Mike or whether I was just reacting to his dislike of me, I can't say. But I hated him, that's for sure. I was not prepared to lose Mike, and I might as well say that I'm still not prepared to lose him. I'm prepared to accept the fact that Jim and I aren't going to have the same kind of relationship as we each have separately with Mike, but the fact that he spelled it out for me will keep me from reading things in that aren't really there. But if it hadn't been for this group, things would have been a lot different. It helped me to see things as they are, not as they appeared to be.

Jim: And I'll sit here and agree that he's right. I thank the group too. How's that for harmony?

Rick: (sarcastically) I'd say Mike's a lucky guy.

Joe: (angrily) What in the hell do you mean by that? Jim and Carlos are levelling with us, and you come in like gangbusters with another one of your cracks. I've asked you before what in the hell was wrong with you today. Now I'm going to ask you again.

Rick: (softly) Maybe I should get it off my mind. (In normal voice) But before I do, I want to say something especially to Mike, Jim and Carlos. Okay?

Joe: Just spit it out. You've been raising hell all afternoon. Just get it out anyway you want to.

Rick: Okay, I will. You guys may have thought I meant something other than words when I said Mike was a lucky guy. Now when I say this I mean that you have two good friends, Mike. Oh, hell, yes, there's a lot more involved. But at least you've got something going in the way of relationships. And this is what I wanted to say to you. I don't see much in a homosexual relation for me, and I just sure as hell don't want to get involved in one. But what I have to say . . . (his voice trailed off.)

Joe: What in the hell are you talking about?

Mike: Leave him alone, Joe. (to Rick) You want me to help you with it, baby? I can get it out in the open for you.

Rick: Thanks, Mike, but I can get it out in the open for myself. But you know that I appreciate it that you offered. No, the group has given me the courage. It's just that I don't want to offend you three guys.

Mike: Don't worry about it, Rick. I get mad only when a guys says queer and means all kinds of bad things going along with it.

Rick: Okay. That's what I needed to know. But the fact about all this is that when I think about Joe it makes me feel like I'm a damned queer. And I'm not. And I need you guys to help spell it out for me. (He breathed a deep sigh of relief.)

Joe: My God, Rick. You can't be serious.

Rick: (to Joe) The hell I can't! And you make it even worse. You make me run after you like, I think the expression was, a bitch in heat.

Joe: (explodes) Now what in the goddamned hell do you mean by that? I don't make you do any running after me.

Mike: (to Joe) Same difference, baby. Rick wants a buddy. He's elected you, but you want to use him as a companion when it's convenient and have him get out of the way when it isn't. (Turning to Rick) Your message comes across, Rick. Loud and clear.

Rick: But there's no sex in it.

Mike: I agree with you. There's no sex in it.

Rick: I guess the thing I can ask you to help me decide is whether to say sayonara to Joe as a buddy. As a friend. I don't really want to, you know. But since I've been thinking about it, it seems like the only thing to do.

Todd: But if you tell Joe what your bitch with him is all about, maybe he will change. Hell, I know I've done some rethinking on my own. Maybe he can do some, too.

Frank: Sure. Look, he's already done some. And he told us about how selfish he used to be when he took a girl to bed. He's kind of done some experimentation there. There's no reason he can't expreiment with you as a buddy.

Carlos: And Jim and I got a lot worked out.

Jim: All that you're saying is true, and I guess that's one of my hopes in telling you. But even a bigger thing is honesty with you guys. I've watched all of you struggling with honest feelings, and I've sat back and been a sanctimonious son of a bitch. That much I want to change about myself.

Telling you this, and asking your help, may help me.

Frank: Sure it will.

Rick: But like I said, I guess that the first thing to do is decide if I even want to continue having Joe as a friend.

Joe: Why not, for Christ's sake? We've been friends for a hell of a long time.

Rick: Correction, Joe. I've been your friend for one hell of a long time. But it's like Mike said, you've used me as a companion. When you wanted me out of the way, you sure as hell let me know it. (He looked squarely into Joe's eyes.) Like last Friday night.

Joe: Hell, I had a date. What the hell do you want? Me have no dates. Just sit around and chum around with you. Hell, that does sound queer. (mutters) You may have been right the first time after all.

Rick: No, Joe, it's not that simple. But we could have double-dated. You never want to double-date.

Joe: Simply because it's harder to make out with a chick when you've got another couple along.

Mike: Bull shit. Hell, you call yourself an operator? You're not, baby. Not unless you can pull it off even if the whole world is watching. I've had it help me as a matter of fact.

Frank: That's the damn truth as a matter of fact. I can recall when I was in high school that doubling was the best way.

Joe: I've never gone that way.

Rick: And you probably never will. You're too goddamn selfish. That's what I'm telling you.

Joe: (defensively) I don't know how selfish gets into it.

Rick: My telling you is not going to make the difference then.

Mike: But there's a lot more than this, Rick.

Rick: You must be some kind of a mind reader, Mike.

Mike: No, It's just that when other people bleed I bleed along with them. I understand because I'm trying to understand. I'm reaching out for you, baby.

Rick: Okay, let me spit it out then. Quick like, so I can get it over with. I'm a virgin, and I've counted one hell of a lot on Joe to help me get out of that condition. (Tears came into his eyes.)

Joe: (yells) What?

Frank: You heard him, Joe. He said he's a virgin, and it bothers him.

Mike: And he's been counting on you to help him get his first piece.

Joe: Gee, what a laugh. First, I don't believe it; and second, if I do believe it, how do I help him get it?

Mike: By letting him double date with you and let him see how the big operator does it, baby.

Rick: (solemnly) I'm sorry if all this embarrasses you, Joe.

Joe: (nodding) Now I know how Mike felt awhile ago.

Mike: No, you don't. It's a completely different thing in the first place. And secondly, I don't give a damn about being embarrassed. You do.

Rick: (crying) I don't really have a friend in the world.

Joe: But you got me, Rick. Regardless of what you say, we've been friends since we were kids.

Rick: Yeah. But I had to get you to play by going over to your house after you. You never came over to my house.

Joe: Damn!

Rick: And in high school, it was me who ran after you all the time. I called you, you didn't call me. And if I didn't call you, I didn't see you. Right?

Joe: (defensively) Hell, I called you. Not that it's all that important.

Rick: It was important to me, but you could not have cared less.

Joe: Then why in the hell didn't you tell me to call you, for Christ's sake?

Rick: Because I know you would have gotten mad, and told me something like if you don't want to call me, you don't have to. And, Joe, I did want to be friends with you. I still want to be friends with you. But I can't see why it can't be a fifty-fifty relationship. Why do I have to make all the moves towards you? Why can't you ever make any moves towards me?

Joe: I will from now on.

Rick: I don't think you will. You're just that kind of person. You take, but you don't give. That's one of the first things anybody said about you in here.

Joe: You could give me a chance.

Rick: I will, Joe. I really want to believe that you'll change. But you won't. I know that too. So it means I'll either go back to chasing you, or we won't see much of each other. And I'm ready for either alternative now, thanks to this afternoon.

Mike: (to Rick) Don't push too hard. Joe's got to get used to the idea and that takes time.

Frank: Okay, Rick. Let's change the subject a little. How about you telling us about your sex life?

Rick: Hell, I told you. There is none.

Frank: That include boys?

Rick: If you're trying to make me mad, Frank, you're not going to do it. Anyway, no girls. No boys.

Todd: Hell, it's not so damn bad being a virgin, Rick. Look at me!

Frank: But you're attracted to Joe?

Rick: Not sexually attracted, Frank. I've always thought of Joe as my best buddy. I guess it's right to say that I've always strongly identified with him. And I guess that part of it is over now.

Mike: Yeah, since he's let you down.

Joe: (shouts) What in hell do you mean let him down? I can't see where I've let him down.

Mike: Of course you can't, Joe. And that's the problem.

Joe: Well, he's my best friend.

Rick: Then why in hell don't you show it?

Joe: What in the hell am I to do?

Rick: Crap! I don't know. I just know that I chase after you all the time just to be with you. And it's not right.

Joe: (snickers) Okay, I'll start chasing you. Will that do the job?

Rick: Let me tell you what I was doing Friday night while you were having your big date, Joe. (He took a deep breath.) I had a very antiseptic date with Claudia Winters. We went to an antiseptic movie, had an antiseptic hamburger afterwards, and then I took her home and gave her an antiseptic kiss on the cheek.

Joe: Well, hell, is it my fault you date girls like that?

Rick: Have you ever thought that maybe I date antiseptic girls because I don't know how to be anything but antiseptic myself? I know no lines, and I know no girls. I don't meet them easy. I guess I kind of figure that since my big buddy is such a clever operator he could kind of help me out.

Joe: By introducing you to girls and by double dating with you so you can watch?

Rick: So I can pick up some tricks myself . . . . So that a climate can be created in which maybe I could function as a stud myself like I would like to, instead of somehow living vicariously in the shadow of your accomplishments. (His voice shook from strong conviction)

Joe: I just don't get it.

Mike: Then try a little harder, Joe. What he's telling you is that he needs your help. To put it plainly, you get girls in bed with you because you're a virile looking stud and you've got a big line.

Joe: I can't help how I look. And I don't know that I've got such a big line.

Mike: Oh, come off it. Modesty doesn't look good on you. All that Rick wants is for you to let him double date with you so that a climate can be created for him. He wants to see how you begin, because he doesn't know how. He's picked on you because he's your friend, and vice versa. He has some kind of an idea that he will make out better if you will only let him double date with you. He thinks maybe the fact that you are seeming to make out will help him. Hell, he might not even be far wrong.

Frank: He might not be at that. Moods are created, you know. I guess he thinks you and your date can create a mood for him and his date.

Rick: Something like that. It sounds crazy as hell now that it's painted out in words though.

Mike: Not necessarily, Rick. Maybe it sounds crazy now, but it didn't sound crazy before you started saying them though. Huh?

Rick: Right! (The tears had receded from his eyes, and he was feeling almost back to normal.) And let me say something else, Joe. After I took Claudia home, I took a ride by your place. Even drove around in back. Your car was in the garage, so I figured pretty wisely that you had your date up there with you. It made me feel funny as hell. I went home and slept in a very sterile bed, I kid you not.

Joe: All right. I see things a little differently now. And maybe you're right about you having to chase around after me. I like you, Rick, and I'll try to be more thoughtful in the future. But I still don't get this business about you and the girls. You've told me how you've made out any number of times.

Rick: Lies. All lies. You heard what Jim said about telling lies he felt he had to tell. Same thing with me.

Joe: Christ. But how in the hell was I to know?

Rick: I can see now that there was no way for you to know. But can you see, Joe, that when you told me about all the great things you were doing that I'd lose face with you if I didn't come up with something?

Mike: Despite all of this, Rick, Joe is a great guy. It probably wouldn't have made a bit of difference.

Rick: I can see that now. But I didn't see it before.

Todd: Score another one for the group massage! But if you're through for the present, Rick, I'd like our champion stud to answer a few questions. (He looked at Joe.) That means you.

Joe: Play it cool, Todd. Remember, I've had a rough day.

Todd: You'll enjoy this. I want you to detail your experiences with that girl that you were with the other night when Rick came by.

Joe: I've already said everything about that that I can possibly say.

Todd: Okay, maybe you did. But it didn't come through to me. Like I said before, I know nothing about sex with a girl. Okay. I'll get a book. And maybe Rick should get one too. But I want to hear the nitty-gritties about going about the job of making out. And I don't think the book will be that explicit. There's a couple of us who can profit from your experience, and I want you to tell me.

Joe: What in the hell do you think I am? A bloody reference book?

Todd: No, but I think you're a guy who's been around in the way that I'd like to go around. If you'll think about it, Rick felt the same way. That's why he said that you let him down. He was counting on you to teach him some of the ropes. Only he didn't come right out and ask. I am asking.

A STRANGE BREED OF CAT

Joe: It's all so damned personal, Todd.

Frank: So what else is new? Do we ever get into anything that's not personal?

Joe: I haven't heard you talking about going to bed with your wife.

Frank: All right, so I haven't. But nobody's asked for one thing. For another, I think we make out okay. But you know, Joe, I still don't think I have the experience that you do. It sounds strange to say it, being married and all; but I suspect it's true. And that may be another reason why Todd's asking you when he didn't ask me.

Joe: How about Denton? Or Mike? (To Todd) Why the hell me?

Todd: It's you I asked.

Joe: But why?

Todd: Look, Joe. Don't play games. Either give me some straight answers, or tell me you're not going to answer the question.

Joe: Christ. I don't see why you're so upright.

Todd: I'm uptight because I'm uptight. You know, you've got a hell of a lot of damn good things going for you. You're sure of yourself, you've got money, and I guess you're handsome. But most important is the fact that you're sure of yourself. I'm not. I've never had a date in my life. I don't even have the guts to ask a girl for a date. Isn't that reason enough to be uptight?

Joe: (laughs) Well hell, Todd! The first thing you've got to do is to ask a girl for a date. You sure are not going to get to first base unless you ask a girl out in the first place.

Todd: (seriously) Don't worry about that. I'll get a date. What I need to know is technique.

Mike: That's putting the cart before the horse, Todd. There's no point in getting bogged down in technique before you even get a girl to try it out on. (laughs) Hell, you're getting to be as analytical as Frank.

Todd: (grins) Well, maybe everything will come together all at one time. That's what I'm planning on anyway.

Joe: Sure, why not? At any rate, Todd, there are some girls who are a lot harder to get than others. You'll have to remember that. If you bat out with one, you've got to go find another. You can't get discouraged. That's the first lesson.

Todd: Got it.

Joe: So I guess the first thing you do is to size the girl up. Find out if she's vain about anything. You know, flatter her in some area she already feels she's tops in. It can work the other way as well. If she's not an especially good looking gal, you can tell her how pretty she is. Every situation is different. But basically what you do is to give her a snow job about something. Get her to trust you. (turns to Frank) Despite what Frank had to say, a line doesn't mean you're using somebody. Not necessarily, anyway. Hell, the girl is just as eager as you are. (To Todd) Remember that!

Frank: (chuckles) I didn't say anything.

Joe: Yeah, but I never know what you're thinking.

Frank: (to Mike) Isn't it interesting how Joe is developing a conscience?

Mike: Maybe there's fine hope for insensitive clods after all.

Joe: I'm ignoring you guys from now on. I'm going to speak directly to Todd.

Todd: Proper thing! Ignore them

Joe: Right! Well, let's say you're driving along in your car, Todd. You've got a girl beside you, so you look for a place you can park. You go through the motion of asking her if she'd like to park for awhile, only you're already parking it. Get the picture?

Todd: Sure.

Joe: If you've got a place to go, that's even better. Always use the excuse about getting off somewhere by yourselves. Just the two of you, or something like that. (wipes his hand across his face) Let's see. Then you start off with a little light hugging and kissing. Then you go into French kissing. (very seriously) Do you know how to French kiss?

Todd: (grins) I've seen it done.

Joe: Good. You're a good student. The first thing you know you have a case of your hands wandering all over the place. First you get them around her waist, and that's a good jumping off place for her breast. We'll assume she still has her clothes on. Anyway, you get your hands moving around her breasts. All the time you're keeping up the kissing, and just for the hell of it you want to get across to her that she's really turning you on. As soon as you can, get your hand on to the bare skin. Use the other hand to gently massage her neck. But get your wandering hand around a teat, and squeeze it softly. Keep up with the heavy kissing until you can tell she's really beginning to enjoy it. The next step is that you want to get your mouth wandering over her breasts. Get a teat in your mouth and nibble on it.

Todd: Sounds simple enough.

Joe: Well, it may sound simple; but sometime's it's a hell of a lot of work to get that far. At any rate, if you do get that far, you're home.

Todd: What does that mean?

Joe: Do I have to spell it out for you? (shakes his head) It's just that if you get this far, chances are all that's left is to get your hand down inside her pants and start rubbing around on her vagina. Take it from me, by this time she's ready for you.

Todd: Well, it sure sounds easy.

Joe: A lot of things sound easier than they actually are. It's not all duck soup. Most of the time any girl will try to argue to the final wire, no matter how much she wants it. The only way you can handle the situation is to keep on going regardless of what she's saying.

Mike: (drily) I can see our buddy Todd getting up on a rape case any day now.

Joe: Well, I'm counting on the fact that he'll realize that if she starts kicking and screaming and hollering like hell he's to give it up for a lost cause.

Mike: (laughs) That's a help!

Joe: Anyway, no rough stuff, Todd. Just act cool. Take your time getting around her arguments, if she has any. But be gentle all the way. Just keep your mind on that hot little hole she has waiting for you, and you'll get to it.

Frank: And of course you'll have to report back to us, Todd.

Todd: (laughs) Hell, if I can pull it off, I sure won't have any objections.

Mike: Well, we've all had a lesson now, haven't we?

Todd: (annoyed) Well, some of us need a lesson more than others.

Mike: Oh, don't get uptight, Todd. I was just kidding. (To Joe) So what was so different about the other night? You said it was the greatest you ever had. (laughs) I'll live vicariously along with the rest of you.

Frank: Christ, what we all need is a key to a communal bedroom.

Jim: Pornographic films are probably the answer. We can all sit around in a circle and hold hands.

Mike: (grins) Yeah, we should try that too.

Frank: I'll be damned if I will. Not with you guys. Somebody will end up getting screwed.

Mike: Sounds like it might be fun. (To Joe) Anyway, tell us about the other night.

Joe: Well, I think it was just a matter of my making up my mind that she was going to have an honest-to-god orgasm. I never thought too much about giving her the orgasm before. But this time I took a hell of a lot of time; just like I was telling Todd. No big variation. I just think time was the answer. I just didn't give it to her until she was jumping around on the bed like a wild woman, begging me for it.

Todd: (deadly serious) Did you kiss her around her bottom, Joe?

Joe: Good god, no! Christ, what a question, Todd!

Todd: I should think you'd want to try it.

Joe: Well, that isn't in my bag of tricks.

Todd: Maybe it should be. It probably would have made it a lot better than it was.

Joe: Hell, I don't see how it could have been better.

Mike: (laughing) Our boy is learning fast. (To Joe) You've got a precocious student on your hands.

Jim: (sarcastically) Or maybe just one hell of a hot stud.

Mike: But you know, Joe, he's right. I'm surprised how you consider yourself such an ace, and yet you've never sucked on a hot cunt. Hell, you've missed one hell of a lot.

Joe: (defensively) I've just never wanted to try it.

Mike: Well, let me ask you something. Has a girl ever suggested to you that you go down on her?

Joe: No. Never.

Mike: Do yourself a favour and try it.

Joe: That I'll have to think about.

Mike: Why, for Christ's sake? Do you think there's something nasty about it?

Joe: Hell, I've never thought about it.

Rick: Joe, has a girl ever sucked you?

Joe: God, no. I wouldn't let her.

Mike: (explodes) My God, you are a puritan underneath all that rugged exterior. Man, you just don't know what you're missing unless you give oral sex a try. That's when everybody goes wild, Joe.

Frank: Okay, Mike. You're the expert. How do you go about having oral sex?

Mike: No big deal. You just wait until the proper moment comes along, and then you get your mouth over her cunt. A good time in Joe's story to bring the mouth into play was when he said she was begging him to give it to her.

Todd: What would you have done?

Mike: Hell, I would have swung around and started lapping on her cunt just as quickly as I could. I would have tongued her clitoris until she was begging me to shoot her and get her out of her delicious misery.

Todd: What's a clitoris, Mike?

Mike: It's a piece of skin that kind of hangs down at the top of her cunt, Todd. The clitoris is anatomically similar to the penis.

Frank: Right. But of course it's a lot smaller. You have to feel around for it. When a fetus starts growth, the penis and the clitoris are designed alike. One just replaces the other is all.

Joe: Your cock rubs against it when you have intercourse.

Mike: Not necessarily, Joe. That's why it's a hell of a lot better for the girl if you get your tongue around it before you put yourself in. Or you can do it with your finger; only not as good.

Joe: I thought the cock always rubbed against it.

Frank: Mike's right. The penis doesn't always massage the clitoris. A lot depends on the guy's technique.

Mike: And that's the reason a lot of people say that there aren't any frigid women; just incompetent men.

Joe: Would you agree with Mike, Denton?

Denton: I think I'd be more prone to agree with him than to disagree. Certainly it might be an oversimplification to say it's always the fault of the male, but I would suspect that in many instances the man's incompetence is at fault.

Frank: How would it come about?

Mike: (chuckles) My God. A graduate psychology student.

Frank: Oh, come on, Mike. There aren't all that many books on the subject, you know.

Mike: I was just kidding.

Denton: (laughs softly) Some textbooks are there, Frank. It's just that it's a not part of the required programming. In any event, I guess I'd try to answer your question by saying that, reduced to its essential, it boils down to how a woman accepts her sexuality. She can't be too aggressive, because her role is more of a passive one. Incidentally, research has shown that aggressiveness in the female can act in an adverse manner on the male's sexuality. On the other hand, the role of the male is aggressive; some men play this role too much, and this contributes to a fear on the part of the woman. Or, I should say, it can contribute. All kinds of conditioning certainly play a part in it.

Frank: Could it be physiological?

Denton: Rare instances have been cited, but in most instances frigidity is a psychological phenomenon.

Frank: So that would make each case uniquely different?

Denton: That's true, although there are probably constellations of experiences which could be suggested as causal.

Mike: (To Frank) You ought to read up on the subject, Frank baby.

Frank: (grins) Right! I'll take your advice.

Denton: Fellows, we'll have to call time now. Okay?

SESSION IX

Joe: (looks at his watch) It's always amazing to me how Denton can keep track of the time.

Frank: He has to.

Joe: Yeah, I guess so. But I get so involved that I lose track of the time Today just flew by.

Mike: (rises from his chair) Yeah, and I always dread the time when Denton says it's time to go. It's always like you're being choked off in the middle of things.

Todd: Yeah. You want to keep going, only you know you can't.

Joe: A mood is broken.

Frank: To be honest about it, I always feel so damned helpless.

Denton: Why do you say that, Frank?

Frank: Simple! After you say it's time, what the hell else is left to say?

Mike: Yeah, I've noticed that. Conversation just comes to a grinding halt. You feel if you even utter another word that you're being dishonest.

Denton: (laughs) Glad you fellows feel that way. If you shut up when I tell you to, it means that some of my conditioning of you must be working. Now, go along with you.

(General laughter and banter as they file from the room)

SESSION X

(The group was assembled when Denton arrived.)

Mike: Hey, Denton, you're late.

Denton: Yeah. Well, sorry about that, Mike, but I had a student in my office.

Joe: You've always got students in your office.

Rick: Denton is father-confessor to the whole bloody student body.

Denton: Not bloody likely! But it does seem I keep busy.

Frank: Well, it's the only way to go.

Mike: It could be worse. Suppose nobody ever came to see you?

Denton: I'd miss that.

Jim: Denton, doesn't it ever grate on your nerves?

Denton: What do you mean, Jim?

Jim: Oh, you know. All the problems you hear.

Frank: He does with his problems in his office just what he's done with himself in here. Everything goes on the back burner.

Denton: (laughs) Frank, you make it sound so desperate.

Mike: But it's true, you know. I don't feel like I know you personally very much better from these sessions. You've stayed out of it as much as you could.

Joe: Right. You didn't share.

Todd: Well, with the rest of us surfacing all the time I guess Denton just hasn't had a chance.

Frank: Go on, Todd. There's more to it than that.

Carlos: You got any problems, Denton?

Denton: (laughs amiably) Thousands of 'em, Carlos! And I'm not talking about the students on this campus if that's what you're thinking.

Jim: How come you've never leveled with us then?

Denton: Mainly because I didn't see it as part of my relationship with you guys to do so. How does that grab you?

Jim: Frankly it sounds like a cop-out!

Denton: No, Jim, believe me. It wasn't a cop-out.

Rick: What would you call it then?

Denton: More like role playing, I'd say.

Joe: You mean you've been playing a role in here?

Frank: Good Lord, Joe. You make it sound like he's got a social disease.

Mike: Hell, we've all been playing roles.

Joe: I haven't. I've been myself.

Mike: Whether you know it or not, dummy, everybody plays roles all the time.

Frank: Right. When you move from one situation to another situation you immediately change your role. You're a student in one role, a lover in another, an obedient son in another. Got me?

Joe: Okay. I just hadn't thought of it in those terms before.

Denton: That's about the size of it, then. I've been behaving like I thought I should have behaved.

Frank: Encouraging us to talk eh?

Denton: In sum and substance, yes; although I would phrase it as encouraging you to relate with each other. And the thing is, Joe, if I talked too much, then the rest of you would not have had as much opportunity to get to know each other.

Joe: Well, it doesn't really matter. Whatever you did, Denton, must have been okay. I've said it before, but this has been a tremendous experience for me. (grins) And I don't mind if you were role-playing.

Denton: (laughs) Thanks for the blessing, Joe. (Becoming serious.) But today I want to bring a problem before the group.

Mike: Shoot!

Denton: Well, it has to do with how much longer the group is going to go on.

Mike: He's telling us he wants to get rid of us.

Denton: (laughs) I'll have to admit that's about the size of it. Except that I truly don't want to get rid of you. It's just that I think we need to give some thought about how much longer the group will go on.

Carlos: This comes as a shock to me.

Jim: Why should it? Did you think we were going to go on like this forever?

Carlos: Actually, I've never thought about it.

Jim: Well, it's obvious that Denton has. It's like Mike says: Denton wants to get rid of us.

Mike: Only I meant it as a joke.

Jim: What the hell do you think I mean by it?

Mike: It doesn't sound as if you're laughing.

Jim: (sarcastically) Laughing on the outside, crying on the inside. Don't you know?

Rick: Now what in hell is that supposed to mean?

Jim: Mean! Mean! Mean! Something always has to mean something to you guys. Me? I'm tired of thinking about what things mean! I'm going out and do something.

Rick: We're all going to go out and do something, Jim.

Jim: Yeah, but later. Me. I'm going out and do something now.

Frank: It sounds like you've got plans, Jim.

Jim: Nope, no plans. Except to leave, that is.

Todd: Can I ask you a question, Jim?

Jim: Sure. Why the hell not?

Todd: It sounds to me like your leaving is pretty definite.

Jim: It is.

Todd: When?

Jim: Well, shortly.

Todd: Before the end of term?

Jim: I think so. I've got nothing to lose. I'm not passing my courses anyway.

Todd: That's what I thought. But I was wondering if you had planned to tell us in advance that you were leaving.

Jim: (grins) Yeah, I see what you're getting at. You thought I'd just slip away into the night.

Joe: That occurred to me too.

Jim: Well, you're wrong. I came in today with the idea of telling you guys. I feel I owe all of you that much. But before I could bring it up, Denton said we should talk about disbanding. (Shakes his head.) Talk about mind-reading!

Denton: (laughs) No, Jim, you're giving me credit where it doesn't belong. I didn't know you - or anyone else - was giving thought to leaving, or otherwise breaking up the group.

Joe: Why did you bring the matter up, Denton? Do you think it's time for the group to disband?

Denton: Joe, I really can't answer that question. Honestly, I can't. Whether it's time or not is something no one ever knows for sure. Actually I guess we could have initially set out the number of sessions we'd have just like we stated the number of hours we'd meet each time. I didn't do that because I felt we'd play the length by ear.

Joe: Then why did you raise the issue at this time?

Denton: If anything, Joe, I was anticipating.

Joe: Anticipating?

Denton: Yes. Basically I guess I had it figured out that people in the group might be thinking it was time to end it.

Todd: Who in the group? Only Jim has said he was ready for it to break up. (Looks around.) Is there anybody else?

Denton: It's not really a question of anyone wanting it to break up, Todd. Some of us might never want it to break up.

Joe: (laughs) I guess I'm one of those.

Todd: Me, too.

Denton: But in terms of objectives, where are we? Have we gone where we want to go? Do we have any further go go?

Mike: Again, how can you tell?

Denton: That's a little easier. Everyone can speak his piece.

Rick: That's a cop-out, Denton. I'm sure I don't know how much longer we should go on. I know I'm not ready to stop.

Carlos: Neither am I! And I don't know if I'd be able to recognize the time when it came.

Rick: If it ever came!

Carlos: Right!

Denton: But Jim recognized it, didn't he?

Joe: Well, then, Jim; how did you go about recognizing it?

Jim: Pardon me?

Joe: How do you know it's time for us to break up?

Jim: Darling! I didn't know you cared.

Joe: (laughs) You silly ass! You know what I mean!

Jim: (soberly) Yes, I know, Joe; but at least I was trying to make a joke. (grins) I guess I've learned from the group what I needed to learn. Maybe I even knew it before, and didn't learn anything at all. (shakes his head) I just don't know. But I do know that my mind is made up. I guess that sums it up.

Mike: What's your mind made up about, Jim?

Jim: I can't hack it around here any longer. The scene gets lousier, so I'm cutting out.

Joe: Just like that?

Jim: No, I've given thought to it. A lot of thought. Now it's time to give wings to my words.

Mike: Where are you going, Jim?

Jim: The bright lights of L.A. first. Then what, I don't know. Depends on what I find.

Carlos: (laughs) Who is better than what, wouldn't you say?

Jim: (grins) What or who. Whatever!

Joe: What the hell are you going to do in L.A.?

Mike: Oh, come on, Joe. Do you want him to draw you a picture?

Joe: (irritated) I just don't want him to make a mistake.

Mike: Mistake! Mistake! How do you know whether or not you're making a mistake unless you try, for God's sake?

Rick: That much is true. Besides, whether he thinks he can or not, he can always retrace his steps.

Frank: What are your plans, Jim? Feel like sharing them?

Jim: (laughs) I would if I could. Really. I just don't know what I'll do. The thing I do know is that the pressures on me are so great that unless I leave home and have the freedom to be myself I simply am not going to be able to keep from going out of my mind.

Mike: But it might be naive of you to think that the pressures on you are going to go away simply because you leave home, Jim.

Jim: You're right there, Mike. The pressures that stem from my homosexual orientation might be just as intense in L.A. as they are here; but one thing I won't have to do is play a role.

Mike: And that's where I'm afraid you're being naive.

Jim: Why, Mike? You of all people? You manage very well. As a matter of fact, it's been you whose made the most impact on me since this group's been going on. I've looked at the way you handle yourself and decided I could do well if I could just get away from my bloody family.

Mike: But I'm with Joe in not wanting you to make a mistake.

Jim: I can't be making a mistake, Mike.

Mike: Can't?

Jim: Christ, Mike. It's like I told you. I want to be like you. I want to learn to handle myself like you.

Mike: And I'm honoured that you feel that way. On the other hand, no one knows better than me how easy it is to kick over the traces completely. You have to be on constant guard if you want to maintain a balance.

Jim: But I'm not interested in maintaining a balance, Mike. I just want to be able to handle my sexual orientation in the same casual way you've learned to handle yours. Stretching a point, I want to feel no more guilt because I like boys than Joe does because he likes girls. Why can't that be?

Carlos: They're both avoiding telling you that what'll probably happen is you'll end up in drag.

Jim: Maybe I will and maybe I won't.

Carlos: Whatever turns you on!

Todd: Well, I don't think it's anything to joke about.

Carlos: I didn't mean it as a joke, Todd. Who knows? I might go that way myself.

Todd: Knock it off, Carlos. Neither you nor Jim are going that route.

Jim: Don't be too sure, Todd. If that's what it takes to make me accept myself, then that's what I'll do. I'm tired of being at loose ends.

Mike: Believe me, Jim, that'll be the day when you'll truly be at loose ends.

Jim: Well, I'm not saying it's going to happen. I am saying that if that's the way I can learn to come to terms with myself then that's the way it will be. (laughs) Who knows though? I might end up as straight an arrow as old Joe.

Mike: (quietly) Don't count on it, Jim. You've tasted the forbidden fruit and you don't go back.

Joe: What the hell is that supposed to mean? You're practically guaranteeing that Jim can go only one way.

Mike: No, I'm not saying that at all. Look guys. I don't want Jim to end up as a simpering twit in drag any more than any one of you do. I've already given my opinion on that subject. But I think the surest way to guarantee that he will move in that direction is for him to totally deny his inner urges. He may have been cracking a joke when he said he might end up as straight an arrow as Joe; but on the other he might be serious about it.

Todd: So what's so wrong about it if he is serious? Mike, I can tell you that it's living hell being in doubt. I think I'm getting my thoughts on the matter sorted out, and I'm not trying to kid anybody when I say I've been playing some kind of sex game. I had myself convinced I was homosexual; now I'm not so sure.

Rick: I'm wondering if any guy can ever be completely sure of his masculinity.

Mike: It all depends on how you define masculinity, Rick.

Carlos: Yeah! Being a homosexual has nothing to do with masculinity.

Rick: I guess I meant a guy can never be sure of his heterosexuality.

Mike: Of course I wonder why any guy would want to seek a constant reassurance of his heterosexuality. It limits his scope.

Joe: (laughs) So you've said, Mike; but I still don't agree with you.

Mike: (laughs) Don't fight it, baby. Let it happen.

Frank: Denton, what do you think?

Denton: About what, Frank?

Frank: Oh, about Jim going off to L.A.! Do you think it's a good idea?

Denton: Well, I suppose if that's what Jim wants to do it's okay.

Frank: But suppose something happens to him?

Denton: I'm a great believer in allowing every human being the freedom to fail, Frank.

Frank: Oh, hell, Denton. This problem isn't one that lends itself to such an analogy.

Denton: (looks quizically at Frank) Maybe you didn't understand, Frank. Or maybe it's not the best analogy I could have made. Whatever, none the less, Jim feels he want to get away. He's contending that he has all kinds of pressures bearing on him that quite literally are getting him down. So, after reasoned deliberation on the matter he resolves to try getting out from under the pressures by moving out. Now there is no guarantee that by moving away from the current set of problems he's not going to inherit some equally awesome ones. That's what I meant by freedom to fail. In a nutshell, he won't know if he can alleviate the pressures until he makes an effort to ease them.

Frank: Yeah, I see what you mean.

Rick: But what about going the in-drag bit? Do you think that's a possibility?

Denton: (laughs) Hey, wait now! I'm not a mind-reader; nor can I forsee the future.

Mike: Well, I think it's a damn good possibility. Even a probability.

Rick: That's a hell of a thing to say.

Mike: Look, we all like Jim. There's no question of that, and certainly not any as far as I'm concerned. But being realistic about the trappings of the gay world, I mention it to Jim so that he can give some thought to what he may be letting himself in for.

Todd: Forewarned is forearmed, eh?

Mike: Something like that.

Jim: (grins) Well, you're a good buddy, Mike, and I know you mean well. But you see, to me that wouldn't necessarily be the end of the world. If I could be happy that way, why not?

Mike: (dogmatically) You wouldn't be happy.

Jim: How in the hell would you know, Mike? Have you ever gone in drag?

Mike: Hell no! And I wouldn't.

Jim: And yet you do admit you get turned on by guys as well as girls? And then there's Joe who's equally sure only girls can turn him on. Do you see what I'm trying to tell you, Mike?

Mike: Sure. You're saying everybody is different.

Jim: Right. And that's the main thing I've come to appreciate in these sessions. Everybody is different. Everybody marches to the beat of a different drummer. I'm just going to find a beat that I can march to. That's all. I sure as hell have never found it in my life before.

Denton: Probably all that Mike is trying to tell you, Jim, is that since you're moving into a different setting you have to be careful to know what it is you are getting into.

Jim: Right. And I can agree with that. But I'm not going to close the door on any possibilities; that's all I can say.

Denton: And certainly no one can expect more from you, Jim.

Frank: When is it you want to leave, Jim? Did you want to wrap up the sessions with this one?

Jim: When I go will that be the end of the group?

Denton: It wouldn't be the same without you, Jim.

Jim: Well, that certainly makes me feel good.

Mike: Oh hell, Jim. We've all developed some pretty strong feelings for each other.

Joe: Yeah. It's been a big surprise to me how it's all worked out.

Rick: Me, too. I've never been closer to people in my life than I am with you guys.

Todd: It's strange that it worked that way.

Frank: But that's how it's supposed to work, I suspect.

Denton: I suppose we could go on without you, Jim.

Frank: But would we really want to? You know, it's like losing one of your good right arms.

Joe: You brought the subject up in the first place, Denton. What do you think?

Denton: Well, like I said, I was kind of anticipating. Also I was trying to get at some feelings about closing off the group if anybody really wanted to.

Carlos: And you hit pay dirt with Jim, huh?

Jim: Hey, guys. Don't put me down like this. I really don't want to leave the group, but I've just got to get away. You can understand that.

Carlos: Sure we can understand. We all understand a lot about each other. But I swear I can't figure out how Denton anticipated it was time.

Frank: Neither can I, but let's think about the alternatives open to us.

Jim: There is none for me. I simply have to get out.

Frank: Okay, we can accept that. But what do the rest of us do?

Mike: Well, let's see. There probably are three. One, we could go on without Jim; two, we could find a replacement for him; or three, we can just let the group go.

Rick: I kind of think it's about time we broke the group up.

Joe: That's stupid as hell. Why would you want to do that?

Rick: No real reason. Or maybe we could just break up for a couple of months. You know, let some time go by so we can digest all the different experiences we've had. Then we could get back together. Maybe even Jim . . .

Frank: That's a lousy idea. Hell, we'd never get back together.

Mike: I agree. I don't think we'd get it together even if we tried.

Jim: (definitely) Besides, once I get out of town you can just bet that I'll never get back again. Or not for a long time anyway. I may be going to nothing, but I sure as hell am leaving nothing too.

Frank: Despite what Jim says about not coming back, we couldn't put it back no matter. A group like this either has to grow together or it soon starts growing apart.

Joe: You may be right. But hell, none of us knew how to get it going this time. Denton helped us once, and he'd help us again. The experiences we'd all have in the meantime would help get things going again. I would think the big obstacle we already overcame.

Frank: Yeah, but I think this would prove to be a very different kind of obstacle. I just don't think we could swing getting together again if we once broke up.

Todd: What do you think, Denton?

Denton: Oh, it could be done. But Frank is right in that it might not be as easy as it sounds.

Rick: So scratch that as an alternative.

Todd: What would be wrong in finding a replacement for Jim?

Frank: I don't think it would work.

Todd: Why not?

Frank: A new guy would be difficult to work in, that's all. Lord, how would you feel coming into a group like this just guessing at all the things that must have gone on before that you know absolutely nothing about? Man, it just wouldn't work.

Joe: A girl might add some colour to our proceedings.

Rick: (laughs) Man, a girl would have to be out of her mind to get involved with a lot like us.

Joe: It wouldn't make any difference. She'd feel just as out of place as any newcomer would.

Todd: Gee, I hadn't thought about it that way. But you're right. Nobody could hope to come in as a replacement.

Joe: Well, how about just keeping on without Jim?

Carlos: As far as I'm concerned, we shouldn't do that.

Rick: Why not?

Carlos: I guess I'm trying to put myself in Jim's shoes.

Joe: What do you mean by that?

Carlos: Just that if for some reason I had to leave the group I think I'd resent it if the group went on without me.

Mike: You've got a point there, Carlos.

Jim: Hell, I wouldn't resent it if you fellows went on without me. That would be selfish as hell, wouldn't it?

Mike: It might be, but I think I'd feel that way too.

Frank: I don't know if I'd resent it or not, but I sure as hell would think an awful lot about what the group was doing without me.

Carlos: Same difference!

Rick: It might be especially hard for Jim if he's out in L.A. trying to make a whole new scene and he's spending time thinking about us.

Jim: I kid you not! I'll be thinking about you in any event.

Mike: Right. All of us will continue to think about everybody in the group. But it'll be a bit different if you think about the people individually as opposed to thinking about the group as an entity.

Frank: Yes, I can see that.

Todd: So can I. So the only alternative is for us to break up the group, eh?

Jim: Damn. I'm sorry I said anything. I should have just wandered off into the night.

Joe: Then you would have really made us feel bad, Jim.

Todd: It's much better that we know, Jim.

Frank: We're at an impasse, Denton. What do we do?

Denton: Well, I think probably the best thing is for us to decide if breaking up the group is what we really want to do.

Joe: We can't do that. No one wants to break up the group.

Jim: Not even me. I just feel that I have to get away.

Rick: And no one is holding that against you, Jim. We understand.

Mike: Well, I think we should go through the formality of breaking up.

Joe: Even if I don't want to?

Mike: It's something we've got to face sooner or later. Why not now?

Rick: But why now?

Mike: Now is as good a time as any.

Joe: What do you mean by that?

Mike: Well, the way I see it is that we now have an excuse.

Todd: Christ, we don't need an excuse.

Mike: Sure we do. And Jim has given us one.

Joe: Oh, that's a crock. If anyone of us ever felt like quitting the group, hell, we'd just come on down and do it. There'd be no problem.

Mike: If there'd be no problem, what do you think we're faced with right now?

Frank: Hey, I see what Mike means. That's exactly what Jim did. He came down to tell the group he was dropping out, and look at the hassle that's come about because of it.

Joe: Damn. It's no hassle. I just don't want the group to break up.

Carlos: And Jim?

Joe: I don't want Jim to leave.

Mike: Right. So we're exerting all kinds of pressure on him to stay.

Joe: No one is trying to pressure him into staying.

Mike: Maybe not directly. But look how he must feel with all this conversation going on around his head.

Frank: Right. He's being made to feel that his leaving the group is causing us to disband. Isn't that right, Jim?

Jim: Well, I've got to admit I feel guilty.

Mike: See. That's exactly what I'm telling you.

Joe: Hey! I don't agree. We're just wanting Jim to make sure he's doing the right thing.

Rick: Right. There's no question of a third degree.

Frank: But there is the question of pressure. Since we don't want him to leave, we're bombarding him with questions as to where he's going and what he plans to do.

Mike: And at the same time we're all beating ourselves over the head trying to find a reason for staying together.

Joe: Hell, we don't need a reason. We've got the reason.

Todd: That's true.

Mike: Okay, we've got a reason. Or at least we had a reason. Now we are struggling mightily to keep that reason alive; and, in my opinion, when the reason becomes the end in itself rather than the means to the end, then the reason is no longer valid.

Frank: Mike's right. We're exerting pressure on each other to keep the group intact.

Mike: Exactly. And no matter what regard we hold for each other, when the time comes that pressure to remain intact is the only real thing that's holding us together, then it's time for the group to break up.

Todd: Well, I'm with Joe and Rick. I don't want the group to break up. Not yet, anyway.

Frank: When will you be ready for it to break up, Todd?

Todd: I don't know. Sometime, sure, but not now.

Frank: How will you know?

Todd: That's a hell of a question.

Mike: No, it's a damn good question, Todd baby. The only thing hellish about it is the difficulty you experience in trying to answer it.

Todd: The only way I can answer it is by saying that I think I would know.

Mike: And then what?

Todd: Well then, I'd come in here and tell you guys of my decision.

Mike: Which is what Jim did!

Joe: Christ, this is getting us nowhere!

Rick: We've already covered this ground.

Frank: We've skirted the issue, Rick. We haven't resolved it.

Rick: Well, how in the name of God can it be resolved? Jim says he's going to leave the group, and you and Mike seem only too anxious for the rest of us to break the group up. It looks like Joe and Todd want to keep going, and I'm not sure where Carlos and I stand.

Carlos: (grins) Gee, that's the honest to God truth. I'm confused.

Mike: (to Rick) It's not that I want to break up the group.

Frank: I sure as hell don't either, Rick. The point is that pressure is now being exerted on us to stick together as a group. And that's not right.

Mike: And look at it this way. If somebody else wants to quit in another couple of weeks we'd find ourselves going through the same bloody examination.

Todd: Maybe it's even better to quit while we're ahead.

Joe: Now what in hell is that supposed to mean?

Todd: Well, I was just thinking that all of us feel that we have gained a lot from participating in the group. How much further along can we go? What else can we do? So that's what I mean. Since we are all happy right now with what we've done and nobody else knows what next we are going to do, maybe it would be a good idea to quit while we're ahead.

Joe: Hell, Todd. That doesn't hold water. We never have known in advance what we were going to do, so how could we now plan ahead?

Rick: Right. I bet Denton didn't ever know what we were going to do.

Denton: (laughs) That's true, you know.

Joe: (interrupts) Denton, do you think we should continue without Jim?

Denton: Why bring me into it? You guys seem to be getting at the problem okay.

Joe: It seems to me we're going in circles.

311

A STRANGE BREED OF CAT

Denton: Maybe it seems that way, but I can't say I agree. It's been noted that there are three alternatives to choose from. You've looked at all of them in fairly decent depth.

Rick: True enough. But we're still up against a blank wall.

Joe: It's the same old thing. You're damned if you don't and you're damned if you do.

Frank: Well, dammit. This is getting us absolutely nowhere. We're all doing a pretty good job of fence straddling.

Carlos: Even though Jim's leaving, he could still have his say. Right?

Todd: That's a damn good point, Carlos. Let's see what Jim has to say.

Mike: No argument there.

Frank: Except there is still a form of pressure on Jim.

Joe: If you look at it that way, it's pressure on all of us.

Jim: The only thing I can say is that I'm beginning to feel like a bastard.

Joe: (laughing) Proper thing!

Mike: Honestly, Jim. Does it make any difference to you?

Jim: It's selfish as hell, but I wish we could have our last meeting together while I'm still here.

Rick: Okay, Jim. That's honest as hell. But why?

Jim: Oh, I think because we all started this thing together and I'd enjoy us ending it together. That's not a very damn good reason maybe, but that's how I feel.

Joe: Okay. I'll buy that. As much as I don't want the group to break up, I'll buy that.

Rick: Well, that kind of wraps it up.

Mike: Meaning?

Rick: Just that if Jim thinks we ought to have a final session while he's here, then that's what we should do. We owe him that, eh?

Frank: You know I just don't believe it. It was a lot easier making the decision to come together than it was to make the decision to break up.

Mike: No comparison, Frank. One was an individual decision, and that makes it easier.

Frank: That's part of it, but I think there's more.

Joe: What?

Frank: When do people separate, Joe?

Joe: Well, when they argue or have a falling out I guess.

Frank: Right. But yet we've not had an argument nor a falling out, and yet we're trying to reach an agreement to go our separate ways. See what I mean?

Todd: It's like I said. Quit while you're ahead.

Frank: Yeah, but that saying is usually applied when you're dealing with situations or things; not when you're dealing with people, eh?

Mike: Well, look! Do we make today the last session or do we prevail on Jim to stick around for another week?

Joe: Let's ask Jim to stick around for another week.

Todd: Yeah. One more session. How about it Jim?

Jim: It's okay with me. If everybody else wants to.

Rick: I'd like to.

Joe: Me, too.

Carlos: What will we do?

Mike: Oh, we'll think of something.

Todd: Sure.

Denton: All right then fellows. If it's agreed we'll meet one more time, let's wrap it up for today. I don't feel too good about today's session, and I would suspect that several of you feel as uptight as I do. We've had a good thing going, but now it's coming to an end! And that's sad. But we've all got to support Jim in his decision, whether we have reservations or not. He's given thought to what he's doing, and you can't expect anybody to do any more than that. As for the rest of us, I think the right decision has been made. I'm comfortable with it, even though I may not like it personally; and that's what I'd like for all of us to give some thought to. Okay?

(The group assembled quietly. There was the usual banter, but the overtones of the finality of the session obviously pervaded the camaraderie.)

Rick: I feel like this is going to turn into a wake.

Jim: Yeah. I've been wondering if having this last session is such a good idea after all. Maybe we should have just come to a screeching halt last week.

Mike: (changing the subject) You've made no change in your plans, eh, Jim?

Jim: (quietly) No, none at all. I still plan to leave.

Todd: How are you going to do it, Jim?

Jim: You mean leave home?

Todd: Right. Are you going to say goodbye, or what?

Jim: I don't want to be melodramatic about it, but I'm going to leave a note.

Joe: Wouldn't it be better to tell your folks what you're going to do?

Jim: (laughs) Boy, that's a laugh. I could just see their faces lighting up when I tell them where I'm going and what I plan to do.

Joe: (annoyed) I don't mean tell them everything, Jim, but couldn't you pass off a story about wanting to get out on your own? It sure as hell would be a lot kinder to them than just walking out and leaving a bloody note.

Rick: It sounds cold to me. I couldn't do it.

Jim: Yeah, but maybe neither of you guys have the scene at home that I do. I've never been able to talk things over with my parents. Believe me, if I were to try now to tell them that I'm taking off it would be a hassle like you've never seen.

Mike: So what's one more hassle in the middle of many, Jim? At least you'd be playing the game cool regardless of what they do. You'd be honest with yourself.

A STRANGE BREED OF CAT

Frank: Besides, they might surprise you.

Jim: That would be the day!

Carlos: Well, you ought to give it a try anyway.

Rick: Sure. It's like Mike says. At least you'd be doing the right thing. They might rant and rave, but at least you're not being deceitful.

Jim: Well, it looks as if you're all in agreement on the subject. Of course, none of you have to go through it either! That makes it pretty easy, eh?

Mike: True enough. But just because they're liable to raise hell with you doesn't mean anything. You've decided in your own mind what's best for you, so just stick to your guns.

Jim: Well, supposing I do tell them I'm leaving; how much do I tell?

Joe: Without lying, I think you should tell them as much as you want to.

Mike: Right. You figure they can't handle the whole truth. Okay. That's no problem. That's part of being kind; and besides, you owe them that much. But leave out the parts you think they can't handle.

Jim: I don't think they can handle any of it without a lot of hassle. That's what I'm trying to avoid.

Todd: Sure. Only look at it this way, Jim. Your leaving is going to be very hard for them to handle whether you tell them or not; but if you give them the reason that you want to go out and find a job and be on your own, at least they can eventually accept that. That's not saying they won't try to argue you out of going. You're just phrasing it so that they can understand. The rest of if you can hold back because they're not going to be able to understand, and that's okay. At least in my book it is.

Jim: I guess you guys are right. It wouldn't be right just to run off.

Joe: That's what I was saying. Whether they agree with you or not is unimportant; at least you're giving them something they can try to understand.

Rick: Right. And just for an example, take us guys sitting around here.

316

SESSION XI

Look how we've begun to understand each other. Communication did it.

Joe: That's true enough. It still doesn't mean all of us see eye to eye on things. I doubt we ever could, but on the other hand we've begun to accept each other regardless of the way we might disagree.

Frank: We don't even shout at each other much anymore. (laughs) I guess that's as good a reason for closing down as any other.

Mike: Yeah. The shouting does seem to be a thing of the past.

Todd: In the light of things as they are now, it seems stupid that we sat around for so long a time slugging it out the way we did.

Frank: No, I don't think it was stupid. It was a process we had to go through. People shout when they attack or when they defend. Each of us has done his share of attacking and defending. You might say we've gotten it all out of our system in here.

Mike: Not all the way. Each one of us will continue to shout outside the group.

Todd: But hopefully at a lower level.

Frank: That's true, of course. Undoubtedly, we've all learned to shout in a lower key. On the other side of the coin 'though, we've learned to trust each other in a way that makes non-shouting possible. I think one thing I've learned from this group is tolerance.

Todd: Hell, I guess we've all learned that.

Frank: But the funny thing is that I thought I knew it before.

Mike: Live and learn, baby.

Joe: Right. Man, I kid you not that things have gone on in here that have really blown my mind. I really feel I'm a different guy from what I was three months ago.

Todd: Why not? I know damned well I am.

317

Mike: Well, now. What are we going to do? Are we going to sit around and all give testimonials?

Frank: (laughs) Mike, you have a way of reducing things to the crudest of essentials.

Mike: Yeah, I know; but what are you going to do? I try to see things as they are and attempt to tell them like it is. It gets me in hot water sometimes, but that's part of life. The good part, I might add.

Frank: I guess it's really up to Denton to assess what we've done in the group, but I know that I think we've all done good things.

Mike: Only I don't see why Denton is the one to assess things. I think he can see only what he thinks he sees, and I don't mean to take anything away from his powers of evaluation. All I'm saying is that each of us is the best judge of what went on.

Todd: Right. There's no way that anybody can measure the total result of how I feel about the new me. Nobody!

Rick: You really feel you've changed that much?

Todd: Only it's not feeling. I know! And maybe it shows, but maybe it doesn't.

Frank: How do you really know, Todd?

Todd: You see, that's it. I do know, and I can tell everyone of you in words. But unless you could get deep down inside of me, all you have to go on are my words.

Frank: And words are inadequate. It's like love. How in the name of heaven do you use the word love? We can use the term; we can tell somebody we love her. (looks at Jim) Or him, for that matter! But how in the world can a word substitute for the reality of the situation?

Mike: Well, of course you can't. You have to show that you love; just like you have to show any kind of feeling.

Carlos: I feel I've gotten some new ways of looking at things also. Maybe the experience for me hasn't been as profound as it has been for Todd and maybe some of you other guys, but I think what has happened is going to show in the way I think and the way that I feel.

Frank: That's what's going to happen in Todd's case too. He's going to show the changes; just not say they've come about.

Mike: This brings me to something I've said previously. I think Denton should write these sessions into a book.

Frank: Yeah. I like that idea. Denton should really do it.

Joe: It's a good idea, but what's the point?

Mike: Look, has anything gone on here?

Rick: Hell, there's unanimous agreement that there has been.

Mike: Okay. Let's share it with the whole wide world.

Joe: But suppose the whole wide world doesn't want to read about it?

Mike: Well, screw them.

Frank: Now, there's a new found healthy attitude.

Mike: It's true, Frank. Screw all the mothers who don't want to read about it. What difference does it make?

Rick: It makes a hell of a lot of difference if it doesn't sell.

Joe: Right. It would be an exercise in futility.

Mike: Crap! Nothing is an exercise in futility. It's an experience. We've all had the experience, and now we want to share it with other people. The whole bloody world for that matter if they'll take the time to read it.

Todd: But how can Denton write it? Or anybody else for that matter? It's like you said, Mike. Not detracting from Denton's ability to assess and evaluate, it is up to each of us to best judge what happened.

Joe: Well, it would be a bloody mess if we all sat down in an attempt to write up the sessions. We'd be spending so much time describing how we felt on a particular occasion that we'd never get any words down on paper

Frank: So we're back to words.

Todd: Right.

Mike: Well, I think we would all have to agree that process is out of the realm of the descriptive. So what we have left is content. That's all we have.

Frank: Then you're suggesting the content be written without any attempt at process?

Mike: Right. If no attempt is made at trying to describe how any of us felt, then there'd be no problem with words.

Frank: You're thinking people might be able to identify with words.

Mike: Empathize is what I mean. Hell, people do it all of the time with the telly and with movies.

Joe: And you think guys would identify with us?

Mike: Sure, we're nobody special. Everyday run of the mill types — every-one of us.

Frank: Only most guys don't have a chance to get in a group like this where ideas and feelings can be really ventilated.

Todd: And learn from it like we did.

Mike: Right. So that's the idea of getting it all written down on paper. Who knows? It might be the next best thing to being here.

Todd: Anybody got any reservations about the idea?

Rick: Well, real names wouldn't be used, would they?

Joe: Yeah, that's a point. Names should be changed to protect the innocent. That's what I think.

Mike: That's an original thought, Joe baby. Hell, you see that goddamn phrase on television all the time.

Carlos: It could just as well read to protect the guilty.

Todd: Oh, go on.

Frank: It's probably a good point though. I feel the same way.

Mike: What way? What do you mean?

Frank: Changing the names. I think that should probably be done.

Joe: No sweat. As a matter of fact, every thing about us could be changed.

Mike: Just so long as the basic message gets across, why not?

Rick: All of us are forgetting one thing in our push to become national heroes.

Todd: What's that?

Rick: It seems to me we've all decided that Denton is going to write this book, and everyone thinks it's a great idea. Only Denton hasn't said what he thinks about it. He may not even want to do it.

Mike: We're just taking for granted that he will.

Todd: Sure. Good old Denton. How could he refuse?

Frank: I don't know. Let's ask him.

Rick: Let me be the one to ask him.

Todd: Why you? It's Mike's idea.

Rick: Big deal! I want to ask Denton if he'll write the goddamn book.

Mike: (laughs) Already yet. Will you ask him?

Rick: (solemnly) Will you write about our cerebral experiences, Denton?

Mike: (laughing) Christ. How about the visceral ones?

Todd: Hold on. One level of experiences at a time.

Rick: Will you, Denton?

Denton: Good Lord, how can I? I've kept no notes. How is it possible to put everything in sequence?

Mike: For what it's worth, we'd help.

Frank: Sure.

Denton: It's a lot easier said than done. For instance, who can recall how the first session went?

Joe: That one I can give chapter and verse about.

Denton: And session two?

Mike: Hell, ad lib as you go.

Denton: (laughs) I thought you wanted this to be a true story.

Frank: It will be.

Denton: Not if I'm ad libbing all over the place

Mike: Seriously, Denton. Will you try?

Denton: Is that what all you guys want?

(Bedlam breaks loose among cries of "hell yes" and "tell it like it is.")

Denton: Okay. I've got some basic remembrances for the outline. It can probably be done.

Carlos: You really will do it then?

Denton: Well, let me say I'll try. But I'm going to have to call on you guys from time to time for editing duties.

Jim: Right. Well, you can reach me in L.A.

Joe: (Shakes his head) I'll be damned.

Mike: Maybe all of us will, Joe baby. In the meantime how about let's all getting together and taking our fearless leader out for a few drinks this afternoon to wind the sessions up in a proper way.

Rick: Proper thing.

(The last and final session ends, with the group adjourning en masse to seek liquid refreshment.)

EPILOGUE

The pages of content which precede this final summation are words which a group of guys in search of a better awareness of self exchanged with each other. Sometimes the words were thrown as if they were rocks; other times they were used as clubs to batter someone with. All humankind uses words as weapons, so it would have been unrealistic to expect that the group — especially in its initial stages — would have been any less brutal with each other; yet through sincere efforts to communicate and to understand, especially in the ultrapersonal realm of sexuality, a bond developed which transcended differences of opinion and divergent perspectives. Love has been said to be many things: the use of the word has even been prescribed, dictated, circumscribed, defined, restricted, enjoined, and frequently perverted. It really doesn't have to mean anything other than "I understand."

Denton watched over the group from the time it struggled with the pangs of birth to attempts to become an adhesive entity through the infighting of adolescence which manifested itself in the brawling which is so common of the postpubescent child. He gloried in the full maturity that the group eventually attained.

Subsequent sessions more often than not attained the appearance of glorified bull sessions, the gut level type of confrontation disappearing as acceptance became more a style of life and less of a bandied about word. When tolerance blocked at the word level, Denton devised games that circumvented hostility and allowed meaning to shine through in a crystal clear fashion. Somehow it became pretty damned obvious that when humans feel the freedom to confront and encounter, they soon learn from freely given antithetical perspectives that commitments on cognitive and affective levels too often are the result of some highly distorted perceptions. Mankind can relate well if it can ever get a lot of the verbal garbage out of the way. Every member of the group came to value every other member as a valuable human being, and collectively they sought wisdom and growth.

Denton White was not God, nor did he play at being a God. He attempted to teach in a very subtle way the beauties of acceptance. One does not need necessarily to like or agree with every other human being, yet there is something to be said for attempting to understand and appreciate the vagaries of man. Acceptance is the first step. Even if change is desirable, acceptance must lead the way before change can be brought about.

324

EPILOGUE

Denton was no God intervening in and manipulating the lives of men. This was the bag of the ancient Greek deities. He was not totally unaware that some change had come about in the perceptions and cognitions of the several group members, but he would have been very hard pressed to have accounted for these changes. And others he was simply unknowledgeable about.

Nonetheless, and for a little while at least, the group served the purpose of dredging love from the depths, understanding from darkness, and tolerance out of misinformed bigotry. It served that purpose beautifully, so what more justification is required? And, who knows, it may indeed have been the most significant thing to occur in several of the lives it touched.

There were many times that the language used by the group members would have done justice to the most hardcore seaman on the New York waterfront. It will offend some people, and of that there can be no doubt; but the business of encounter is a serious one. When a guy is tense and hostile he rarely uses anything other than the vernacular which best describes these emotions. No apology intended, but that basic fact should be kept in mind by anyone who feels compelled to condemn the level of language. My personal feeling is that what the whole human race needs to do is learn to shout in a whisper and love with a roar!

But there were times when the basic goodness inherent in humankind shone through as well. A few more lines in this vein would render the entire experience maudlin. In retrospect some of the memories might really degenerate to that level, but it's a safe bet that if the group got together for any length of time and some clown decided to wax eloquently sentimental that he would be brought up short by a healthy outburst of the selfsame waterfront language.

So the group is gone, and the time has passed, but everybody is a little bit richer, eh? Who the guys were is unimportant, but if anyone can read himself into a part — then that's what he should do. None of the guys would mind, for in fact that was the reason these pages came about. Where have they gone? Well, hell! Would you believe Toronto and Los Angeles, Monterrey and Asheville, and points in between?

Finally, let's hope the content was agreeably reported. Take my word for it, baby. The process was great as hell!